TERROR AND VIOLENCE

Anthropology, Culture and Society

Series Editors:
Professor Thomas Hylland Eriksen, University of Oslo
Dr Jon P. Mitchell, University of Sussex

RECENT TITLES

TERROR AND VIOLENCE

Imagination and the Unimaginable

Edited by
ANDREW STRATHERN, PAMELA J. STEWART
AND NEIL L. WHITEHEAD

PLUTO PRESS

First published 2006
by PLUTO PRESS
345 Archway Road, London N6 5AA
and 839 Greene Street,
Ann Arbor, MI 48106

www.plutobooks.com

British Library Cataloguing in Publication Data
A catalogue record for this book is available from
the British Library

ISBN 978 0 7453 2399 2 hardback
ISBN 978 0 7453 2398 5 paperback
ISBN 978 1 8496 4275 0 PDF

Library of Congress Cataloging in Publication Data applied for

10   9   8   7   6   5   4   3   2   1

Designed and produced for Pluto Press by
Chase Publishing Services Ltd, Fortescue, Sidmouth EX10 9QG, England
Typeset from disk by Stanford DTP Services, Northampton, England

CONTENTS

LIST OF FIGURES

ACKNOWLEDGEMENTS

We want to thank the set of people who contributed essays to this volume. Each of them was invited, by ourselves as editors, to discuss the topic of terror and violence in relation to the imagination and the unimaginable. They have all done so admirably.

Andrew Strathern and **Pamela J. Stewart** want also to thank the Center for West European Studies (University of Pittsburgh) for support of our research; the University of Aberdeen's Research Institute of Irish and Scottish Studies (RIISS), where we were provided with affiliations and office space in 2004 to work on this project as well as others; the Institute of Ethnology (Academia Sinica, Taipei, Taiwan) for affiliations and office space during parts of 2002, 2003, 2004 and 2005; and the Dong-Hwa University (Hualien, Taiwan) and Peking University (Beijing, China) for the opportunity to provide lectures and discuss our thinking on these topics and others during 2004. We thank the Harry Frank Guggenheim Foundation and the Hewlett International Grant Program (University Center for International Studies, University of Pittsburgh) for support of research that fed into our chapters in this book. We especially thank our friend and colleague, Prof. Richard Feinberg (The Kent State University), for inviting the two of us to the Central States Anthropological Society's 2004 meeting where Andrew Strathern presented some of our thoughts on the topic of terror and the imagination in the Keynote address to the Society (Andrew Strathern and Pamela J. Stewart (2005), 'Witchcraft, Sorcery, Rumors, and Gossip: Terror and the Imagination – A State of Lethal Play', *The Central States Anthropological Society Bulletin*, 40(1): 8–14). We especially thank also all of our interlocutors in Ireland, Papua New Guinea and Taiwan.

Neil L. Whitehead wishes to thank the participants in the *Legacies of Violence* research group at the University of Wisconsin-Madison for the opportunity to present many ideas on this topic, and the International Institute of the University of Wisconsin-Madison for funding to support the *Legacies of Violence* project: (http://www.intl-institute.wisc.edu/ResearchCircles/LOVindexpage.htm). Thanks are also due to Philippe Descola at the Collège de France, Anne-Christine Taylor at the Ecole des Hautes Etudes (Paris) and the participants in the *Cultures of Violence* conference series at Mansfield College, Oxford, as well as my fellow panellists for the session 'The Violence of Representation', at the American Anthropological Association, Chicago, November 2003.

Pamela J. Stewart, Andrew Strathern and Neil L. Whitehead
1 March 2005

INTRODUCTION: TERROR, THE IMAGINATION, AND COSMOLOGY

Andrew Strathern and Pamela J. Stewart

DEFINITIONAL PRELIMINARIES

Terror and violence are topics that are deeply emotive, are widely written about, and have come to occupy a peculiarly prominent place in the images and experiences that surround the everyday lives of people in many parts of the world. In its essentials, the situation is not new, since violence and fears of violence have probably been a part of human life as long as humans have existed (see Laqueur 1987). However, each historical period tends to bring with it a new opening of various themes surrounding this topic.

In the world today, the major conflicts between the communist and the capitalist regimes, signalled as the Cold War, have been replaced by a 'hot war' of conflicts ideologically centring on the imputed actions of Al-Qaeda and the various sovereign states that see themselves in different ways as involved in 'the war on terror' – which means 'the struggle against terrorists'. This hot war has witnessed fewer words and more actions: enactments of violent destruction and death that have often caught people by surprise, going beyond their earlier imaginations of how events would turn out. And they have subsequently given rise to seismic shifts of perceptions, policy, and ideological responses, as governments and peoples attempt to encompass such events within not only their imaginations but also their assessments of how to confront them in the present and if possible prevent their recurrence in the future.

As with the global Cold War period, these efforts are accompanied by new written commentaries, dramas, poetry, art, television programmes, and film-making, which are all a part of the collective and individual constructions of a political life that now takes into account what was formerly unimaginable but rapidly becomes almost a part of everyday experience. The development of imaginaries of this kind takes place on both sides of any given conflict, often with nearly identical but politically opposed rhetorics supporting them.

1

Without such frameworks of thought and emotion the conflicts would not proceed in the same way or at the same levels. Media sources, by their very immediacy, we might say, can greatly intensify and magnify the perceptions involved of events; but they do so not only by presenting visual images (which are nonetheless devoid of other sensations such as heat, dust, cold, intense smells – see Sontag 2003), but by appealing to, and conforming with, basic scenarios in people's minds, mental habitūs in the terms of Pierre Bourdieu (Bourdieu 1977), connected to cosmic schemes of 'good versus evil' and 'the lessons of history'.

We should make it clear here that our principal concern in this volume is with terror and the imagination as important concepts that *impinge upon* the specific issues that are covered in the present outpouring of research and discussions regarding terror*ism* and 'how to deal with it'. Our contributors do address aspects of our topic in ways that often, for empirical reasons, foreground acts classified by governments or individuals as terrorism; but the book as a whole is not meant to be a general survey of all the places in the world where relatively intractable issues of terrorism are constantly being played out. We are concerned with the concept of terror, which is a universal and global condition that many peoples live with on a day-to-day basis.

We have included contributions from writers on places that form far less a part of the media reporting in the so-called 'Western world' (a term that is itself not well suited to the complex global realities of today but continues to have rhetorical currency in the terror-related struggles themselves), while not attempting, simply for the sake of coverage, to assess various well-documented situations, for example, in the Middle East, about which media reports and stories emerge regularly in the morning newspapers and television shows in many parts of the world. This is not because we regard some areas as more or less important for our argument than others. It is rather because our approaches and interpretations have merit and applicability in general and can therefore be used to explore many situations, from small-scale to large-scale.

It is worthwhile to draw on a less familiar case and give it a central place where it can help to illuminate other cases that are more familiar and apparently better known but have not been previously analyzed in the ways that we advocate. It is this intellectual endeavour that allows comparisons to be offered between small-scale processes in a place such as Papua New Guinea in the Pacific region and larger-scale processes between nation-states in the international sphere, ultimately because many of the same human processes of thought and action are involved, regardless of scale. For the same reason we have stressed here a range of ideas that have been deployed by anthropologists, bringing these to bear on our topic. Our discussions clearly overlap in theme with many that have been written by political scientists and historians who are experts on 'terrorism'. We have been concerned, however, to see what we can especially contribute to these broad discussions from our own disciplinary insights. (For a selection of political science references, see the bibliographies in Juergensmeyer 2000, e.g. Rapoport 1988; Wilkinson and Stewart 1987.)

We have been involved in this exploration of 'terror' as a theoretical construct for some time. Two of our recent books, *Violence: Theory and Ethnography* (Stewart and Strathern 2002a) and *Witchcraft, Sorcery, Rumors, and Gossip* (Stewart and Strathern 2004) explore violence and terror using case studies from Sri Lanka, Rwanda-Urundi and elsewhere in Africa, India, Indonesia, Papua New Guinea, and Europe. We also organized and held an interdisciplinary workshop at the University of Pittsburgh in March of 2005, which brought together an international set of scholars in political science, history, psychology, anthropology, and media studies to discuss the topic of *Global Terror and the Imagination*.

Early on here, also, we wish to introduce another point, acting as a caveat. Much analytical and rhetorical energy has been spent on trying to define in absolute terms what is meant by 'terrorism'. Whereas 'terror' is a term that refers to an emotional response, even though its more specific components, manifestations, and triggers may vary culturally and historically, 'terrorism' at once evokes political rhetoric. Components of a definition may be offered, such as 'deliberate attacks on civilian non-combatants in a conflict situation'. This component, for example, can be useful in trying to set a baseline for the 'ethics' of military action in times of acknowledged and open war. But attacks of a clandestine kind may also be made against military forces, and function to produce terror and fear in much the same ways as when they are directed at civilians. Examples abound from Northern Ireland, where Irish Republican Army (IRA) attacks were often made on the occupying British military forces. (Here it is also, in passing, important to note the use of the term 'army', which aims to legitimize IRA actions as those of one army against another and therefore as 'war'. War may be defined as 'legitimate', while violence may not be, in people's minds.)

For the purposes of any given participant in a conflict, it may be important to define what constitutes a terrorist act and terrorism in general. Analytically, however, it is clear that whatever components of specific meaning enter into the definition of terrorism, the application of the term 'terrorist' is relative and situational. One person's meat is another's poison; and what to one person may be a terrorist is to another a freedom fighter – as it has become almost conventional to acknowledge. More significantly, the reason why this is so is that everyone's viewpoint depends on their situation, and more specifically 'whose side they are on'; and it is one of the effects of a world deeply caught up in the violence of acts and the imaginaries that surround, reflect, and further engender these acts that there is a pressure on everyone to 'take sides'; not least the pressure exerted by powerful nation-states and the demands placed by governments on their own citizens and vice versa. As a result of these processes and their global ramifications, the ideological conditions of the Cold War, in which binary divisions of the world were made on one basis, have rapidly been duplicated in a new context, in which the principal feature is the contextual ambiguity of 'inside' versus 'outside' relations. It is this characteristic that makes comparisons between the fear of sorcerers or witches in small-scale clan-based contexts such as in Papua New Guinea (see Stewart and Strathern 2004) and the fear of terrorists in the USA, UK or elsewhere, not only feasible but illuminating.

This example also holds the key to examining the relationship between individual/personal and collective imaginations, which come together in the context of the experience of and response to terror. Two very different mechanisms can be identified here. At one level there is the obvious effect of government actions in centralized polities, for example statements by political leaders regarding 'the war on terror' and 'the price of freedom', or the public dissemination of classifications of levels of threat, in colour codings, that the US Homeland Security authorities began to issue after the 11 September (9/11) 2001 attacks in the US. These responses are comparable to declarations by clan leaders about visible and known enemies. But such declarations are made much more effective, that is frightening, if they are accompanied by a flow of informal rumour and gossip that may amplify, reduce, contradict, support, or give a new twist to government-based communications.

In the Papua New Guinea Highlands these processes of rumour and gossip are constantly at work in face-to-face contacts, as people try to obtain the best intelligence they can about threats to themselves. In the worlds of literate communication, one analogue of this is e-mail and internet postings, which are a major source of alterity, confusion, and resistance to government edicts and whose effect may often be to raise general levels of suspicion and fear, just as happens through gossip in village or clan contexts in places such as Papua New Guinea. These are themes we have explored in our previous thinking and writing (Stewart and Strathern 2004) in our work on witchcraft, sorcery, rumours, and gossip.

Essentially, rumours and gossip, while seeking to establish or base themselves on a concept of 'facts', are acts of the interpretive imagination, trying to bundle together an account of what is happening, has happened, or will/might happen with a further interpretation and evaluation of such an account. Rumour and gossip are therefore prime political instruments and can be used either to support or to oppose authority in the context of discussions about violence and terror.

Although we have pointed out that it is difficult to define 'terrorism' because of the term's intrinsic situational and rhetorical sense, it is nevertheless worthwhile to consider in a broad sense the relationship between violence in general and terror. Are all acts of violence equal producers of terror? And how do we define violence? This latter point is one that we have discussed earlier, drawing and commenting on David Riches' earlier work (Riches 1986; Stewart and Strathern 2002a). The value of Riches' work on this topic was twofold: first, and fundamentally, he stressed both the immediate efficacity and the interpretive ambiguity of acts classified as 'physical violence'. Such violence is in principle available to anyone. In its primordial form, represented endlessly in media depictions, it depends only on the use of the body itself.

The mystique of Kung Fu traditions brings this together with concepts of mind control. Gunpower amplifies this primordial capability. A lone rebel can thus kill a political leader. In such an extreme context, most people will declare the act of violence to be illegitimate and an act of terror. But many acts of violence are seen differently by different people. Riches argues that an essential feature of violence is that its legitimacy may be contested. His model of the situation of violence explains this further. His second contribution to the theme of violence was to distinguish between performers, victims, and witnesses of violence. In our work (Stewart and Strathern 2002a: 35–51) we have called his characterization 'Riches' triangle' or more generally the triangle of violence.

In developing this concept further, we have argued that the arguments about the legitimacy of violence are distributed differently around this triangle and that in particular the category of the witness may be complex and contain within it persons who evaluate the act of violence and its results quite differently (ibid.). People's responses may also be linked to the amount of damage or destruction an act causes. Broadly speaking, a slap on the face or a fist pounding a table will incur fewer arguments about its legitimacy than a murder, although this also depends on who has done what to whom and who gets to know about it.

Not all acts of violence, however, are equal producers of terror. Those acts of violence that produce terror, not only on victims but also on a wider world of witnesses, are those, we suggest, that contain certain elements that relate to political 'archetypes': they are surprising, surprisingly damaging, reveal a powerful will on the part of the performers, and suggest a world of meanings beyond the acts in themselves. Above all, terror may consist in the realization, on the part of witnesses who identify with the victims, that an act of violence is seen as legitimate by its performers and those 'on their side'. This is particularly so when the act is concatenated with a perception that it is executed in pursuit of revenge and revenge is by the performers of violence equated with, rather than separated from, justice.

This point of revenge is one that we have argued extensively before (Stewart and Strathern 2002a: 108–36), pointing out how pervasive, deep-seated, and widespread the theme of revenge is as a prime motivation for violence, acting as both motivation and justification for the action and so revealing the 'powerful will' we have referred to here. Cursory experience of viewing popular televison serials in the US indicates clearly that revenge is constantly cited as a salient 'folk model' to explain action, overriding conventional legality or conventional morality in many instances and revealing ambiguities in the moral relations between people and between people and the state. This is one of those motifs that links together small-scale interpersonal interactions and the large-scale interventions of nation-states in international contexts: colonial 'punitive expeditions' were acts of revenge, just as acts of uprising against colonial powers themselves often were. And punitive trade sanctions exemplify the same process, outside the immediate context of lethal violence, but often with equally powerful effects.

Here we build further on these points about violence and terror by stressing another factor: the importance, through all the contexts of violence and terror, of the imagination. Crucial, then, to our viewpoint in this volume is that terror implies the imagination, and often the more general realm of 'the imaginary' as such, that is, the world of ideas that shapes people's response to events in terms of cosmologically established or recreated themes. This aura of ideas, strongly imbued by emotions, quickly surrounds the material acts involved. Terror is thus in the mind and in the interaction between the mind and the world at large. Acts of violence link the two: Mark Juergensmeyer, in his survey and analysis of religiously inspired violence (or violence that includes religious ideas as a part of its justification) strikingly includes the putative 'mind of God' in this nexus between thought and action, since God is often appealed to as the ultimate justification for violent projects by some people (Juergensmeyer 2000).

God, in this sense, is clearly an important part of the aura of ideas that we have identified as the imaginary. 'The imaginary' here does not signal that the thoughts involved are either factually 'true' or 'untrue' with respect to the world. It simply indicates that people's thoughts about the world often run far beyond its obvious empirical manifestations, and that the frameworks that are built out of people's thoughts become as important as, or even more important than, their everyday empirical observations, especially where their emotions and their own sets of values are strongly present. These frameworks can then be rhetorically and ideologically played upon, augmented, or transformed in the pursuit of particular political agendas or missions to shape history at large, and to shape people's memories.

Terror is thus based on an interlocking feedback between memory and anticipation, the same nexus that makes possible continuity in human interaction generally. Here, however, the feedback is based on a sense of rupture. Terror consists precisely in intrusions into expectations about security, making moot the mundane processes on which social life otherwise depends. Repeated ruptures shift people's perceptions and render them progressively more anxious and vulnerable to disturbance. At this point the imaginary may enter, often by way of images that nowadays are globally diffused through information technology. Once the imaginary has taken hold, polarization between the parties to a dispute may set in, so that mediation of conflicts becomes harder. Finally, if conflict reaches a certain level of terror, people's basic identities themselves become challenged.

A processual model of this kind, which can at the same time be used in historical studies, enables us to see how terror proceeds from specific acts that rupture normative expectations, polarize parties, and ultimately challenge their identities. These identities may be reasserted and hardened in the sequence, or they may disintegrate. The circulation of images leads to a heightened sense of terror, but satiation may also take place. The repeated incursion of physical acts of violence into this cycle of the imaginary refuels the whole recreation, and at times escalation, of senses of terror. Physical actions at different points in the world enter into global circulation and give an increasing sense of the place and problematics of violence and terror.

THE IMPORTANCE OF THE IMAGINATION

In this section we expand on the definitional and interpretive issues already raised by exploring further the significance and crucial role of the imagination in the generation of terror. At the outset here it is relevant to ask: whose imagination are we discussing? Bearing in mind the triangle of violence model outlined above, we note that the imagination brought into focus may be quite different from the viewpoints of the performers, victims, and witnesses.

In the US the case of the Unabomber (Juergensmeyer 2000: 141), who targeted scientists with whose actions he disagreed in terms of his own complex ecological ideas, clearly shows how even a lone agent may develop a cosmological viewpoint that justifies his actions as means to an end without anyone else sharing in the exactitudes of his mind-set: a performer with a philosophy all of his own, which he nevertheless followed with a zeal and pertinacity equivalent to upholding a shared religion. His philosophy, and indeed his whole life, became a work of the imagination, with devastating consequences for those he targeted, and ultimately for himself when he was eventually identified and captured.

The imagination we are dealing with, then, is one that may or may not be shared among performers, victims, and witnesses. What is nevertheless circulated between them is a set of anticipations and feelings about the effects of violent acts and their meanings. These anticipations and feelings further enter in one way or another into wider fields of circulation, because terror and violence are a part of life for nearly everyone in one degree or another. Some persons are victims, some are perpetrators, and others are observers of violent acts or acts that terrorize. Observers may think themselves safely removed from the impact of terror and violence until something happens to them, perhaps unexpectedly and shockingly.

Terror and violence can be immediately tangible or they can gradually and unobtrusively eat their way into the psyche, only to be physically expressed or enacted at a later time. Schröder and Schmidt (2001: 9) note the importance of what they call 'violent imaginaries'. Analogous points are made by Göran Aijmer (2000: 3–8), when he expresses his interest in the 'symbolism of iconic codes and their use in the visionary building of possible worlds, forming the *imaginary order* of a society' (p. 3). Violent acts, Aijmer argues, may embody complex aspects of symbolism that relate to both order and disorder in a given social context, and it is these symbolic aspects that give violence its many potential meanings. This is a particularly important point when we consider the violent acts taken by peoples around the world in the name of a particular religion or in a belief that these acts conform to a set of 'moral' teachings directly linked to specific cosmological ideologies.

Schröder and Schmidt argue that 'violence needs to be imagined in order to be carried out' (2001: 9), and they go on to point out the importance in this context of historical memory, which 'can be represented through narratives, performances and inscriptions' (ibid.). This argument is further underpinned by Aijmer's analysis of symbolism and 'iconic codes', that is, codes that are embodied or expressed 'outside language' (2000: 3). Aijmer also emphasizes the imaginary character of symbolism here, expressed in ways that he says cannot be verified in terms of 'referential meaning' (ibid.). Put more simply, this means that people create their own fears out of the imagination of possible horrors. To this we can add that when actual horrors take place, as they frequently enough do, these in turn feed into the world of the iconic imagination.

The present collection of essays explores the role of the imagination, and we extend this to include 'the unimaginable', that is, the shocking and potentially violent response to an event that jars people into acting because of the unique and unimaginably disturbing nature of the originating event. Vincent Crapanzano's concept of 'imaginative horizons' and 'frontiers' is relevant here, especially when he writes of frontiers 'that postulate a beyond that is, by its very nature, unreachable in fact and in representation' (2004: 14). Shocking events reveal these frontiers, but they also shift them.

In assessing the impact of activities seen as terrorizing or 'terrorism' around the world, then, we have to take into account that their effects are magnified through the workings of the emotions and the imaginative capacities of people. These imaginative capacities are strikingly engaged in extreme circumstances involving bomb blasts, the collapse of buildings, dismemberments, mutilations, and acts of torture. Imagination is involved also in cases where people envisage themselves as the performers of violence as well as on the part of victims and witnesses.

Problems posed by terrorist activity have come to occupy the centre of the stage in world politics. Terrorist actions are seen as actions involving violence against a state and its civilians in the name of a particular ideological cause. This is a part of global everyday experience as reflected in the media, principally televison, radio, and newspapers. Yet deeper questions of what constitutes terror and what actions are recognized as acts of violence do not form a part of the daily presentations of images. Our basic argument is that the power of ideas regarding terror does not rest solely on the events of terrorist actions, destructive as these may be. It rests also on the great multiplications of reactions to these acts and the fears that these acts arouse in people's imaginations. The imagination is therefore crucial to our conceptualization of terror in this volume.

Contemporary theoretical interests in the imagination stem from a number of sources. One strand of thought goes back to Benedict Anderson's concept of the nation as an 'imagined community' (Anderson 1991). For Anderson the important thing about the nation was that its members could not know one another face to face but imagined themselves as members of a community through symbolic means such as newspapers and media generally. We should add here that all communities, regardless of scale, are actually to some extent imagined; for example, a kin group's members imagine their own solidarity by means of notions about ancestral figures. Mythology

is a prime arena for the imagination in this regard (for an example
from Papua New Guinea, see Stewart and Strathern 2002b).

Another line of thought has to do with the imaginative work
of interpreting ethnographic materials. John and Jean Comaroff
wrote about this in *Ethnography and the Historical Imagination* (1992).
Their argument is that the historical imagination is a prime means
of understanding how to integrate fragmentary perceptions into
cohesive schemes of interpretation. 'The meaningful world', they
write, 'is always fluid and ambiguous, a partially integrated mosaic
of narratives, images, and signifying practices' (p. 30). They propose
a historical approach 'that is dedicated to exploring the processes
that make and transform particular worlds' (p. 31). The arena of
studies concerning the global topic of terror and the imagination
corresponds very clearly to these viewpoints.

Another prominent writer who has stressed in general the
significance of the imagination is Arjun Appadurai. Appadurai has
approached this topic from a number of angles. He refers to the
process of deterritorialization of populations in the contemporary
world, leading them to reinvent the idea of 'the homeland', which
may 'exist only in the imagination of the deterritorialized groups, and
it can sometimes become so fantastic and one-sided that it provides
the fuel for new ethnic conflicts' (1996: 49). Here we gain a glimpse
of the relationship between the imagination, senses of identity, and
violence, emerging out of social disruption. A prime example would
be Liisa Malkki's portrayal of Hutu refugees in Tanzania and their
mythico-histories and stereotypes regarding the Tutsi (Malkki 1995;
Stewart and Strathern 2002b: 18–34). Elsewhere, Appadurai notes
that the imagination works to produce change in contexts of social
action generally (p. 185). Specifically, he refers to the effects of the
internet, which 'allows debate, dialogue, and relationship building
among various territorially divided individuals who nevertheless are
forming communities of imagination and interest that are geared
to their diasporic positions and voices' (p. 195). Most generally, and
strikingly, Appadurai asserts that 'the imagination has now acquired
a singular new power in social life' (p. 53), which he links to the
accelerated transnational flow of images. Such flows in turn create
the 'spectacle' of violence, in which relations between persons are
realized purely through images. Media representations of violence
are therefore not just a passive part of imagination but are very much
active constituents as well.

This active role of what we call representations is not new, although,
as Appadurai points out, the internet and other media have led to
an immense speeding up of the circulation of motivating images.
Spectacles of violence, whether as acts of resistance, of torture, or
of tyranny and subjugation, have played an important role in the

reproduction of violent relations themselves, whether mimetically or dialectically. These spectacles may themselves embody political or cultural power and act to break down or reproduce senses of identity. The ancient Roman circuses, presided over by the emperors, are an obvious case. Ritualized violence in bullfighting is another example (Bouroncle 2000; Martin 1986 – both studies appearing in well-known collections of essays on violence in general). Virgil Kit-yiu Ho, in the same collection as Bouroncle's chapter (namely, Aijmer and Abbink 2000), presents a discussion of public executions in late Imperial China (Ho 2000), beginning with some assertions about the cultural variability of what constitutes violence itself. He cites Cantonese martial art movies, which, he says, 'lure their fans with highly explicit scenes of blood-spattering fighting' (p. 142).

The circulation of media practices may have outdated this observation, with the production of Quentin Tarantino's film *Kill Bill* (compare also Stephen Chow's *Kung Fu Hustle*, which we saw when it was shown in Taipei, Taiwan, in early 2005). The point about the scenes of violence in these films is perhaps not so much that they are very violent (having seen both films we can attest that they are), but that the violence itself is framed stylistically, and in many of the Chinese Kung Fu films that we have watched over the years, violent acts are accompanied by much mystery and magic, locating the episodes firmly in a historical imaginary of values that partake of a folklore or legendary character and are thus removed from a distinct sensation of immediacy.

Ho's remarks on Kung Fu are made in passing. His main point is that the public executions of criminals can be seen as aesthetic shows or images that are designed to reinforce, rather than subvert, social order, and are therefore not classified as violence as such. One detail, however, reveals ambivalence: one official, according to a mid-nineteenth-century observer whose account is drawn on by Ho, was given the task of paying respects to some deities whose temple was near to the place of execution. These deities were 'regarded as having the power of preventing the spirits of decapitated criminals being hurried by revengeful feelings into inflicting injuries on the judge, magistrates, and others who have administered the law' (Gray [1878] 1972: 64, quoted in Ho 2000: 147). Later, Ho suggests that perhaps this act of paying respect to the deities could be seen as a mode of thanking them for their assistance in apprehending the criminals (p. 150); but, given the cross-cultural prevalence of ideas about vengeful spirits and the perception of needs to propitiate them that exists also in Chinese customary ideas, we may suggest that the deeper reason is as Gray suggested. There is always some uneasiness about punitive justice and an inchoate recognition of the alternative primordial order of revenge that it is supposed to replace. Fears of vengeful ghosts represent a persistent extension of the same violent imaginary that justifies public executions as an instrument of coercive control over people's imaginations. The general point here is that spectacles are indeed instruments of control reinforced by aesthetics, and the same is the case for contemporary media representations.

Appadurai's use of the term imagination overlaps with his use of 'imaginary', referring to a realm or dimension of life in which the imagination is at work, for example the relationship between neighbourhoods and 'a wider territorial imaginary'. His usage here is similar to that of Aijmer referred to earlier on 'the symbolism of iconic codes and their use in the visionary building of possible worlds, forming the *imaginary order* of a society' (Aijmer 2000: 3). Aijmer's point is that images can take on a life of their own in relation to other images and symbols and can exercise influence outside the realm of discursive language (ibid.). Since Aijmer's discussion is in the context of his theorizing on the domain of violence, his identification of the imaginary is particularly relevant to our theme in this collection of essays.

What has not been done explicitly is to apply the partial and separate insights of these and other authors to the topic of terror. By linking terror to the imagination we intend to produce a synthesis of thoughts that joins together, rather than separates, the realms of physical events and imagined events by showing how these feed into one another. We have earlier demonstrated at length the general validity of this point in our book on witchcraft and sorcery, showing how gossip and rumour play into and magnify ideas and actions regarding witchcraft and sorcery, and how they can in themselves be instrumental in generating violence (Stewart and Strathern 2004; see further below). A parallel between 'rumor' as 'news in search of verification' and the intelligence operations of governments can be aptly made here, especially in those instances where it turns out that policy decisions are made on the basis of information that is unverified or unverifiable but corresponds to the ideological mindset of those who receive and manipulate it.

The novelty of our overall approach in this volume, then, partly lies in our application of the concept of the imagination to the study of terror and violence. Although Crapanzano's extended essay on imaginative horizons is not explicitly concerned with issues of violence, his general scheme of thought and several of his specific observations provide a useful framework of theorizing for our topic. First he locates imagination at the centre of social life and links it, as Appadurai and others have done, to 'the social imaginary' (Crapanzano 2004: 7). Citing the philosopher Charles Taylor, he remarks on the constitutive character of the imaginary in society, and notes that it 'is carried in popular images, stories, and legends' (ibid.).

In considering his own approach to imagination, Crapanzano says that he has chosen a processual approach, meaning that he is less concerned with a structural account and more with the recurrent ways in which the imagination enters into life through imagery and expressive culture in general (p. 8). The themes he deals with include 'body, pain, hope, memory, transgression or death' (p. 9). In passing, he notes that contradictory imaginaries pose a severe challenge to each other, and he characterizes the 'war with Iraq' as an attempt to obliterate those who pose such a challenge, describing the war as, *inter alia*, a *Kulturkrieg* (p. 11). (He locates his observation here in the year 2004 when his book was published.)

In his third chapter, on 'body, pain, and trauma', Crapanzano explores the issues of pain, and 'the use of pain in determination of truth' through torture (p. 89), as well as the links between pain and memory. He remarks that 'torture instils fear, pervasive fear, and terror, the object of which is more than pain or suffering, mutilation and death' (p. 88) (see Christopher Taylor 1999 on the 'sacrifice' of victims via mutilation). 'It creates uncertainty and unpredictability – a sense of the fully contingent that lies neither with a god nor destiny, but squarely in human hands' (p. 88). The torturer therefore is one who imagines a set of ways to inflict pain in order to demonstrate power, the extraction of information perhaps being used as a rationale for this existential action, as was ostensibly the case in the abuse of prisoners in Abu Ghraib in Iraq during 2004 (Danner 2005).

In Crapanzano's observations, what is particularly interesting is his stress on the unpredictable character of torture. That which is unpredictable is also at the horizons of the imagination. If it moves across those horizons, it produces shock, not only in its victims, but also in those who later become witnesses of the torture. In some cases the extreme emotional response of complete numbness, or lack of ability to even feel shock, may be experienced. This contingency and unpredictability, inflicted on the bodies and minds of the tortured, mirrors in some ways the contingency and anxiety that accompanies situations of heightened alert against terror.

A *New York Times* article from 11 January 2004 reflects on the conditions brought into being by such alerts, and the response of government by increasing security checks at borders and stepping up the collection of information from all over the world, leading some critics to 'wonder whether the whole process has become a bit of self-fulfilling prophecy, with an apparatus that has an incentive to report terrorist threats, based on solid information or not' (Eric Lichtblau, *New York Times*, Sunday, 11 January 2004, Week in Review Section, p. 3).

The parallels with cargo cults and millenarian movements seem clear here (see, e.g., Stewart and Strathern 2000). The imagination is at work, and running overtime, in these examples. Fingerprinting incoming passengers on flights to the US is one response; and a strange parallel is found in torturing prisoners to obtain a hidden 'truth' from them. Both processes are attempts to extract a 'truth' by ineluctable bodily means from persons whose identities and loyalties are seen as potentially ambiguous or dangerous. Generalizing here, we may say that the most important point for our topic of terror is that the imagination, which is essential to social life in general, flourishes in particular when there is uncertainty. The point was also central to our earlier discussion on rumour and gossip (Stewart and Strathern 2004). We would now join rumour, gossip, and the imagination together as social forces; or we may regard the former as in large part the product of the latter.

The imagination also comes into play when violent acts are deliberately used to stimulate further violent acts. Mark Juergensmeyer (2000: 196) tells the story of a young Sikh woman activist who 'broke into the house of a Hindu shopkeeper whom she suspected as having reported her to the police'. Unmoved by the shopkeeper's pleas she shot him dead, and reported that 'one of her purposes was to spur Sikh men' into acts of greater courage, since if 'girls could be so brave', boys could follow suit (Juergensmeyer 2000). We see here how the young woman played on gendered expectations. Even more strongly we see how gender here was harnessed to extend the horizons of imagination about what kinds of violent acts could legitimately be carried out in the name of a cause. Mechanisms of this kind drive escalations of violent acts over time, spurred on by competitive emulation.

Another finding by researchers and theorists of rumour is also interesting here. This is that rumour sometimes trumps 'facts', because rumour can appeal more to the imagination and a desired mind-set than facts may do. The by-now well-known case of the claim by both the British and the US governments in 2003 that Saddam Hussein had weapons of mass destruction that could be deployed against targets within 45 minutes illustrates this point in classic fashion. Expensive and diligent searches for such weapons after the invasion and occupation of Iraq in 2003 and 2004 did not yield evidence of such weapons existing, and subsequently it was suggested that the quality of US intelligence should be reviewed in relation to this matter. During the inquiry held by Lord Hutton in the UK into the death of Dr David Kelly, a British weapons inspector and expert on Iraq, British intelligence officials admitted that even the claim itself related only to battlefield weapons, not internationally usable missiles (see Strathern and Stewart 2004a for a further discussion of these materials). While the Hutton Report eventually exonerated the British government of any outright dishonesty with regard to the case for war presented to Parliament and the British people, placing blame instead on the BBC for unverified reporting, this in no way rebutted the basic assertion made in the media that the intelligence itself was not well founded and would be better classified as a form of rumour. Rumours about terrorism may therefore certainly themselves produce terror and may give rise to massive military action. Such an observation gives a sobering perspective on the world of the imagination about which, as we have noted above, Vincent Crapanzano has eloquently commented (Crapanzano 2004: 19). Like the iconic images discussed by Aijmer (2000), imagination transcends reality and its rational articulation; but in doing so it can bring further realities into being.

WITCHCRAFT, SORCERY, AND TERROR: A COMPARISON

Our book, *Witchcraft, Sorcery, Rumors, and Gossip* (Stewart and Strathern 2004) and Neil Whitehead's *Dark Shamans* (2002; see also *In Darkness & Secrecy*, Whitehead and Wright 2004) have taken the topic of violence in a number of further directions.

For Whitehead the ability of sorcery to project itself through the fundamental categories of cultural imagination underwrites the political and social power of sorcerers and even suggests their entailment in the wider processes of cultural reproduction. In a similar way the inchoate and threatening 'terrorist' is a figure that can be deployed to sustain and enhance power relations, as it invokes the imagination of insecurity and so licenses new regimes of 'homeland security' and the repression of dissidence.

In *Witchcraft, Sorcery, Rumors, and Gossip* (Stewart and Strathern 2004), we deal with the realms of witchcraft and sorcery, and then we move directly into the arena of the imagination and its fears as these have produced witch-hunts and apprehensions regarding occult sorcery in many parts of the world. The book specifically asks how such fears are produced, and it concentrates on rumour and gossip as processual forces instrumental in generating both fear and violent responses to such fears in physical executions of suspected witches. We stress the power of rumour and gossip in this context. This gives the analysis a new twist, flowing from a general processual approach to the interpretation of anthropological and sociological data. In the arena of rumour and gossip, as in others, some people have more power to influence courses of action than do others. But rumours also tend to break out of the confines of power. In parallel to our argument about witchcraft, we point out that rumours and gossip are often at the heart of subversive movements that lead to violent protests against political authorities. Correspondences are found between rumours that generate witch-hunts and rumours that authorities in government are perpetrating malign acts. The globalized world of

Figure 1   A leader in the Mount Hagen area, Western Highlands Province, Papua New Guinea, in the 1960s. He is orating over a present of sides of pork from a group with whom there had been fighting in the pre-colonial past. He wears a mixture of introduced and indigenous clothing. His steel axe is available either for garden work or as a weapon. Leaders 'control the talk' between friendship and hostility. His dramatic gesture marks his commanding presence in local politics. From the 1970s onward, fighting between groups re-emerged, with its disturbances and temporary creations of 'terror'. (Stewart/ Strathern Archive)

rumour has produced parallel fears and concerns in many regions of the world, linked by reactions to significant events, such as the destruction of the twin towers of the World Trade Center in New York on 9/11/2001. In these reactions imaginative responses to the events themselves play a central role.

Figure 2   Two senior men watch the development of a dispute over pigs given away between groups in the Mount Hagen area, Papua New Guinea, 1960s. Minutes after this picture was taken, a physical fight broke out. (Stewart/Strathern Archive)

Equally, it is the case, as Whitehead has stressed, that government forces may themselves play on people's imaginations and fears, and may also disseminate rumours, as a means of increasing their control and power over the populace at large. The opposing sides in a conflict may therefore contribute to each other's social reproduction because of the factor of mutual fear, manipulated by rumour and fuelled by the invocation of cosmological powers and the imperatives of revenge that are fostered by those in authority.

When put in this way, it is quite evident that the production of rumour goes hand in hand with the reproduction of social and political relationships. It is essential to stress here the fluidity and

Figure 3 Two men enter into an altercation over pigs in an exchange. Others holding long staves attempt to intervene. Mount Hagen, Papua New Guinea, 1960s. Stick-fights of this kind were common in pre-colonial times, and would escalate into wider conflicts in the event of blood being drawn. Intervention was uncertain, and the commotion spread both fear and interest quickly. (Stewart/Strathern Archive)

multiple potentialities of rumour, because it is in such fluidity that its connections with terror can be made. Rumour is also very much a part of history. It comes and goes and may be recurrent, or new rumours replace old ones as new constellations of power, fear, and anxiety capture people's attentions. We make here a comparison between some materials of our own on Papua New Guinea (the Duna, Hagen, and Pangia areas of the Highlands) and Neil Whitehead's work on the history of a particular sorcery complex among the Patamuna

Figure 4   A truckload of riot police drawn up on the site of a battle between major groups in the peri-urban area near to Mount Hagen, Papua New Guinea, 1970s, prior to Independence in 1975. Riot police were often viewed at this time as a 'third tribe', interfering between two groups engrossed in fighting. (Stewart/Strathern Archive)

people (and others) in Guyana, Amazonia. While our own emphasis has been on a processual model of rumour and gossip as these relate to witchcraft, and Whitehead's focus has been on images of assault sorcery and how they have changed historically, there is a strong overlap between the materials themselves based on their connections with ideological formations and social processes over time.

Whitehead's focus is on a particular kind of assault sorcery known as *kanaimà*. The idea of 'assault' gives to this version of sorcery attack a greater aura of terror than might pertain to sorcery by food pollution ('poison') or even leavings sorcery (in which the sorcerer picks up an item imbued with the victim's life force and uses it to make an attack). Assault sorcery combines the imagery of direct, physical violence, and mystical or cosmological ideas about the efficacy of magic. The idea of 'ritual murders' that turns up from time to time in Euro-American contexts conveys this same sense of fear that is magnified because of the killer's putative adherence to some scheme of thought that 'justifies', or even demands, this violent act. These characteristics are found also in New Guinea ideas.

Kanaimà sorcerers are said to give ambiguous and obscure signs of their presence along trails and to stalk their victims whom they hunt for food as prey. Their place is the forest, although sometimes they might approach the house of an intended victim, making bird-like

Figure 5 A riot police commander, helmeted, and an Australian government officer (Assistant District Officer) watch the potential movement of enemies across an old mission airstrip. Behind the two Australians are two old pre-eminent leaders of one of the groups involved. Other men watch the officials. Mount Hagen, Papua New Guinea, 1970s. Later years saw an increase in problems of fighting and violence through the Highlands region. Large-scale mining projects, bringing government revenue, both precipitate such conflicts, in part, and have to cope with them. (Stewart/Strathern Archive)

sounds indicating their intent to kill. In the Pangia area in Papua New Guinea assault sorcerers (*uro, maũa*) were also originally thought to frequent remote forest areas between settlements on the fringes of the Wiru-language-speaking region. Like the *kanaimà*, they were thought to be tricky and stealthy, and their presence was inferred from an unusual sense of heat in the forest.

Kanaimà are said to search for victims to kill for ritual food, and to stuff the mutilated bodies with herbs that eventually produce a

Figure 6 The aftermath of a death. Women, their bodies plastered with yellow and white clay, gather round a pole on the top of which the ceremonial head-dress and bark belt of the dead man are suspended. Funeral speeches often inflamed tensions between groups owing to suspicions that the deaths of leaders were caused by sorcery. Cycles of fear, grief, revenge, and compensation for killings ensued from such suspicions, spread by rumour. Mount Hagen area, Papua New Guinea, 1970s. (Stewart/Strathern Archive)

special aroma, like a kind of cooking, which leads the sorcerers back to the place where they are said to bury the victim until putrefaction sets in. Shifting their shape if necessary, it is said that they then revisit the grave, insert a stick into the corpse, and suck its juices, which are said to taste like honey (Whitehead 2002: 96). They may remove pieces of bone material and place these in caves as gifts to senior sorcerer-adepts who may use them to 'cool' down their ritual 'heat' or to help them locate their next victim (p. 97).

In New Guinea, shape-shifting abilities are often attributed to 'cannibalistic witches', who are said to seek to kill victims in order to disinter and consume their corpses. The *kanaimà*'s putative practice of 'cooking' their victim's bodies finds a particular parallel in Duna (Papua New Guinea) ritual practices of the past in which a ritual victim's body was left for the victim to die before it was distributed along a ritual trackway to promote fertility of the earth (Stewart 1998). Whitehead points out that the *kanaimà* is not simply seen as a sorcerer. The *kanaimà* is also seen as a 'shaman', with access to forms of magic that in other contexts are used for healing rather than killing purposes. The body of the victim is in some sense like that of an animal sacrificed to spirit powers, becoming part of a cosmological cycle between humans, animals, and the spirit world.

As shamans, however, *kanaimà* are seen as the descendants of an original trickster spirit, Makunaima, whose brother Pi'aima was the ancestor of the *piya*, the shamans who cooperate with chiefs to create social order (p. 103). *Kanaimà* may be seen as waging secret warfare to destroy village life, while *piya* attempt to restrain or control them. This complex of ideas explains why Whitehead calls the *kanaimà* 'dark shamans'.

In Duna cosmology, 'witches' (many of whom are said to be females) are seen as descendants of a male cannibal trickster figure also; while male assault sorcerers are seen as marauders from a different language area altogether, Oksapmin, across a large river (the Strickland) to the west of the furthest reaches of Duna settlement (see Stewart and Strathern 1999). The Duna raided Oksapmin for victims to use in their fertility rituals in the past; in contemporary times Oksapmin assault sorcerers are said to intrude on Duna settlements and kill women and other people (although not to eat them). Interestingly, in the Duna language witchcraft and assault sorcery are categorized together. Witchcraft is *tsuwake kono*, which we may gloss as 'the magic of the mind', while assault sorcery is *tsuwake tene*, 'the original or root kind of magic'.

These comparative details show interesting overlaps and differences between our materials from Papua New Guinea and Neil Whitehead's materials from Amazonia; but the main analytical point of Whitehead's discussion is to show how ideas about *kanaimà* have changed over time and how in nineteenth-century colonial times chiefs were sometimes said to co-opt *kanaimà* sorcerers in order to help them kill specific targeted enemies (Whitehead 2002: 130). (Female 'witches' were also said to have been co-opted in pre-colonial times among the Duna for similar purposes.) Each *kanaimà* sorcerer was said to have 'familiars disguised as predators or raptors' that could engage in killings for them. The histories of warfare between groups were therefore concerned not just with 'material, physical events but a hidden dimension of struggle for the order of the cosmos' (p. 131). When guns were introduced from the outside world in the nineteenth century, the *kanaimà* were said to have become especially useful for their abilities in covert tracking of dangerous foes, and it was in this context that the *kanaimà* came to have the reputation of 'secret avengers' (p. 139).

At a later stage, as a result of the impact of Christian revivalistic movements emerging out of Spanish evangelizing, a split occurred between 'modernizing' factions centred on the 'alleluia' Christian sect, and 'traditionalizing' factions, one of whose symbols became the *kanaimà* sorcerers and the chiefs who used their services. Over time again, in the twentieth century *kanaimà* ideas have become reified as authentic or premodern tradition, or, as Whitehead puts it, a form of hypertradition (2002: 182), whose agents are now seen as attacking the dominant black officials in the Guyanese government and encroaching Brazilians employed in mining camps that threaten Patamuna territoriality.

Whitehead's historical account demonstates cogently the historical transformations of ideas and practices in the *kanaimà* complex and especially their role in struggles over power. The sorcerer-shaman is a weapon that can be used to serve a local polity or undermine it, and comes over time to stand for resistance to 'modernity', forming a rhetorical foil to 'modernizing' policies. Significantly, this latter development had its roots in Christian evangelism with its efforts to dichotomize the world and picture tradition as 'evil'. But *kanaimà* is also an indigenous symbol of terror, conjured up this way and that by the imagination over time.

While we cannot trace an exact parallel here from our own research materials on New Guinea, we can corroborate the association between assault sorcery and changing notions of danger and insecurity over time. We offer here a pair of observations from two of our research areas. First, with regard to assault sorcery in the Pangia area, in 1967, only a few years after the imposition of Australian colonial control over fighting between groups living within the area, assault sorcerers were said to belong only to a small peripheral area within the Pangia district, furthest from the administrative station and nearest to great stretches of uninhabited forest. We understand this to represent also the situation in immediate pre-colonial times. By the early 1980s this situation had changed drastically – the assault sorcerers were said to be at work in all the new colonially established villages, menacing even those close to the government station. Why the change? Colonial government, for one thing, had made travel in general between villages easier, by the creation of roads and the abolition of warfare. It was thought that if ordinary people could move about in these new circumstances, so could sorcerers. But also, since 1975, Papua New Guinea had become an independent country, and regular administrative control had been loosened. This newly volatile situation, coupled with the freer movement of people that was by now habitual, increased fears of the assault sorcerers passing through the area. Fears of assault sorcerers thus became expressions of a discourse of anxiety about the new state and the threat of invasion of new centres by old peripheries.

Our second case from our research materials is from the Duna area. In the 1990s in our research locale, the Aluni Valley, fears of both the internal depredations of 'cannibal witches' and the external attacks of assault sorcerers from Oksapmin became intensified. The loss of indigenous ways of dealing with witchcraft among the Duna and the inadequate access to introduced medicine help to explain the former syndrome; while the latter has to be looked at in the contexts of both political space and gender relations. The Aluni Valley and Oksapmin were in pre-colonial times linked both by mythology and by trading expeditions. Ritual ties were cut off by missionization, and trading was curtailed by the availability of trade goods from other sources. Hence the Oksapmin became more 'the Other' than they had been before. Their male assault sorcerers were said particularly to menace women who strayed outside their settlements and gardens. These sorcerers were said also to place young women in their front ranks as a way to lure Duna men, rendering them also vulnerable to attack. Duna leaders used these images as ways to warn people to control their movements and behaviour: homegrown versions of 'homeland security', based strongly on a cultural imaginary (for further discussions of related themes see Whitehead and Wright (eds) 2004, including their Introduction to that set of studies, pp. 1–19, and the Afterword by ourselves, 2004b, pp. 314–20).

SUICIDE BOMBERS, RELIGIOUS VIOLENCE, THE COSMOS, AND THE STATE

Violence flourishes in flux and feeds on many levels of conflict. As Whitehead puts it for *kanaimà*, we are dealing with discourses that refer 'simultaneously to the dynamics of the spirit world, physical aggression by individuals, the tensions and jealousies between villagers and family members, and the suspicions of distant enemies and outsiders' (2002: 1). Equally, he notes, in a manner consonant with our own emphasis on the power of rumour, 'one is simultaneously dealing with convincing case histories, wild rumors, considered attributions of blame, false accusations, ungrounded gossip, and justified suspicion' (ibid.).

If these characterizations capture well the currents of conflict in which violence is nurtured, our discussions of assault sorcery and witchcraft have also made it clear that cosmology is important; and cosmology is very much a product of the same impetus to create a cultural imaginary that we have pointed to earlier. What must also be stressed here is that state authorities may be deeply involved in both creating and feeding off such an imaginary. States and cosmologies may be symbiotic or in conflict; and aspirants to possess their own state may draw on cosmic imagery to drive an independence movement forward, thereby earning for themselves the term 'terrorists' from the point of view of those they oppose. Both sides in any such conflict depend on the production of fear and terror against their enemies.

The suicide bomber can be seen as an extreme agent for such a production, a human engine of terror combining the ultimate of self-sacrifice with the ultimate of hidden destructiveness towards others. The extreme character of the image here should not, however, deflect us from noting that in essence such a bomber is in many ways not different from those who risk their lives to defend their country against its enemies. In both cases an imagined community is involved, and a cosmos of order that discursively constitutes such a community. The shock inherent in the suicide bomber's actions is in the conversion of risk into certainty and in the self-inflicted as well as inflicting nature of the act itself. By blowing himself/herself up, the suicide bomber appears like an altruistic sorcerer or witch, willing to die in order to cause death to others.

The mentalities involved can be seen in a number of ways. One book-length study carries the striking title *My Life is a Weapon* (Reuter 2004). This succinctly conveys the idea of ultimate symbolic and embodied condensation that is at work in the concept of the suicide bomber. In war, the fighter and the gun are closely identified. In suicide bombing the identification becomes all-consuming. The imaginative groundwork for these actions is already present in the images of war generally, where the individual is trained to sacrifice himself/herself for the 'greater good' and this sacrifice may involve the death of others.

Israel Orbach has explored the specific historical and cultural factors that have gone into the Palestinian intifada, for example: indoctrination, promises of rewards in heaven, the glory of martyrdom, the results of better status for the families of those who kill themselves in this way, and the place of all this in a national imaginary founded on the notion of an 'intrepid warrior' who is thought not to be afraid of death (Orbach 2004). Orbach also makes use of the idea of dissociative trance in relation to suicide bombers (ibid.). Richard Kearney (2003), speculating on the 'meanings' of the 9/11 attacks, cites Kant's philosophical use of the idea of the 'sublime' as a mixture of inwardly experienced pleasure and horror aroused by the spectacle of such attacks, and he raises the possibility of seeing the emotional mind-set of the suicide bomber as akin to such a notion.

Imagery of what some would call 'heroism' marked by dying with wounds sustained in the front of the body are not peculiar to any one context. They are to be found in many traditions of thought surrounding warfare. For example, in Papua New Guinea, a leader of the Kawelka people in Mount Hagen (Western Highlands), Ongka-Kaepa, gave an oral account of a standard speech made by fighters among his group in one moment of pre-colonial history:

Let them try to kill us one by one until we were all finished off and a visitor
to our land could later tell the story of how the Kawelka all stood together
as one man and were annihilated at this spot . . . Let us stand here and face
them, let us take the wounds in our fronts and not in our backs fleeing, let
our women escape with their small sons at the breast, and later bring them
back to show them the place where we, the men of Kawelka, fought and died
to the last man, so they will know who their fathers were and who it was that
killed them [and so take revenge]

(Strathern and Stewart 2000: 47)

In the case of the Chechens' occupation of a theatre in Moscow in
October 2002 and their attempt to bargain for the lives of some of
their own people with those of the hostages they took (resulting
in disaster for most of those involved), the Chechen leader Movsar
Barayev videotaped a message that was broadcast from the Al-Jazeera
station in Qatar. In the message one of his followers said, reportedly,
'Each one of us is willing to sacrifice himself for the sake of God
and the independence of Chechnya,' adding 'I swear by God that
we are more keen on dying than you are on living' (The Moscow
Times.com, Saturday, 26 October 2002, www.themoscowtimes.com/
stories/2002/10/26/302.html).

Such an invocation of God, and the swearing of oaths, have become
hallmarks of religiously motivated violent acts, often connected with
nationalist causes. It should be noted, though, that some Muslim
commentators stated that Barayev himself was more of a bandit than
a religious zealot, and one mufti of the southern Russian border area
near to Chechnya commented of Barayev that 'he never read a single
line from the Quran, and he doesn't undertand the true meaning of
jihad (holy war)' (The Moscow Times.com). In this instance, some
twenty-five of the fifty hostage-takers were women, who had become
fighters. Some media commentators suggested that these women were
widows and relatives of persons killed by Russian soldiers, and were
seeking revenge. We see here how an elementary and nearly universal
imperative such as the desire for revenge can become intertwined
with nationalist and religious dimensions. Broadcasting videotapes
of the sort mentioned here on Al-Jazeera is also significant in this
regard, linking Chechnya symbolically to similar events in parts of
the world such as Palestine.

The role of women in the Chechnyan case is paralled from Palestine
by the emergence of young women as suicide bombers (*New York
Times*, Sunday, 14 April 2002, International Section, pp. A1 and
A12), in one instance apparently trained by Hezbollah from the Al
Aksa Martyrs Brigade. The *New York Times* (Saturday, 13 April 2002,
International Section, p. A6), noted that 'the active involvement of
women . . . marks a clear departure from practices of the past and
from a tradition-minded society where the men did the fighting

and the women – as so often in war – did the grieving . . .'. This change was linked to a period of conflict between the Israelis and the Palestinians over settlement areas and the search for 'terrorist' elements within these areas.

Clearly an escalation of shock on both sides of the conflict was involved, creating one of the situations in which both the imagination and practical actions push beyond previous horizons. At this time also the wife of the then Palestian leader, Yasir Arafat, speaking from Paris, was reported as saying that if she had a son she would be honoured to sacrifice him for the Palestinian cause (*New York Times*, Monday, 15 April 2002, International Section, p. A11). A scholar at the University of Cairo was also reported in the same newspaper article as declaring that such 'martydrom operations' were the 'highest form of jihad operations' (ibid.) and should be regarded as an 'Islamic commandment'.

A senior fellow at the Council of Foreign Relations involved in promoting Arab–Israeli peace, Henry Siegman, was reported to say, 'I fear that for the Israelis and Palestinians the goal is no longer security or the creation of a state but vengeance' (ibid.). These exchanges indicate that while shock is expressed on both sides, the cultural imaginary works within a number of primordial-sounding concepts, applied situationally: sovereignty, the right to land, aggression, occupation, martyrdom, and in the bluntest of terms, vengeance. More than a year after these reports, with the problem of suicide bombing continuing, a commentary section in the *New York Times*, Week in Review, Sunday, 24 August 2003, was headed 'The Terror Industry Fields Its Ultimate Weapon', that is, the suicide bomber, pointing out that 'of the terrorism industry's two raw materials – bombs and people – people are far easier to come by'. An economic argument is thus applied to the routinization of the practice. The same article, however, also remarks on the 'element of surprise that has an incredible and devastating shock value'. This article also notes that in Iran over a century ago a group known as the Assassins became notorious for stabbing political figures at close range, virtually ensuring their own death.

The production of mental and visual images is an integral part of the reproduction of violence. The circulation of images is itself a device for strengthening a particular view of what 'order in the world' should be and can function as an instrument for the use of violence in pursuit of such an order: an order that is discursively projected and legitimized in cosmological terms. An extensive discussion of this theme as a whole has been given by Mark Juergensmeyer (2000, e.g. chs 1 and 4). Juergensmeyer provides a striking quotation from Mahmud Abouhalima, an associate of Sheik Omar Abdul Rahman, with whom he spoke in 1997 while Abouhalima was on a lifetime sentence in a federal jail in the US. Abouhalima compared a life without religion to a pen without ink (Juergensmeyer 2000: 69).

Juergensmeyer further notes the words of the Egyptian Abd al-Salam Faraj, author of a pamphlet 'The Neglected Duty' dating from the 1980s, who grounds the activities 'of modern Islamic terrorists firmly in Islamic tradition', and argues that the Qur'an is 'fundamentally about warfare. The concept of *jihad*, struggle, was meant to be taken literally, not allegorically' and 'the true soldier of Islam is allowed to use virtually any means available to achieve a just goal' (Juergensmeyer 2000: 81). This kind of scheme of thought is replicated repeatedly throughout Juergensmeyer's case histories dealing with various religions, sects, and geographical locales. The pervasive use of military terminology is also shared by Christian and Islamic adherents alike, for example in the Christian imagery of 'Onward Christian Soldiers', as Juergensmeyer points out (Juergensmeyer 2000, ch. 2).

It is interesting to note here how often the globalized struggles involving religious imagery are intertwined with the secular equivalent of a religious ideal, the nation-state. Palestine comes to have a synecdochal position in this regard for other struggles. Insurgents struggle for 'freedom', citing larger religious imperatives such as the 'will of God'. Conversely, state authorities may use the same expressions to justify their own coercive actions.

Resonating with Michael Taussig's well-known work on terror and 'epistemic murk' (Taussig 1987), Monique Skidmore has discussed fear, vulnerability, and terror-making in urban Burma (Myanmar) (Skidmore 2003; see also Campbell and Brenner (eds) 2000 on 'death squads'; and Sluka 1999). One of Skidmore's concerns is how the state forces deliberately instil fear as a part of their policies of control, thereby routinizing it in people's everyday lives. A concomitant of this process in people's responses is an element that corroborates our own emphasis on rumour and gossip: in a set of liminal circumstances during Skidmore's fieldwork, the city of 'Rangoon was ablaze with rumors' (p. 6). The military government claimed control over both 'culture' and 'progress', and reinforced its presence with spectacles of weapons and troops, urging 'vigilance' on the part of the people against outsiders who might 'interfere' with the internal affairs of the nation. The state is therefore heavily involved in a construction of public affect (p. 8), founded on fear.

Fear is not just something immediate, but has a temporal aspect, relating to the future (p. 10), and preventing people from imagining any future other than their subjugation to the military state (ibid.). One expression used by people appealed to an image of a small stream of water released from a hole in a rock, referring to 'a tiny release of fear' that emerged not 'as a result of anything physical or from an actual event, but rather from thinking – from the mind' (p. 11).

People mostly kept their fears to themselves, because government informers were said to be everywhere, and any expression could lead to their arrest, detention, and interrogation (ibid.).

Skidmore continues by pointing out that much news is government propaganda and knowledge of government actions is important, so that rumours flourish, allowing people a space in which to speculate, 'to gamble on courses of action, to assess options, and to weigh probabilities' (p. 13). Rumour 'presents an impression of clarity' (ibid.). It helps people make sense of their lives in the city, and because it is a matter of public circulation about others, not oneself, it is more safe than personal narrative. With stories about the arrests of dissidents, 'it is, however, also a carrier of terror' (ibid.). People feel 'crushed' (p. 15), and 'vulnerable' (p. 16). When the military visit a house, they make an inventory of all its contents, and then take the occupants away in a prison van (p. 18). People lose expectations because they do not know what to expect. No future can be imagined. To express all this, Skidmore quotes an old Burmese proverb: 'What is darker than midnight?' (p. 19).

Studies such as Skidmore's raise many questions about the inchoate character of various dangers and also the implications of fieldwork itself in dangerous places, also examined in the collection *Fieldwork Under Fire* (eds Nordstrom and Robbens 1995), on which Skidmore draws in her own account. Danny Hoffman has examined the problems of 'frontline anthropology research in a time of war' (Hoffman 2003); and Murray Wax and Hugh Gusterson have discussed the question of anthropological work and military intelligence (Wax and Gusterson 2003). For our purposes here, it is the analysis of how state governments may induce terror not only by their actions but by propaganda and the creation of dysphoric affect that is of interest. The same may be said of insurgency movements that seek to topple governments.

The Burmese military appear to have incorporated State Buddhism into their programme, although Skidmore does not emphasize this point. Elsewhere, with the aim of legitimizing acts of violence, both state authorities and those who oppose them frequently invoke an image of God. David Domke, among many other political commentators, has pointed to the importance of the invocation of God and of the image of 'good' and 'evil' in the discourse of the George W. Bush Administration in the US, entitling his book on this topic *God Willing?* (Domke 2004; see also Kaplan 2004). In Iraq, although there was a large turnout for the vote for a new government on 30 January 2005, some Shi'ites pointed to the fact that their local religious leaders had not told them to vote: 'God willing, I will not be voting,' one man said (*New York Times*, Saturday, 29 January 2005, A1). God, via their clerics, was for these Iraqi citizens the ultimate arbiter of what they should do. It is particularly notable that the opposed sides in an escalating conflict may employ similar rhetorical tropes involving religion, but in contradiction with each other.

Osama bin Laden's speech of Monday, 1 November 2004 illustrates this observation clearly. He begins with 'Praise be to Allah who created the creation for his worship and commanded them to be just and permitted the wronged one to retaliate against the oppressor in kind . . . security is an indispensable pillar of human life . . . and free men do not forget their security . . . We want to restore freedom to our nation, just as you lay waste to our nation. So shall we lay waste to yours' (www.scoop.co.nz/mason/stories/WO0411/S00034.htm).

Here we see that the words of bin Laden are ones that appeal to a similar narrative of 'value of freedom' and the imperative of retribution that has formed the leitmotiv of the agents of action and policy since 9/11 in countries such as the US.

Magnus Ranstorp has surveyed the trends in recent years of religious terrorism, based initially on his studies of the Hezbollah and Hamas organizations, and he points out how such movements combine a framework of religious ideology with practical and precise political action in Lebanon and Palestine (Ranstorp 1996). Again, exactly the same observation holds for many governments whose leaders invoke both rational planning and religious justifications for their actions. Competing imaginations that invoke similar claims to a 'moral order' or 'human values', or appear to do so, can lead to the most intractable of contests, since they are essentially claiming exclusive possession of the same ideological 'turf', which implies a zero-sum situation of prospective winner takes all.

THE CHAPTERS IN THIS COLLECTION

The chapters in this book, all based on careful ethnography, make nuanced use of the basic ideas that have formed the foundation of our project here and which we have expanded somewhat in our introductory remarks above. In multiple and overlapping ways these chapters draw attention to a variety of themes that emerge from our stress on rumours, imagination, cosmology (and demonology, as Neil Whitehead puts it in Chapter 6), state violence and the relevance of ideas regarding sorcery and witchcraft to the ontogenesis of terror generally.

The chapters explore themes that link violence, terror, and the imagination together in a wide variety of settings around the world: Africa, Greece, India, Fiji, Ireland, Guyana, and Indonesia. Each author brings a particular perspective to bear on general questions of what constitutes terror, what are its roots and its results, and what parts it plays in human experience and history, with special reference to the effects of the imagination in its dialectical relationship with experience. While psychological processes as such are not at the forefront of the topics explored in most of the papers, we recognize that an integrated perspective must take such processes into account, and the final paper in this volume, by Michele Stephen, boldly tackles this difficult question with the aid of Kleinian theory.

We have arranged the chapters both thematically and with reference to geographical areas. The first chapter, by Misty Bastian (Chapter 1) considers a less well-known counterpoint of the 9/11 attack on the World Trade Center: the violent conflictual responses to the event generated in Kano, Nigeria. Bastian also argues that the concept of terrorism has been used to play on the imagination at a global level and to fight terror with terror, perhaps with the aim of reconstituting and revalidating moral worlds. The risk involved here, Bastian argues, is that violence takes the centrestage of action whichever side one is on and the concept of terror loses its specificity. Chapter 2, by Elisabeth Kirtsoglou, shifts us from Africa to Athens, in Greece, where Kirtsoglou, like Bastian, takes up the question of local consequences and local discourses following from 9/11. Greek responses in Athens were conditioned by the country's own turbulent political history and in particular by narratives of the 1975 assassination of a British army officer by the terrorist organization known as 17th of November. Cynicism and suspicion of government versions of events mark the urban Greek political consciousness here, and stories of conspiracies and cover-ups allow people to feel that they have their own imagined interpretations of world political events. Similar forms of consciousness emerge in Britain, the US, and elsewhere whenever scepticism regarding government actions prevails.

Both of these chapters reveal the importance of currents of rumour running through communities and their potentials for creating violence, as well as the globalization of violent media images and the ambiguities involved in the concept of the 'war on terror'. Bastian stresses the fragmenting impact of events on collective memory, and the ideological skewing of memory that results from this. She also shows how the response to news of 9/11 was influenced by aspects of local histories that occurred long before 9/11 itself. This is an example of how selective aspects of the past may invade and recolonize the present in a time of crisis, fluidity, and liminality.

Searching for meanings, people find these in templates that belong to their own symbolic repertoire of historical images and experiences, making what is discontinuous in some ways seem continuous in others. Bastian also illustrates the mimetic mirrorings in the mutual use of the term 'terrorist' by opposing sides in disputes that engendered clashes between Christian and Muslim populations. In such a situation a dialectic emerges in which each side elicits

and feeds off the statements and suspicions of the other, leading
to the possibility of an escalation into overt violence. All this is in
accordance with the processual models we developed in our 2004
book on witchcraft (Stewart and Strathern 2004). It corresponds, in
a context outside witchcraft itself, to processes that have occurred
in parts of Africa and elsewhere, leading to modern witch-hunts and
witch-killings. Bastian's own further reflections on the situation in
Kano are sombre. She wonders if the universal use of the epithet
'terrorist' leads to a view of the world as a space of ineluctable
violence. This is the 'horror' that Kearney, in the article cited earlier,
tries to combat (Kearney 2003).

Kirtsoglou's chapter shows the particular twist that imaginative
rumour can take in a context where there is suspicion and distrust of
government and its imputed transnational connections, in this case
between urban Athenians in Greece, their government, and images of
the US. Kirtsoglou also shows how perceptions of earlier Greek terrorist
activities undertaken by or attributed to the 17th of November group
influenced responses to 9/11. As other commentators on Greece
(Herzfeld 1987) have noted, she remarks on the ambivalent feelings
of peripheral inclusion versus exclusion that Greeks in general feel
with regard to the larger region of Europe and the world-order beyond
it. Kirtsoglou argues that rumours of conspiracies on the part of
greater powers are a part of the way Athenians try to negotiate their
own senses of identity and citizenship: in other words, how they
try to imagine and reimagine themselves in old and new contexts
of violence and state authority.

Chapter 3, by Joyce Pettigrew, further takes up the problematic
questions of state violence and definitions of terror in relation to India
and the treatment of Sikh citizens in the Punjab. Her focus is on police
violence and the problems of living with the experience of violence
on a regular basis. Pettigrew defines terror succinctly as 'organized
political crime'. If so, it is crime that is structured by particular
conflicting imagined definitions of the nation and the state.

Chapters 4 and 5, by Susanna Trnka, and by Pamela J. Stewart and
Andrew Strathern, respectively, examine further contexts of divided
states and communities in which episodes of political violence have
affected the way people perceive their world. Trnka's chapter deals
with the attempted political coup in Fiji in May 2000, in which
George Speight, a Fijian businessman with financial problems, played
a central part, for which he was later imprisoned. The attempt by
Speight to take over the government reopened old divisions between
Fiji's Pacific Islander population and the Indo-Fijians originally
brought to Fiji by the British colonial government to work on sugar
plantations. Indo-Fijians later became prominent in business and
in agricultural enterprises, while native Fijians retained control of

land ownership and the modified chiefly structure of their own society. Speight's coup attempt was intended *inter alia* to stop the Indo-Fijian-controlled government of Prime Minister Mahendra Chaudhry from changing the rules of land ownership. Following it, urban areas became staging grounds for the mass looting of Indo-Fijian owned shops and businesses, while in rural areas disaffected native Fijians physically attacked Indo-Fijians in settlements and villages. Trnka's chapter traces how perceptions and fears between these two categories of people changed over time during the conflict, influenced by their imaginative constructions.

Stewart and Strathern similarly explore narratives of conflict in the divided society of Northern Ireland, adding a discussion of ways in which organizations have been developed with the aim of ameliorating conflict between categories of people labelled as Protestants or as Catholics. Divisions whose roots go back to the seventeenth century and the colonization of Ulster, but which have emerged very sharply since the partition of Ireland in 1920 and the violence known as 'the Troubles' dating from around 1968, plague the most recent peace process instituted since 1998 with the Good Friday Agreement in Belfast between the British and the Irish governments. Stewart and Strathern's discussion shows how narratives are founded both on the immediacies of experience and on the categorical background senses of identity that belong to the political imagination, an imagination that is responsive to change in some ways but locked into a particular set of presuppositions on the other.

'Divided societies' is how one could describe Fiji, Ireland, and India, in very broad terms. Within India, the Sikhs are a special case, an interstitial group left without anchoring by the Partition of India in 1947 (compare the 1921 'Partition of Ulster'). Sikh separatism resulted from the Sikhs having no particular area of their own within the divided area of the Punjab, and this led to the Sikhs' attempt to declare a separate state for themselves in 1986, met by continuing counter-insurgency responses by the Indian state authorities. A 'war of terror against terror', in Misty Bastian's terms, thus seems inevitable and is perpetuated by the narrative creation of collective memory, as much a work of the political imaginary as a historical record, although based on actual atrocities and punishments. The chapter overall vividly shows the effect of imagination in the interpretations people placed on events, based on their hopes, fears, and suspicions.

Fiji, with its post-colonial legacy of the separation between indigenous Pacific Islanders during colonial times and the Indians as workers on sugar-cane plantations, provides another breeding ground for the development of rumours, suspicions, and physical violence. The ambiguous position of government police in the upheaval caused by George Speight's coup attempt is one theme that emerges from

Trnka's nuanced account. Another is the rapid spread of narratives (= rumours, gossip) as people moved about and tried to understand events. Ambivalent perceptions of 'others' also emerged in the liminal time of the coup. Seen from the perceptions of the Indo-Fijians, who could not own land but often had a higher socio-economic class than their indigenous Fijian neighbours, Trnka's chapter indicates that the transformation, or escalation, of local disputes into ethno-nationalist ones was not absolute. The experience of people at local levels led them to balance, or try to balance, contradictory images of 'others' as either hostile or friendly. Local experience can thus enter into 'the imaginary' and help to modify the march to violence.

Northern Ireland, and the wider historical region of Ulster to which it essentially belongs, contains similar complexities of perception. In our chapter we approach some of these complexities via narrative forms that we encountered in our fieldwork. Our chapter considers and contextualizes three forms of narratives in the fractured identity politics of North–South and Protestant–Catholic relations in Ireland. The first 'form' is that of narratives of *bombing* and being 'blown up'. We discuss here an account of the bombing in Claudy in the 1970s and another of the Omagh bombing in the 1990s. The first account is highly personal, but is framed by political values and assumptions. The second is also personal but, stemming from a later period of history, it carries a different set of political messages.

The second 'form' encompasses narratives of *burning*: the burning of large bonfires at times of Protestant celebrations and the retaliatory burnings of Protestant-related buildings around the time of the 'marching season', primarily 12 July with its celebration of William, Prince of Orange's, victory over James II at the battle of the Boyne in 1690. We give an example of an event in County Donegal, just across the border from Northern Ireland, in July 2003, and the interpretations people placed on it. Here political and personal interpretations were at odds with one another, depending on how people wished the issue to be imagined by the community at large.

The third form of narrative has to do with *borders*, and stories of violence that takes place across them. These stories are highly prevalent in the context of North–South relations. We contrast here the narratives of which we have knowledge in County Fermanagh with those we know from County Donegal, and interpret these again as representing different imagined positionalities within the overall context of conflict and peace-making. The Fermanagh stories stress violence, murder, and 'ethnic cleansing'. The Donegal stories stress the nostalgia for Ulster balanced against cross-border initiatives for peace centred on a celebration of the newly reconstructed Ulster-Scots identity. The Ulster-Scots movement quintessentially demonstrates the significance of the reimagining of political space that often accompanies attempts to redefine conditions of conflict and peace-making in divided circumstances.

At the back of people's minds the memory of the time of the Troubles endures, as a kind of screen through which experience is filtered, whether consciously or not. One couple with whom we spoke in Belfast during June 2004 told us, among other things, of their fears when a British Army/Police Land Rover vehicle came to their doorway one night. Their son was out, and they were afraid that the authorities had found him dead. Fortunately, he had been discovered unconscious by the roadside and the police had rescued him and brought him home. The arrival of a Land Rover at one's doorway was proverbial, the couple told us, almost always portending the announcement of a violent death. The example shows the pervasiveness of fear in so many of the contexts that we and other authors examine in this volume. Fear, like hatred, or a desire for revenge, can take over the whole mind and body, and memories of such a syndrome become deeply embodied within people. We cite this case to show the point (and also because it is among the minority of stories we heard with a sense of relief rather than horror in its ending). Our narratives also include episodes that indicate mixed feelings of hostility and alliance between people on opposite sides of conflicts.

Chapters 6 and 7 explore questions of the imagination and the roots of violence in depth, with implications for both ethnography and psychology. Neil Whitehead's chapter (6) delves deeply into Guyanese history as a means of explaining entrenched notions regarding *kanaimà* sorcery, which requires that victims be maimed in order to transform them into a kind of divine food. The image of *kanaimà* as a practice has changed over time. It was used by colonial explorers and missionaries to constitute the local people as 'savages', obstacles to progress. Whitehead strikingly calls this a demonology of development, compounded also by ideas about cannibalism. Later, it came to be viewed as a kind of ritual of revenge. Most recently it has become a vehicle for discourses about indigeneity and resistance to the exploitative features of 'modernity'. Throughout these transformations, the imaginative fascination exerted by *kanaimà* as an image of occult violence has ensured the persistence of ideas regarding it.

Michele Stephen's exploration (Chapter 7) into the depths of Balinese notions of witchcraft parallels Whitehead's exploration of *kanaimà* sorcery; but whereas Whitehead's treatment is primarily historical, with some psychological overtones, Stephen's approach is psychological, but grounded also in Balinese mythology and history generally. Uniquely among the chapters in the volume, Stephen applies the psychology of Melanie Klein, centred on the image of the mother with its good and bad aspects, both to Balinese ideas regarding female witchcraft and the goddess Rangnda/Durga, and to notions regarding terrorism in contemporary world politics. Her argument provides a fittingly challenging final component to the chapters in our volume.

Both of these concluding chapters can be seen as explorations into aspects of the psychology of violence and its representations in popular and specialist discourse. Their handling of this topic differs somewhat. Whitehead concentrates on history, without skirting the details of the imagery of assault sorcery among the Patamuna. He shows both the persistent power of occult images and the mutability of their political and social interpretations over time (see our comparative reprise of his analyses and our materials from New Guinea, above).

Guyana, like the remote settlement we discuss from the Pangia area in New Guinea, becomes, in Whitehead's own terms, 'the end point of exploration, the counter point of modernity and the obstacle of development . . . In this way *kanaimà* becomes the metaphoric equivalent of the Conradian "heart of darkness" . . . veritably a land of mystical terror and savage violence' (from Whitehead's chapter, this volume).

Michele Stephen also deals uncompromisingly with horror and its limits. Her touchstone, however, is not history (or historicity) but the psychoanalytical work of Melanie Klein. She draws on the idea that the psyche seeks to repair emotional damages by means of 'reparations', so that it can maintain its 'good objects', its feelings of self-worth. Violence is prevalent, revenge is important, but reparation takes place as well. Beyond the imagination of violence, and the unimaginable lengths to which it seemingly can go, there is the imagination of making amends, according to Klein. Stephen argues, in turn, that imagined figures of terror in Bali result (in accordance with Melanie Klein's theories) from infantile rage against the 'terrible mother', and also produce accusations of witchcraft (mostly) against women.

Pursuing links between these arguments and the issues of terrorism, Stephen, drawing on our own work on witchcraft and sorcery, proposes that:

the theme of bodily invasion . . . provides a link between imaginary violence and modern terrorism. Threats from an external enemy that can be identified and acted against by conventional military means are one thing, but when attacked by unknown assassins who have invisibly penetrated the interior of the body politic, then the likelihood of provoking the most primitive levels of paranoid fears and defences seems obvious. The terrorist throwing bombs and poison gas becomes the infant attacking the parental imago with explosive faeces and poisonous urine – and expecting terrible vengeance in return. Both victims and aggressors are thrown back into the paranoid schizoid position of early childhood in their extreme emotional responses. The task of controlling or breaking the cycle of violence and the need for revenge is thus even more difficult to achieve than in conventional, even nuclear, warfare.

Yet if this is so, a Kleinian perspective on human aggression indicates that although such is inherent in the human psyche, so also is the urge to repair and make good the damage done. We need to find the cultural means to make reparation, and thereby confront and deal with our own persecutory fears and guilt.

When on 12 October 2002 terrorist bombs killed over 200 people in Kuta, a tourist district in Bali, the Balinese response was not to seek revenge or to give way to despair. Instead, after an appropriate interval, Balinese performed a series of *caru* rituals. Such rituals (of which there are many levels) are, as described earlier, directed to transforming the dangerous and disruptive forces in the world generated by the goddess Durga and her spouse, Kala Rudra, back to their pure and benign forms. Some might object that such actions can have no effect on terrorists, and I could not dispute this, but for the Balinese who had experienced the horror, the rituals served an important psychological need, preventing an escalation of paranoid fears and helping people to begin the difficult psychic process of restoring their good inner objects and rebuilding their inner world through making reparation. (Stephen, Chapter 7, this volume).

A challenging conclusion to Stephen's chapter and to the individual case-study chapters in our book, this idea of 'reparation' as a fundamental human act in counterpoint to 'violence' suggests the imaginative vistas that many people seek.

REFERENCES

Aijmer, Göran (2000) 'Introduction: The Idiom of Violence in Imagery and Discourse'. In *Meanings of Violence: A Cross-Cultural Perspective*, ed. G. Aijmer and J. Abbink. Oxford and New York: Berg, pp. 1–22.

Anderson, Benedict (1991) (rev. edn) *Imagined Communities. Reflections on the Origins and Spread of Nationalism*. London and New York: Verso.

Appadurai, Arjun (1996) *Modernity at Large. Cultural Dimensions of Globalization*. Minneapolis and London: University of Minnesota Press.

Bourdieu, Pierre (1977) *Outline of a Theory of Practice*, transl. by Richard Nice. Cambridge: Cambridge University Press.

Bouroncle, Alberto (2000) 'Ritual, Violence and Social Order: An Approach to Spanish Bullfighting'. In *Meanings of Violence*, ed. G. Aijmer and J. Abbink. Oxford and New York: Berg, pp. 55–76.

Campbell, Bruce B. and Arthur D. Brenner (eds) (2000) *Death Squads in Global Pespective: Murder with Deniability*. New York: St Martin's Press.

Comaroff, John and Jean Comaroff (1992) *Ethnography and the Historical Imagination*. Boulder: Westview Press.

Crapanzano, Vincent (2004) *Imaginative Horizons. An Essay in Literary-Philosophical Anthropology*. Chicago: University of Chicago Press.

Danner, Mark (2005) *Torture and Truth: America, Abu Ghraib and the War on Terror*. New York: New York Review Books.

Domke, David (2004) *God Willing? Political Fundamentalism in the White House, the War on Terror, and the Echoing Press*. London and Ann Arbor, MI: Pluto Press.

Gray, J.H. (1972) (1878) *China: A History of the Laws, Manners and Customs of the People*, 2 vols. Shannon Island: Irish University Press.

Herzfeld, Michael (1987) *Anthropology through the Looking Glass: Critical Ethnography in the Margins of Europe*. Cambridge: Cambridge University Press.

Ho, Virgil Kit-yiu (2000) 'Butchering Fish and Executing Criminals: Public Executions and the Meanings of Violence in Late Imperial and Modern China'. In *Meanings of Violence*, ed. G. Aijmer and J. Abbink. Oxford and New York: Berg, pp. 141–60.

Hoffman, Danny (2003) 'Frontline Anthropology: Research in a Time of War', *Anthropology Today*, 19(3): 9–12.

Juergensmeyer, Mark (2000) *Terror in the Mind of God. The Global Rise of Religious Violence*. Berkeley: University of California Press.

Kaplan, Esther (2004) *With God on Their Side*. London and New York: The New Press.

Kean, Thomas H. et al. (n.d.) *The 9/11 Commission Report: Final Report of the National Commission on Terrorist Attacks Upon the United States, Authorized Edition*. New York and London: W.W. Norton & Co.

Kearney, Richard (2003) 'Terror, Philosophy and the Sublime: Some Philosophical Reflections on 11 September', *Philosophy and Social Criticism*, 29(1): 23–51.

Laqueur, Walter (1987) *The Age of Terrorism*. Boston: Little, Brown.

Malkki, Liisa H. (1995) *Purity and Exile. Violence, Memory, and National Cosmology among Hutu Refugees in Tanzania*. Chicago: University of Chicago Press.

Martin, Garry (1986) 'Honour, Integrity and the Problem of Violence in the Spanish Bullfight'. In *The Anthropology of Violence*, ed. D. Riches. Oxford: Basil Blackwell, pp. 118–35.

Nordstrom, Carolyn and Antonius C.G.M. Robbens (eds) (1995) *Fieldwork under Fire: Contemporary Studies of Violence and Survival*. Berkeley: University of California Press.

Orbach, Israel (2004) 'Terror Suicide: How is it Possible?', *Archives of Suicide Research*, 8(1): 115–30.

Ranstorp, Magnus (1996) 'Terrorism in the Name of Religion', *Journal of International Affairs*, 50(1): 1–9.

Rapoport, David C. (1988) *Inside Terrorist Organizations*. New York: Columbia University Press.

Reuter, Christoph (2004) *My Life is a Weapon. A Modern History of Suicide Bombing*. Princeton: Princeton University Press.

Riches, D. (ed.) (1986) *The Anthropology of Violence*. Oxford: Basil Blackwell.

Schröder, Ingo W. and Bettina E. Schmidt (2001) 'Introduction: Violent Imaginaries and Violent Practices'. In *Anthropology of Violence and Conflict*, ed. B.E. Schmidt and I.W. Shröder. London and New York: Routledge, pp. 1–24.

Skidmore, Monique (2003) 'Darker than Midnight: Fear, Vulnerability, and Terror Making in Urban Burma (Myanmar)', *American Ethnologist*, 30(1): 5–21.

Sluka, Jeffrey (ed.) (1999) *Death Squad: The Anthropology of State Terror*. Philadelphia: University of Pennsylvania Press.

Sontag, Susan (2003) *Regarding the Pain of Others*. New York: Farrar, Straus, & Giraux.

Stewart, Pamela J. (1998) 'Ritual Trackways and Sacred Paths of Fertility'. In *Perspectives on the Bird's Head of Irian Jaya, Indonesia*, ed. J. Miedema, C. Odé and R.A.C. Dam. Amsterdam: Rodopi, pp. 275–90.

Stewart, Pamela J. and Andrew Strathern (1999) '"Feasting on my enemy": Images of violence and change in the New Guinea Highlands', *Ethnohistory*, 46(4): 645–69.

—— (eds) (2000) *Millennial Countdown in New Guinea*. Special Issue of *Ethnology*, 47(1) (Durham, NC: Duke University Press).

—— (2002a) *Violence: Theory and Ethnography*. London and New York: Continuum.

—— (2002b) *Remaking the World. Myth, Mining, and Ritual Change among the Duna of Papua New Guinea*, Smithsonian Series in Ethnographic Inquiry. Washington, DC, and London: Smithsonian Institution Press.

—— (2004) *Witchcraft, Sorcery, Rumors, and Gossip*, New Departures in Anthropology Series, no. 1. Cambridge: Cambridge University Press.

Strathern, Andrew and Pamela J. Stewart (2000) *Collaborations and Conflicts: A Leader through Time*. Fort Worth, TX: Harcourt College Publishers.

—— (2004a) 'Violence: Conceptual Themes and the Evaluation of Actions'. Special Issue, 'The Meanings of Violence and the Violence of Meanings', *Polylog* 5 (electronic journal, http://them.polylog.org/5/fss-en.htm)

—— (2004b) 'Afterword: Substances, Powers, Cosmos, and History'. In *In Darkness and Secrecy: The Anthropology of Assault Sorcery and Witchcraft in Amazonia*, ed. N.L. Whitehead and R. Wright. Durham, NC: Duke University Press, pp. 314–20.

Taussig, Michael (1987) *Shamanism, Colonialism and the Wild Man: A Study in Terror and Healing*. Chicago: University of Chicago Press.

Taylor, Christopher C. (1999) *Sacrifice as Terror. The Rwandan Genocide of 1994*. Oxford and New York: Berg.

Wax, Murray and Hugh Gusterson (2003) 'Defending the Nation? Ethics and Anthropology after 9/11', *Anthropology Today*, 19(3): 23–6.

Whitehead, Neil L. (2002) *Dark Shamans: Kanaimà and the Poetics of Violent Death*. Durham, NC and London: Duke University Press.

Whitehead, Neil L. and Robin Wright (eds) (2004) *In Darkness and Secrecy: The Anthropology of Assault Sorcery and Witchcraft in Amazonia*. Durham, NC and London: Duke University Press.

Wilkinson, Paul and A.M. Stewart (eds) (1987) *Contemporary Research on Terrorism*. Aberdeen: Aberdeen University Press.

1 'TERROR AGAINST TERROR': 9/11 OR 'KANO WAR' IN THE NIGERIAN ELECTRONIC PRESS?

Misty L. Bastian

DATES IN (AND OUT OF) OUR COLLECTIVE MEMORY

There are deep continuities with the past, despite the claim that September 11 represented a major historical rupture both because the United States was attacked and because it announced merely the beginning of a campaign of terrorism that fundamentally threatens global well-being.

(Lutz 2002: 731)

September 11, 2001 is now a date in our collective memory, but who knows tomorrow?

(from a Nigerian editorial commemorating 9/11, 2001; Anonymous 2002)

As most media-connected people in the world know, on 11 September 2001, in the commercial heart of one of the most powerful of global centres, New York City, two commandeered jetliners crashed into the twin towers of the World Trade Center. Just over 2,000 people died as the towers collapsed, while more thousands barely escaped and hundreds were injured as they ran away from the site of the devastation. At roughly the same time, almost 200 military and civilian workers at the Pentagon in Washington, DC also lost their lives when a third commercial jet dived into the side of their well-fortified building. Yet more people died on a fourth flight that crashed during what we are now told was a struggle between passengers and hijackers over rural Pennsylvania. Almost simultaneously powerful members of the US government and North American media pundits proclaimed these tragic events an 'Attack on America' and began to speculate about the identity or identities of those responsible, who were denounced as terrorists and madmen.

Before night fell on 11 September, people in the US were being assured that this was the day that 'everything changed'. By 12 September plans were clearly underway not only to attempt to rescue

40

whoever was alive in what remained of the three destroyed buildings but also to move towards a more militarized or, depending on one's ideological stance, a more secure 'homeland'. Throughout the North American media during the weeks following what became known simply as '9/11', working-class men in dangerous jobs were lionized – not insignificantly the very class of men who would a short time later be expected to make up the bulk of the newly marshalled fighting force for the country – and women of all classes, but particularly those of the Euro-American middle class, were portrayed as suffering but stoic wives (now widows) and mothers of the 'heroes of September 11th'.[1]

Attention in the US, never very international in its scope, became fixed on internal damage and the moralizing rhetoric of retribution against those perceived as 'against us'. This discourse of alterity quickly fastened itself onto the Muslim world in general and to one 'terrorist mastermind' in particular, the wealthy Saudi militant Osama bin Laden. Again, as the world is all too well aware, the US began a campaign 'to crush bin Laden and his Al Qaeda organization' – which manifested itself in the subsequent, officially undeclared but nonetheless brutal war in Afghanistan. Finally, the Taliban regime of Afghanistan was officially ousted from power, but the whereabouts and ultimate fates of Taliban leader Mullah Omar, bin Laden and several of his key lieutenants remain a mystery over two years later.[2]

As fewer people in the world know – because, even when it was covered in the global press, it was as a strictly 'local' event – on 13 October 2001, in the commercial heart of the northern region of one of the United States' allies and peripheral trading partners, Kano, Nigeria, hundreds of *'yan daba*[3] (ethnically Hausa) Muslims marched through the streets around the city's Sabon Gari (foreign quarter), singing the praises of Allah, holding up posters decorated with the image of Osama bin Laden and, according to some reports, brandishing machetes.[4] This, in turn, led to violent confrontations between the bands of *'yan daba* and their young, southern Nigerian Christian counterparts (mostly Igbo but including a smattering of Yoruba-speaking youth) who came out of Sabon Gari to 'defend' their territory.[5] Shops were looted and burned, as were local offices of national media houses, and mosques as well as churches were wrecked. Both the police and the armed forces stationed in Kano were called out to deal with the rioters. These official, government-sanctioned 'peacekeepers' felt no compunction about using live ammunition against people they found on the streets, although they later claimed that they tried tear gas first and found it ineffectual (Musa 2001a). The violence was not completely quelled until the 14th, or thereabouts, and scattered incidents of trouble between inhabitants of Sabon Gari and other sections of Kano continued well into the next year.

A couple of years after what some Nigerians called the 'Kano War', the death toll from the incident remains in dispute but has been placed unofficially at around 200. Nigerians are sceptical about that number, however, since they are aware of the federal government's desire to downplay what occurred in Kano that weekend – particularly as it followed hard on the heels of another, even deadlier moment of urban unrest in Jos (a city to the south of Kano with a large population of both Christians and Muslims). To many southern Nigerians, the events of 13 October, alongside the pre-9/11 carnage in Jos, represent yet another example of what they like to call 'Muslim extremism' in the northern states.[6] Because of the supposedly local character of the events, then, it is necessary to give a more detailed description of the 'Kano War' (or 'Kano Riots') than I have above of the events that have been abbreviated in global discourse simply as '9/11'. In the following description, I will attempt to demonstrate how the supposedly local was necessarily entangled with the global from its beginning.

THE 'KANO WAR': HOMEGROWN HEROES OR HOMEGROWN TERRORISTS?

On Friday, 12 October 2001, after Jama'at prayers in Kano, the one-month anniversary of the fall of New York's 'twin towers' was commemorated by a series of rousing sermons from Hausa Shi'ite scholars, some of whom may or may not have used the term jihad (in this instance, meaning a disposition towards holy war) to describe the state of local Muslim discontent with a perceived southern, Christian Nigerian disrespect for Shari'a law.[7] It seems clear from published reports and interviews with participants given directly after the 'war' that the immediate American judgment of Osama bin Laden's guilt was used by these *mallams* as an example of Christian hypocrisy and wrongful power in the world. There were certainly specific remarks in the sermons aimed at how such Christian hypocrisy was currently manifesting itself even in Kano, historically one of the most Muslim of Nigerian cities.[8]

According to most of the Nigerian media, northern and southern, the march that took place on Saturday, the 13th, following people's overnight consideration of the sermons, was meant to be a peaceful assembly – more along the lines of a demonstration of support for the Muslims' Afghani brothers-in-religion than the beginning of jihad itself in the city. However, a quarrel of some sort between Hausa Muslims and Igbo Christians near the Sabon Gari Market, and the rumour that Muslims were fleeing from the Sabon Gari quarter in fear of their lives, energized the *'yan daba* marchers and brought them into the vicinity of Sabon Gari, carrying weapons. There they were met by youthful, male inhabitants of the quarter who, having heard of the proximity of *'yan daba*, had picked up their own weaponry and were prepared to fight. By the evening of the 13th, a number of churches and mosques, along with places of business, media houses, private residences and automobiles, were charred ruins; over one hundred people were officially considered to be dead or missing; hundreds more were being treated for their wounds or were hiding in Sabon Gari police stations and the nearby army barracks.

In the next couple of days, Nigerian President Olasegun Obasanjo, speaking from Paris, where he had gone on a diplomatic trip, would declare, 'I don't worry'[9] about the violence and would return at his leisure to tour Sabon Gari on foot and ringed by bodyguards: not because he was also generally 'unworried' about the mood of his constituents, but because his bulletproofed vehicle had a flat tyre. In Sabon Gari Obasanjo talked with looted businessmen, religious leaders and refugees from the 'war'. He would also find himself on at least one occasion surrounded by a large and indignant Igbo-speaking group who chanted, 'Give us Biafra!' and other, anti-federal government slogans.[10] Directly replicating some of the North American discourse around 9/11, Nigerian media would dub those people who sheltered others of a different ethnicity during the riots the 'heroes of October 13th', while the *'yan daba* were stigmatized as homegrown 'terrorists' in the largely Christian south while being represented mainly as 'undesirable elements', 'street hooligans', or 'unemployed youths' in the Muslim north.[11] Northern media also explicitly included the Christian inhabitants of Sabon Gari in their discussion of hooliganism, sometimes passing over any suggestion that Muslims had initiated the violence. Southern media initially heaped blame on both camps but soon came to a more defensive posture and identified most of the 'terrorists' with a particular religion, Islam, and most of the 'heroes' with another, Christianity.

During the time that has passed since both 11 September and 13 October 2001, these initial discursive tropes have grown even more complicated as different segments of the Nigerian population have reacted to the outcome of the US invasion of Afghanistan and the subsequent war with Iraq. There are also deepening tensions between northern and southern Nigeria over the continued implementation of Shari'a law in northern states and a growing concern over how Nigeria as a nation should position itself towards the US and that country's supposed enemies, the majority of whom appear to be Muslim. A country largely made up of people who, today, associate themselves with reformist versions of both Islam and Christianity, and who maintain close ties with co-religionists across the world

(Marshall-Fratani 2001), Nigeria's multiple understandings of the 'war on terrorism' offer us a particularly salient example of the ways that '9/11' has, indeed, become a part of what the Nigerian editorialist above calls 'our collective memory', while also raising the problem of why an event as telling of global temperature as the 'Kano War' and its aftermaths should be largely ignored – or dismissed as more 'ethnic tension' on a continent infamous, among Western nations, for that easy-to-apply but ultimately empty sobriquet.

The sections below will therefore explore how Nigerian reactions to 'the global war against terrorism' and '9/11' blended into local media representations of the 'Kano War' or 'Kano Riots' of 13 October 2001, then explicate how these representations continue to be significant for Nigerian print media discussion of the country's political economy and religious life. I am particularly interested in how an historical event in the supposed metropole was incorporated into everyday discourse and made familiar to African people with global ties and interests, even though those ties and interests are rarely recognized in the metropole itself. The chapter will therefore focus on how global media sources reverberate – and certain events leave indelible impressions – within local media, helping to shape even the internal, political discourses of what Mbembe (2001) calls the 'postcolony'. I will also consider how terms like 'terrorism' have different valences in different locations and, indeed, how global wars become – in the understanding of people in places like Nigeria – very much subsumed into local ones. The next section will look specifically at how northern and southern Nigerian editorial reactions to the 'Kano War' offer an important insight into the penetration and reshaping of '9/11' tropes in a place where reformist religious struggles are not abstract but can become a matter of life and death on any day, not simply on two days in September and October of 2001.

REPORTING THE 'KANO WAR' IN A CLIMATE OF '9/11'

[The Nigerian Minister of Foreign Affairs, Alhaji Sule Lamido] 'came and was arrogantly speaking Hausa to announce to us why the government was in support of the strike [on the Taliban government of Afghanistan]; he was not persuasive, he was not diplomatic about it, he did not try to educate the people that it was a fight against terrorists. So most commoners immediately saw it as an attack against Islam. I think that was partly the reason why the otherwise peaceful demonstration [of 13 October 2001] degenerated into violence.'
                    (Anonymous 'Hausa respondent', talking about the Kano disturbances
                    to *This Day* newspaper reporters, quoted in Momodu and Musa 2001)

[Dr Ibrahim Datti Ahmed, President-General of the Supreme Council for Shari'a in Nigeria] should realize that with the terrorism unleashed on civilisation on September 11, 2001, nobody is safe anywhere in the world. Making ridiculous claims to distract the world from the business of extirpating terrorism is now his personal delusion. Datti Ahmed must be the lone educated Moslem defending bin Laden. And nowhere else in the Moslem world had demonstrations for Afghanistan led to loss of lives except in Kano. But according to Datti Ahmed 'in Kano, Kaduna, Zamfara and other places, bin Laden is celebrated as a quintessential mujaheedin'.... It is regrettable that Datti Ahmed has chosen to fan the embers of disunity by making inflammatory statements at a critical point[.] Nigeria is in need of national reconciliation and democratic strengthening. Democracy allows the freedom of expression but this right ought to carry along a high sense of responsibility with it.

> (Anonymous editorialist for the southern newspaper
> *The Comet*, n.d., but clearly written after 13 October 2001)

In the two quotations above – one from an 'on the street' interview with a Hausa-speaking man in Kano a few days after the disturbances and the other an unbridled opinion piece written by a southern Nigerian sometime around the same period – competing paradigms for the causes and consequences of the 'war' are already under construction. These paradigms are hybrid, not monolithic impositions from global media or geopolitics. As such they require careful contextualization, not a snap moral judgment that might suggest that one of the speakers is unabashedly *for* the US 'war on terrorism', while the other is *against* it. For instance, while each uses the term 'terrorism' or 'terrorist', and means by that English usage to conjure up all the horror of violent, politically charged acts against innocent persons, neither is using the notion exactly as might an ordinary person in the US.

Both speakers appear to be old enough to have lived through a period that could be described as 'state terrorism' during the late 1980s and 1990s, under the regime of the late General Sani Abacha. They also both, in all probability, regularly apply the term 'terrorism' – as do many speakers of Nigerian English today – to the continuing tyranny of armed thugs who kill and maim honest citydwellers, opposition politicians and would-be voters trying to register for local and national elections. While the regularity in use of the term may now be greater than ever before in Nigerian public discourse, it is hardly a recent, alien, or abstract concept to most anglophones in the country.

These urban, literate Nigerians were not newly awakened to what Slavoj Zizek (2002: 15) describes, quoting the internationally popular film *The Matrix*, as 'the desert of the real', even by such a spectacular, global media event as '9/11'. Some understanding of the world certainly did change for Nigerians on 11 September 2001 – in that they were as startled as the rest of world to see the carnage in New York and generally were as sympathetic as any of the US' allies to the horrors of that event – but what changed for Nigerians was emphatically *not* their comprehension that real terror and violence could be visited upon any unsuspecting person, at any time. This twenty-first-century North American terror was already an old, twentieth-century acquaintance of people who had directly experienced colonialism, neocolonialism, one of the most brutal civil wars of the last hundred years, the militarization of every aspect of the national culture since independence and an insatiable kleptocracy that was nurtured by it all.[12]

The localized quality of an already global style of terrorism is echoed in both quotations by the targets the speakers chose to excoriate. In the first, a Nigerian government minister (and fellow Muslim) is claimed to be responsible for the transformation of a peaceful demonstration of solidarity with co-religionists into a riot, threatening the lives of everyone within range. Foreign Minister Lamido actually did defend the Nigerian government's position of enlisting on the 'side' of the US in the forthcoming war against Afghanistan, although he did not do it in person – as it sounds – and in the face of *'yan daba* marchers on 13 October. Instead, Lamido gave a Hausa language radio interview earlier in the week, explaining the government's official stance towards the war on terrorism. This interview was not well received by the largely Shi'ite religious scholars and politicians who arranged the Saturday demonstration.[13] The cardinal mistake of Lamido's supporters was to place a truck equipped with signs printed with the face of the minister and the name of his party, the PDP (People's Democratic Party), near the site of the original, peaceful protest gathering (in some accounts, a mosque).

Foreign Minister Lamido's virtual presence therefore became, in the minds of many who attended the gathering, a governmental intrusion into religious business. As the government's expressed policy of support for the US was construed by members of the crowd as a threat to their religious freedom, it was a short step for poor, bored, and youthful men in the crowd to seek revenge for the perceived governmental slight to the larger community of Islam. After an American flag was burned, possibly along with an effigy of President Bush, *'yan daba* members of the crowd rushed the truck and torched first the signs with Lamido's portrait, then the vehicle itself. After the PDP truck, *'yan daba* moved on to shops in the main street leading to Sabon Gari and soon met their southern, Christian counterparts coming out of the quarter.

The sheer clumsiness of the Lamido/PDP political intervention into the sensitive space of Muslim protest later caused many Nigerians, particularly in the south, to wonder if it was not a deliberate provocation. In terms of who would benefit from such a provocation, however, there were several, not very coherent theories – although all theorists agreed that southern Christians living in Kano would be the ultimate losers in any series of pitched street battles in the city because of their minority religious and ethnic status.[14] This feeling was exacerbated by the highly visible presence of Hisba (a group whose purview is the proper implementation of Shari'a in every Muslim Nigerian state) at both the 12 and 13 October events. Such a presence could hardly calm Christian anxieties, already high over how Shari'a would make an impact on their future lives as immigrants in Kano.

This national struggle over Shari'a also haunts the anonymous southern editorialist as he writes bitterly about one of Muslim law's best-known Nigerian proponents. Although the editorialist frames his anger against Dr Ahmed in terms of the international 'war against terrorism', coming near to calling Ahmed a terrorist himself for celebrating Osama bin Laden in the face of 'civilisation's' pain on 9/11, the deeper subtext of the editorial has to do with fear that the northern states' moves to make Shari'a the law within their borders might be expanded – although Nigeria has a strong federal system of government – gradually towards the nation as a whole. The notion that an 'educated Moslem' like Dr Ahmed would not only embrace the cause of Shari'a but more extreme forms of Muslim militancy represents to the editorial writer the emerging standardized nightmare of equally well-educated southern Nigerian Christians and secularists.

That standardized southern nightmare can be summed up in one word: jihad. Its mirror image – crusade – is, however, just as potent among deeply devout northerners.[15] While most northern Muslims are loath to use the term jihad in print, southern Nigerian evangelical Christians feel little compunction about advertising 'crusades' to be held in various northern cities. Indeed, the last time a disturbance of similar magnitude took place in Kano – almost ten years to the day of 13 October 2001 – the riots were sparked by the arrival in the city of controversial German evangelist Rheinhard Bonnke (Falola 1998: 211–13) and the Christian Association of Nigeria's (CAN) desire to hold Bonnke's self-described crusade in the city's Race Course, a legacy of British colonialism in the Kano cityscape. Bonnke had previously enraged northern Muslims by preaching (in the south) that the streets of Kano would 'run with the blood' of the sinful, according to southern Nigerian friends of mine, so it was with little surprise that the culmination of this 'crusade' was, indeed, violence.

In comparison to such ardent 'crusaders' as Bonnke and his Nigerian adherents, publicly proclaimed 'jihadists' are actually scarce on the Nigerian ground. Yet Dr Ahmed's defence of bin Laden, above, was not the only one heard in the year following 9/11 and the 'Kano War'. Posters of bin Laden became bestsellers throughout the Nigerian north as well as in large cities in the south-west, notably in Lagos and Ibadan.[16] And questions were constantly raised about the good faith of religious organizations like CAN and Jama'atul Izalatul Biadi'ah Kamatus Sunnah (otherwise known as Izala; cf. Umar 1993) at the time of the riots. CAN members, along with the police, accused the Izala in Kano of staging the violence as a means to eradicate Christians, and Izala accused CAN of sending 'saboteurs'[17] out to dress as Muslims and burn churches in order to incite Christian violence against Muslims (Kazaure 2001e; Musa 2001c). Each group charged the other with acts of 'terrorism', seeking a local moral high ground – as we have seen for other discursive participants in the 'Kano War' – by using the global rhetoric of the war on terrorism.

'Terrorism', whatever its local connotations within Nigeria, now resonates there in slightly new ways: that is, it is more highly valued than before, or has been revalued through its global usage, and is certainly now ubiquitous within the Nigerian mainstream press. But in being newly valued, has the term also been made somehow more *meaningful*? In the next section we will address the issue of how the term terrorism was specifically used in the Nigerian media after 11 September and 13 October 2001, seeking to discover some of its hybridized meanings for Nigerians who understand themselves to live in both local and global contexts.

EDITORIALIZING TERROR, RELIGION, AND SECULARITY IN NIGERIA

The Qur'an tells us how Allah favoured many former superpowers with intellect, skill, power and resources. Yet for their sins, Allah destroyed them (Qur'an 6:6, 29:38 and 46:26). Such destruction may come at the hands of any agent of Allah's choosing. The present unipolar world order, which is unfortunately based on inequity, injustice and hypocrisy, should retrace its steps for the good of all.

(Ja'afar 2001)

Two types of terrorism or terrorists are discernible in Nigeria: state, and socio-political terrorism or terrorists. State terrorism is the use of instruments of state power to inflict acts of injustice, oppression and suppression on citizens ... In the life of this administration [Obasanjo's presidency], state terrorism has been exhibited on a number of occasions with reckless abandon. The demolition of Odi community in Bayelsa State by government soldiers in 1999, which has now been revisited on several villages in Benue State in 2001[,] is a vivid testimony that state terrorism is an art of governance in Nigeria.

(Oni 2001)

As in the two quotations that opened the previous section of the chapter, the Nigerian editorialists quoted directly above may appear to set out two, antithetical worldviews: one deeply religious and possibly anti-Western, or even anti-modern, the other secular and politically activist, responding not to some holy text but to the peculiarly modern analytic discourse of Western social sciences. It might thus be easy for an outsider to assume that Samuel Huntington's (1993, 1996) well-known and grandiose 'clash of civilizations' must be playing itself out here on the local, Nigerian level, with southern Nigerians standing in for the west and northern, Muslim Nigerians taking the fixed role of 'the rest'.[18] Nothing, however, could be further from the truth. Religion frames both editorials, as do secular notions drawn from the rubrics of global modernities, and they do not compete (much less clash) so much as co-exist, representing Nigeria's ambiguous realities better than does a strictly adversarial model of modernity versus tradition.

Southern Nigerian editorialists, like Oni above, are more likely to invoke the neutral-sounding secularism of social science literature in their post-2001 discussions of global and local terrorisms. They talk about nationalities and citizenship, invoking the rubrics of political science and international affairs, describing how terrorism 'is detrimental and inimical to ... international peace and security' (Ayobolu 2002). Yet in even so determinedly westernized a paper as *The Guardian* – Nigeria's elite newspaper of record, usually compared within the country to *The Times* or to *The New York Times* – the editorial page could not resist, in 2002, looking back on '9/11' in highly moralizing, religious terms, terms that sat comfortably with its standard, political analysis. Paraphrasing the English divine and poet John Donne, *The Guardian* noted that:

No nation, after all, is an island unto itself; when the death bell tolls in one part of the world, the echo travels far and wide. In combating terrorism, therefore, the whole world, including America's old power rivals such as Russia and China, suspended their differences ... On the anniversary of the event, what we are compelled to remember are a set of existential dualities: life and death, hope and hopelessness, courage and fear; patriotism and treason; innocence and guilt; humanity and inhumanity; and good and evil. We would recall also as we reflect on these ... the historical meeting of minds between the American state and the people, and the whole world on the question of terrorism and its threat to modern civilisation. What has triumphed, however, is the hope that in the face of evil, the world can find real cause to stand together on a high ground.

(Anonymous 2002)

Later in the same editorial, *The Guardian* takes the Nigerian government to task for not actively pursuing the interests of its own citizens whose lives have been lost in the interim, whether from events like the Kano War or the still mysterious bomb blast that levelled part of the Lagosian suburb of Ikeja in January 2002.

On this painful topic, the anonymous editorialist looks both to North American forensic science and to what he perceives to be a peculiarly modern ideological 'faith in human lives; the accepted thinking that every American life is worthy of protection'. The editorialist clearly counts Nigeria as part of 'modern civilisation', the entity that he perceives to be under threat from global and local terrorism. Why, then, the editorial asks, does its government not put into practice all the ideologies of modernity, including that 'faith in human lives' that Nigeria ought to share with the US? Like many propounding religious questions, *The Guardian* petitioner goes unanswered in his own editorial text.

The long history of Christian rhetoric and theology – even if couched in the supposedly secular philosophy of existentialism – is displayed in southern Nigerian political discourse in examples like that of *The Guardian* editorial. There is little new in that, since political discourse in the West was formulated in direct relation to that religious history, and since many parts of southern Nigeria were missionized along with their administration by the British colonial authorities. As Tariq Ali (2002: xi) points out, religious fundamentalism itself is a product of modernity (and now, we might add, has become a defining feature of many different modernities; cf. Almond et al. 2003), crafted by Western societies and their colonized others, developing at the same time as the grand secularisms of the Enlightenment. Terror was conceived as a political strategy at the same moment, even if it now seems meant to destabilize the 'smooth surfaces' (Hardt 1995) of capitalism and the globalization that social and economic system has helped to create.[19]

Northern (and generally Muslim) editorialists during this period took many positions towards terror and religion in the aftermaths of 9/11 and the 'Kano War', including one that criticized the very notion of Nigeria – or any contemporary country, for that matter – as a secular state. Abdullahi Abubakar (2001) noted the importance of oath-taking within Nigerian jurisprudence as a sign of the civil government's religious background, and went on to argue, quoting the Bible, that

[t]he concept of secularism is a Christian doctrine which is principally aimed at separating the state from religion and emanates from the Biblical injunction: render unto Caesar the things which are Caesar's and render unto God the things which are God's – Matthew 22:21, and the statement attributed to Jesus thus: My kingdom is not of this world – John 18:36.

From this editorialist's point of view, Nigeria had never been secular; it has always been Christian at its base, because this was the religious background of its colonizers. To become a truly 'multi-religious state', therefore, southern Christians would have to learn to accept the coeval status of Muslims – which covertly appears to be an argument for the implementation of Shari'a law in the north, one of the flashpoints of the events in Kano during October 2001. Abubakar is not prepared to talk about Muslim terrorism in the 'Kano War'; his is the voice of a person who perceives himself and his co-religionists to be fighting for religious freedom within an oppressive theocratic (Christian) regime.

Hassan Karofi (2001), on the other hand, faces the issue of purported Muslim 'terror' in Kano and defends the young Muslim men who took to the streets on 13 October. Not only does he question the evidence for bin Laden's guilt in the 11 September terrorist actions in the US,[20] he propounds a theory of North American conspiracy, in which the US government 'hide[s] behind terrorism to fight Islam'. The problem, as Karofi sees it, is that Muslim liberation activities are always understood by those who control the global (and particularly Nigerian) media as 'terrorism', while others, as long as they are not Muslims, are given the benefit of the political doubt. For Karofi and probably for many of his Nigerian readers, terrorism only means oppression of Muslims; it has no other reality. This interpretation appears to be in basic agreement with Huntington: there is a 'clash of civilizations', and aggressive Christendom will have to learn that in 'the selective injustice on Islam lies the course of its greatness'.

The lack of a similarly overt Christian commentary among Nigerian editorialists probably speaks more of the Christian hegemony over much of the country's print media than anything else. Certainly 'born-again' Christian Nigerians I have spoken to since 2001 profess more loyalty to the political positions of the US government than do most, equally vehement Muslims. Perhaps, as Abubakar suggests above, there is little need to spell out a Christian position on terrorism and the events of '9/11' or the 'Kano War'. That position is already implied through its media privileging and Christians – even supposedly secularized ones – are already implicated in it.

However, there has been a good deal of anti-war rhetoric in the southern Nigerian editorial columns since the beginning of the Afghanistan and, more recently, Iraq wars that has been in line with that of northern editorialists. In this, Nigerian writers continue to demonstrate their shared position as, in Baudrillard's (2002: 6) phrase, 'those who have ended up on the wrong side of the global order'. And, as Nigeria has been represented in North American political discourse after 2001 first as a trusted and valued ally (who just happens to be sitting on large oil reserves), then as a possible harbour for 'terrorists' (whose oil reserves are under threat by activists from the Delta), the general southern Nigerian propensity to 'side with' the US has taken a beating. As Nigeria is learning, it has become a good deal easier to be labelled in the latest fashions of alterity (terrorist, terrorist sympathizer, terrorist state) than to prove the label wrong, even when the terms of global engagement are contested within the nation itself.

CONCLUSIONS: TERROR AGAINST TERROR

This is terror against terror – there is no longer any ideology behind it.
(Baudrillard 2002: 9)

None of this will serve America's interests globally and the consequence of
their use of terror to overcome terror might be in the end the rise of greater
terror. If this occurs no one knows what level of legitimate political dissent
will survive in the world as a means of containing the exploitative politics of
governments who can impose their power on the weak and small.
(Barrett 2001)

Hardt and Negri (2000: 32–3) tell us that communication, in the
time of what they call 'Empire', 'expresses the movement and
controls the sense and direction of the imaginary that runs through
... communicative connections; in other words, the imaginary is
guided and channeled within the communicative machine'. I have
tried to suggest above how a national imaginary, that of Nigeria,
can be influenced by global events – although I do not want to take
as monolithic a position towards 'the global' as that suggested by
Hardt and Negri in their work. What, I would have us all ask, is the
content of the communication that moves between and among us,
here in the world?

While the idea of '9/11' certainly had resonance for Nigerian
journalists as they went about trying to report on the events of '10/13',
the war on terrorism was not the only frame they used to make sense
of otherwise senseless violence. And, I would add, the contours of
even the framing device of 'terrorism' were shaped not only by global
experience – or the dominance of global media – but very much by a
local set of histories and experiences. As Stewart and Strathern (2002:
32) note: 'history as it is inscribed cannot be separated from history
as it is experienced'. Those experiences that *feel* most immediate are
necessarily those one experiences at first, rather than second, hand.
Terror, even on a global scale, becomes more locally meaningful when
it has local, as well as global, referents.

The Nigerian 'mediascape' (Appadurai 1996) I have only begun to
unpack above is just that, Nigerian, but should not be underestimated
because of that fact. What we can learn about the 'Kano War' shows
us something about what it means to be on the periphery of two
currently important global centres – caught betwixt and between
Euro-American and Muslim modernities. It is, perhaps, useful to
remember here what Victor Turner (1967: 97) once called such
liminality: the 'realm of pure possibility'. How Nigeria manages its
religious and political dilemmas in the post-9/11 era may well point
to ways the larger world may also take, for good or ill.

The problematic term in this chapter – and, much more importantly,
in the everyday lives of people all over the globe today – is terror.

Looking at how the discourse of terror and terrorism has been seized upon since 11 September 2001, whether in Nigeria or in the US, we discover that terror's semantic content has been radically transformed, made both less and more historically and culturally specific. Terror's meaningfulness, on one level, now resides in whatever use the powerful discursively choose to put it to: that is, pre-emptive (also known as preventative) warfare against a potential 'terrorist threat', developing a hierarchy of 'rogue states' or political adversaries who have 'ties to terrorist organizations', or vilifying former allies as 'soft on terrorism'. Using terror against terror, as both Baudrillard and Barrett suggest above, has cancelled out some of terror's experiential potency and turned it into an object, rather than a subject, of power. If any act can be construed as terroristic, then there is nowhere to turn. The world itself has become a place of absolute, inescapable violence, or perhaps something like a 'non-place.'

According to Marc Augé (1995: 77–8), 'If a place can be defined as relational, historical and concerned with identity, then a space which cannot be defined as relational, or historical, or concerned with identity will be a non-place.' The non-place set up by throwing away some of the meaningfulness of terror – by trying to erase all its historical connections with modernity and therefore its connections with people living under conditions of late modernity – attempts to reconfigure and even to negate human agencies and social ties. However, Augé and the Nigerian media, as well as the work of theorists of violence like Stewart and Strathern, remind us that the non-place of terror against terror is necessarily partial and incomplete. As it struggles to come into (non)being, the imaginaries, the material realities, and the shared histories of real people resist and tinker with its development. The human need to be and work with others asserts itself, even after fear and pain. Social experience can be rediscovered, and terror can be restored to its rightful place as a word that means particular things to particular people rather than an abstract regime of power and control.

What is being contested in Nigeria, as elsewhere, is whether local people can make meaning – even out of violence – in their societies, or whether the means of meaning-making, like so many other 'means' in late modernity, now reside inexorably outside any local context. It is encouraging to note that the 'Kano War' continues to have resonance for thoughtful Nigerians, as they attempt to come to grips with the nation's ongoing troubles,[21] even while '9/11' has taken on local, not only global, significance. The state of 'terror against terror' does not yet fully exist, anywhere, and the Nigerian press and its readers continue to fight its implications through lively discourse and argument.

NOTES

1. These representations of men's and women's roles are, of course, very old ones in the West. See Enloe (2000) and Lutz (2001, 2002) on the gendered as well as class costs of militarization in the US and elsewhere.
2. The same, of course, was also, until very recently, true for Saddam Hussein, his dead sons and many high Ba'ath Party officials after the so-called end of 'major hostilities' in Iraq. In mid-2004, while this chapter is being revised, hostilities in Iraq continue unabated.
3. The term is translated by Nigerians – both by Hausa-speaking and members of other linguistic groups – as 'hooligans' or 'thugs'. Other categories used in internal Hausa discourse about those who participated in the 'war' are *'yan kato da gora* (vigilantes) and *'yan tauri* (hunters, see Musa 2001b). Douglas Anthony, an historian colleague at Franklin & Marshall College who has done fieldwork as well as archival work in Kano, tells me that the term generally is applied to young, immature men 'up to no good'. These young men take an active part in Kano's street life and have been associated with unrest at various times during the past two decades. In the past they were also conflated with youthful religious students, sometimes called *almajirai*, who studied and sought alms on the streets for their own maintenance as well as that of their religious teachers (Anthony, personal communication, 31 October 2001). See also Barkindo 1993 for more on the disenfranchised Muslim youth of Kano from the 1970s onward.
4. Descriptions of the 'Kano War' come from various newspaper accounts of the events of 12–14 October 2001, but particularly from Ajani and Ikyur 2001; Enweremadu et al. 2001; Kazaure 2001a, b and c; Ikyur 2001; Ikyur and Nnadozie 2001; Ikyur and Usigbe 2001; Momodu and Musa 2001; Musa 2001a and b; and Sulaiman 2001. Another important indigenous Hausa analysis can be found in Ado-Kurawa 2001, although one should also take note of a bitter Web rebuttal to this author from a Yoruba-speaker, Awoniyi n.d.
5. Sabon Gari (literally, 'New Town') was a colonial addition to Kano – a place where southern Nigerians, often Christians, have lived since the early years of the twentieth century. See Barkindo 1993 and Larkin 2002 for a fascinating analysis of how Sabon Gari and its westernized sites of pleasure (notably cinemas, bars, and brothels) came to figure in the Kano Muslim imaginary as a place of sinful 'sexual and ethnic intermixing that were deeply disruptive of Hausa moral practices' (Larkin 2002: 326).
6. Officially, 915 lives and 3.3 billion naira's worth of property were lost in the Jos 'ethno-religious uprising' (Obateru 2002). At the time of writing, the naira-to-dollar exchange rate is around 125: 1. For an excellent description of the events of September 2001 in Jos, see Danfulani and Fwatshak 2002. Violence between Muslims and Christians continued in Nigeria – and particularly in Kano – in 2004.
7. Shi'ism is an important part of Muslim life in contemporary Nigeria, although it has played a problematic part in that life (see Umar 1993 on what he calls 'anti-Sufism' in northern Nigeria). According to Falola (1998: 203), 'Each year [in the decade of the 1990s] there has been at least one violent incident involving Shi'ites, mostly occurring in Kaduna, Kano, and Zaria. The movement's ability to mobilize in large numbers,

sometimes of over ten thousand, on a moment's notice makes their actions difficult for the police to anticipate.' Important Shi'ite teachers and leaders are believed to receive monetary support from Iran, and they have frequently expressed their allegiance to as well as taken their political positions from the religious leaders of that country. See Falola (1998: 194–5) for an example.

8. It is also safe to say that Kano has been at the forefront of radicalized Muslim discourse in Nigeria – as well as the setting for some of Nigeria's most notorious religious conflict – for most of the twentieth century. See, e.g., Watts (1992) and Falola (1998: chapter 5) for two clear and useful discussions of the 1980 Kano Maitatsine riots and their social and historical contexts.

9. One northern journalist, Danlami Baban Takko (2001), took the time to unpack the possible semantic content of what would become President Obasanjo's most infamous verbal gaffe of 2001. Takko learned that there could be several meanings of 'I don't worry' in the Nigerian English context – including one that suggested that the president was unconcerned; another that suggested the president had no room for despair over the events and a third, more optimistic meaning of 'I am hopeful that all will be well.' Takko expressed his own hope in the editorial that Obasanjo simply wished the people of Kano well, but the overall tone is one of doubt.

10. 'Give us Biafra!' is a cry that clearly references the unsettled period in mid-1960s Kano immediately before Nigeria's devastating civil war. It is also particularly derisive when levelled at President Obasanjo, who was, in the late 1960s, one of the Federal commanders who led the war against Igbo-speakers and other south-eastern secessionists. The call for 'Biafra' speaks, as well, to a current resurgence of Igbo ethnic nationalism throughout Nigeria and its global diaspora. To understand the complexities of Igbo immigrant life in Kano during and after the civil war period, see Anthony 2002.

11. Youth militias and other, less political youth criminal gangs are an important part of the Nigerian political and social scene in the early years of the twenty-first century. While bands of young people have historically played important parts in, at least, southern Nigerian groups, the transformation of mobile, urban, and generally poor young men (along with some girls) into paramilitary and parapolitical forces is a development of the post-independence period. For some of the history and current activities of such militant youth groups, see Osaghae 2002 and Momoh 2002.

12. Zizek would not, of course, be surprised to hear this. As a Slovene, he lived through one of the most frightening periods of his own people's history. This is why the subtitle of *Welcome to the Desert of the Real* is *Five Essays on September 11 and Related Dates* (my emphasis).

13. One might note that this sort of interview was Lamido's job, particularly as President Obasanjo was out of the country on a diplomatic trip to Paris. However, the spectacle of a Hausa-speaking high government official making an apology for the policies of what is perceived in more radical Muslim circles as a southern and Christian regime was taken as yet another slap in the face by the faithful.

14. Rumours also abounded that the riots were pre-planned ahead of time and that the Lamido/PDP truck was planted by rival APP party members.

Certainly the APP chairman of Kano State, Alhaji, Ibrahim Al-Amin, lost no time in blaming the PDP for all civil unrest in the city and throughout the country: 'If you take stock of all the killings that have been taken place within these two and a half years, it is more than the total deaths recorded since our independence in communal clashes. At no time in our history have human lives been wasted as in the reign of the present governments of the PDP' (quoted in Kazaure 2001d).

15. See Falola 1998: chapter 9 for a cogent discussion of the hate literature that has grown up around these two terms. An anti-Muslim and anti-Christian pamphlet and audiocassette conflict escalates with each new mass religious meeting in church or mosque, as representatives of each religion offer scriptural and social 'evidence' for the bankruptcy of the other's practice.

16. Such posters worried the Governor of Lagos State, Bola Tinubu, so much that he called in Hausa leaders and Muslim scholars on 17 October to berate them for undermining security in the state: 'If we must exist, we must co-exist. One religion must not extinguish the other. Islam must not extinguish Christianity and Christianity must equally not extinguish Islam. Similarly, nobody, Igbo, Hausa or Yoruba can tell the other to leave Lagos' (quoted in Usigbe and Ehigiator 2001).

17. A particularly loaded term in Nigerian history, connected with espionage and pilfering during the civil war period and later with any attempts to undermine public peace and safety.

18. For a southern Nigerian critique of Huntington's position, see Anonymous 2001; for an even more trenchant northern, Muslim Nigerian critique, see Haruna 2001.

19. As Baudrillard (2002: 9) notes about terrorism on 9/11, 'It was the system itself which created the objective conditions for this brutal retaliation.' By 'system' here, I believe he does not mean the government of the US in 2001 (although that is implicated as well), but the larger, historical system of Western modernity itself. What Baudrillard calls, later in the same paragraph, 'the singularity' comes from within the system, not from outside of it.

20. During October 2001, Al-Qaeda had not yet taken responsibility for the destruction in New York, Washington, DC and Pennsylvania.

21. It is less encouraging to note that violent riots continue to shake the city of Kano periodically, one of the worst in history having taken place on 12 May 2004. Over 600 people died in this latest violence, and the recriminations between Christians and Muslims continue along the lines noted for the 'Kano War'. For southern Nigerian media descriptions of the 2004 riots, see Asoya 2004 and Anthony 2004a, b, c.

REFERENCES

Monographs and articles

Ado-Kurawa, Ibrahim (2001) 'Some Causes of Kano Riots and Solutions Based on Stimulating Economic Growth'. Electronically published paper prepared for Inuwar Jama'ar Kano (Kano Forum). http://www.kanoonline. com/publications/pr_articles_kano_riots_01.html. Accessed 20/9/02.

Ali, Tariq (2002) *The Clash of Fundamentalisms: Crusades, Jihads and Modernity*. London: Verso.

Almond, Gabriel A., R. Scott Appleby and Emmanuel Sivan (2003) *Strong Religion: The Rise of Fundamentalisms around the World*. Chicago: University of Chicago Press.

Anthony, Douglas (2002) *Poison and Medicine: Ethnicity, Power, and Violence in a Nigerian City, 1966–1986*. Portsmouth, NH: Heinemann.

Appadurai, Arjun (1996) *Modernity at Large: Cultural Dimensions of Globalization*. Minneapolis: University of Minnesota Press.

Augé, Marc (1995) *Non-Places: Introduction to an Anthropology of Supermodernity*. London and New York: Verso Books.

Awoniyi, Femi (n.d.) 'Fulanis, Yorubas, Islam and Political Power in Nigeria: Re: The Role of "Resource Control" and Restructuring in the Political Economy of Nigeria by Ibrahim Ado-Kurawa'. Electronically published paper. http://www.famji.com/NEWS1083.htm. Accessed 22/9/02.

Barkindo, Bawuro M. (1993) 'Growing Islamism in Kano City Since 1970'. In *Muslim Identity and Social Change in Sub-Saharan Africa*, ed. by L. Brenner. Bloomington: Indiana University Press, pp. 91–105.

Baudrillard, Jean (2002) *The Spirit of Terrorism and Requiem for the Twin Towers*. London: Verso.

Danfulani, Umar Dadem and Sati U. Fwatshak (2002) 'Briefing: The September 2001 Events in Jos, Nigeria'. *African Affairs*, 101: 243–55.

Enloe, Cynthia (2000) *Maneuvers: The International Politics of Militarizing Women's Lives*. Berkeley: University of California Press.

Falola, Toyin (1998) *Violence in Nigeria: The Crisis of Religious Politics and Secular Ideologies*. Rochester, NY: University of Rochester Press.

Hardt, Michael (1995) 'The Withering of Civil Society'. *Social Text*, 45: 27–44.

Hardt, Michael and Antonio Negri (2000) *Empire*. Cambridge, MA: Harvard University Press.

Huntington, Samuel P. (1993) 'The Clash of Civilizations'. *Foreign Affairs* (Summer): 22–49.

—— (1996) *The Clash of Civilizations and the Remaking of World Order*. New York: Simon & Schuster.

Larkin, Brian (2002) 'The Materiality of Cinema Theaters in Northern Nigeria'. In *Media Worlds: Anthropology on a New Terrain*, ed. F. Ginsburg, L. Abu-Lughod and B. Larkin. Berkeley: University of California Press, pp. 319–36.

Lutz, Catherine (2001) *Homefront: A Military City and the American 20th Century*. Boston: Beacon Press.

—— (2002) 'Making War at Home in the United States: Militarization and the Current Crisis'. *American Anthropologist*, 104 (3): 723–35.

Marshall-Fratani, Ruth (2001) 'Mediating the Global and Local in Nigerian Pentecostalism'. In *Between Babel and Pentecost*, ed. A. Corten and R. Marshall-Fratani. Bloomington: Indiana University Press, pp. 80–105.

Mbembe, Achille (2001) *On the Postcolony*. Berkeley: University of California Press.

Momoh, Abubakar (2002) 'Area Boys and the Political Crisis in Nigeria'. Paper presented at a conference on 'Youth Policy and the Policies of Youth in Africa', Program of African Studies, Northwestern University.

Osaghae, Eghose E. (2002) 'Youth Generational Ethnicity in Nigeria'. Paper presented at a conference on 'Youth Policy and the Policies of Youth in Africa', Program of African Studies, Northwestern University.

Stewart, Pamela J. and Andrew Strathern (2002) *Violence: Theory and Ethnography*. London and New York: Continuum.

Turner, Victor (1967) *The Forest of Symbols: Aspects of Ndembu Ritual*. Ithaca, NY: Cornell University Press.

Umar, Muhammed Sani (1993) 'Changing Islamic Identity in Nigeria from the 1960s to the 1980s: From Sufism to Anti-Sufism'. In *Muslim Identity and Social Change in Sub-Saharan Africa*, ed. L. Brenner. Bloomington: Indiana University Press, pp. 154–78.

Watts, Michael John (1992) 'The Shock of Modernity: Petroleum, Protest, and Fast Capitalism in an Industrializing Society'. In *Reworking Modernity: Capitalisms and Symbolic Discontent*, ed. A. Pred and M.J. Watts. New Brunswick, NJ: Rutgers University Press, pp. 21–64.

Zizek, Slavoj (2002) *Welcome to the Desert of the Real: Five Essays on September 11 and Related Dates*. London: Verso.

Media accounts

Abubakar, Abdullahi Salihu (2001) 'Is Nigeria a Secular State?' *The Daily Trust* (Abuja, Nigeria). http://www.allafrica.com. Accessed 17/10/01.

Ajani, Jide and Nathaniel Ikyur (2001) 'No Worry Over Kano Killings – Obasanjo'. *Vanguard* (Lagos, Nigeria). http://www.allafrica.com/stories/200110160391.html. Accessed 12/8/02.

Anonymous (n.d.) 'Why Kano Burns – Datti Ahmed's Vituperations'. *The Comet* (Lagos, Nigeria). http://www.cometnews.com.ng/08112001/ed86501.htm. Accessed 22/9/02.

Anonymous (2001) 'Week of Terror: America's Place in the World'. *Vanguard* (Lagos, Nigeria). http://www.vanguardngr.com. Accessed 14/1/02.

Anonymous (2002) 'September 11, 2001: One Year After'. *The Guardian* (Lagos, Nigeria). http://www.ngrguardiannews.com/. Accessed 12/9/02.

Anthony, Tina (2004a) 'We'll Never Forget These Evils, Victims Lament'. *Vanguard* (Lagos, Nigeria). http://www.allafrica.com/stories/printable/200405170277.html. Accessed 9/6/04.

—— (2004b) 'How Ethno-Religious Crisis Again Shattered Kano'. *Vanguard* (Lagos, Nigeria). http://www.allafrica.com/stories/printable/200405170446.html. Accessed 9/6/04.

—— (2004c) 'Kano Riots: Non-Natives Shun Calls to Return'. *Vanguard* (Lagos, Nigeria). http://www.allafrica.com/stories/printable/200405171100.html. Accessed 9/6/04.

Asoya, Sylvester (2004) 'Madness in the North'. *The News* (Lagos, Nigeria). http://www.allafrica.com/stories/printable/100405171231.html. Accessed 9/6/04.

Ayobolu, Jide (2002) 'Terrorists Are Around'. *Daily Times of Nigeria* (Lagos, Nigeria). http://www.dailytimesofnigeria/Daily Times/2002/October/23/Terroristsarearound.asp. Accessed 23/10/02.

Barrett, Lindsay (2001) 'Terror Against Terror: What Will Survive?' *Vanguard* (Lagos, Nigeria). http://www.allafrica.com/stories/200110180513.html. Accessed 13/8/02.

Enweremadu, Goddy, Peter Umar-Omale, Donald Andoor and Ikenna Emewu (2001) 'As Obasanjo Visits Scenes Today ... FG Blames "Discredited Politicians" for Kano Riots, May Declare Emergency Rule in Benue, Taraba'. *This Day* (Lagos, Nigeria). http://www.allafrica.com/stories/200110160250. html. Accessed 12/8/02.

Haruna, Mohammed (2001) 'September 11 and Huntington's Prophesy'. *The Daily Trust* (Abuja, Nigeria). http://www.allafrica.com. Accessed 27/9/01.

Ikyur, Nathaniel (2001) 'Kano Refugees – Help, We're Dying Here'. *Vanguard* (Lagos, Nigeria). http://www.allafrica.com/stories/200110220513.html. Accessed 13/8/02.

Ikyur, Nathaniel and Emma Nnadozie (2001) 'Death Toll Rises to 122 in Kano Riots'. *Vanguard* (Lagos, Nigeria). http://www.allafrica.com/ stories/200110150229.html. Accessed 12/8/02.

Ikyur, Nathaniel and Leon Usigbe (2001) 'Kano: Obasanjo Goes Tough, Sharia Council Blames Government'. *Vanguard* (Lagos, Nigeria). http://www. allafrica.com/stories/200110170645.html. Accessed 13/8/02.

Ja'afar, Abu (2001) 'Perspectives on Terrorism'. *The Daily Trust* (Abuja, Nigeria). http://www.allafrica.com/stories/2001110030087.html. Accessed 13/8/02.

Karofi, Hassan A. (2001) 'Of Islam, Beard and Terrorism'. *This Day* (Lagos, Nigeria). http://www.allafrica.com. Accessed 21/10/01.

Kazaure, Musa Umar (2001a) 'Kano Riots: Calm After Weekend Violence'. *The Daily Trust* (Abuja, Nigeria). http://www.allafrica.com/stories/200110150046. html. Accessed 12/8/02.

—— (2001b) 'Kano Riots: How a Peaceful Demonstration Turned Violent'. *The Daily Trust* (Abuja, Nigeria). http://www.allafrica.com/stories/200110170324. html. Accessed 12/8/02.

—— (2001c) 'Aftermath of Kano Riots: Uneasy Calm Reigns'. *The Weekly Trust* (Kaduna, Nigeria). http://www.allafrica.com/stories/200110190397. html. Accessed 13/8/02.

—— (2001d) 'APP Blames Government for Kano Riots'. *The Weekly Trust* (Kaduna, Nigeria). http://www.allafrica.com/stories/200112190335.html. Accessed 13/8/02.

—— (2001e) 'Group Wants CAN Probed'. *The Weekly Trust* (Kaduna, Nigeria), 7 December. http://www.allafrica.com. Accessed 13/8/02.

Momodu, Shaka and Yakubu Musa (2001) 'Heretics of Faith on the Loose'. *This Day* (Lagos, Nigeria). http://www.thisdayonline.com/archive/2001/ 10/20/20011020speo2.thml. Accessed 22/9/02.

Musa, Jamila Nuhu (2001a) 'The Riot Is Not a Religious Matter – Kano Police'. *The Weekly Trust* (Kaduna, Nigeria). http://www.allafrica.com/ stories/200110190402.html. Accessed 13/8/02.

—— (2001b) 'Kano Riots: Police Blamed for Extortion'. *The Weekly Trust* (Kaduna, Nigeria). http://www.allafrica.com/stories/200110250587.html. Accessed 13/8/02.

—— (2001c) 'JTI Denies Involvement in Kano Riots'. *The Daily Trust* (Abuja, Nigeria). http://www.allafrica.com/stories/200110300060.html. Accessed 13/8/02.

Obateru, Taye (2002) '915 Lives Lost in Jos Crisis – Panel'. *Vanguard* (Lagos, Nigeria). http://www.allafrica.com/stories/200209180631.html. Accessed 18/9/02.

Oni, Tunde (2001) 'Caging Terrorists in Our Midst'. *This Day* (Lagos, Nigeria). http://www.allafrica.com/stories/200111050082.html. Accessed 13/8/02.

Sulaiman, Aliyu M. (2001) 'Kano Riots: People's Reactions'. *The Daily Trust* (Abuja, Nigeria). http://www.allafrica.com/stories/200110150052. Accessed 12/8/02.

Takko, Danlami Baban (2001) '"I Don't Worry"'. *The Daily Trust* (Abuja, Nigeria). http://www.allafrica.com. Accessed 30/10/01.

Usigbe, Leon and Kenneth Ehigiator (2001) '150 Arraigned Over Kano Killings, Governor Raises Alarm on Bin Laden's Posters in Lagos'. *Vanguard* (Lagos, Nigeria), 18 October. http://www.allafrica.com. Accessed 13/8/02.

2 UNSPEAKABLE CRIMES: ATHENIAN GREEK PERCEPTIONS OF LOCAL AND INTERNATIONAL TERRORISM

Elisabeth Kirtsoglou

INTRODUCTION

It was Thursday 9 June 2000 and I was in a taxi, stuck in the exasperating traffic on one of the busiest Athenian avenues, Leoforos Kifissias. On that same road, the previous day, the terrorist organisation 17th of November, acting in Athens since 1975, had assassinated a British army officer and diplomat named Steven Saunders. The cover stories in the Athenian newspapers indicated that the attack was the work of *agents provocateurs* and, while the radio was broadcasting the latest news, the driver was nodding disapprovingly. 'Terrorism!', he said, 'who buys these tales? We are sweating blood over moving a hundred metres down the Kifissias and they are trying to persuade us that two guys just killed a man here and vanished; not a pair of trained commandoes, just two terrorists. And how did they know about Saunders? Poor us! God knows what kind of games they are playing at our expense this time round!'[1]

As far as I could remember, there always was a 17th of November, and the different explanations about its role and composition were rehearsed again and again after each successful or unsuccessful strike. The very predictable character of the local-level commentary became the objective of my long-term fieldwork in Athens, on perceptions of local and international terrorism upon which the present work is based.[2] My main aim has been the study of Athenian explanatory narratives of terrorism, for I treat these narratives as 'political cosmologies' (Theodossopoulos n.d.); and 'dynamic systems of cultural justification and accountability' employed by citizens as a means of composing expedient and coherent explanations for the disappointments and paradoxes of local-level and international politics (ibid.). The manner in which discourses promoted by political parties, intellectuals, and everyday-commentators alike merge in Athens, supports Papadakis' claim that there is 'no private space separable from wider social and political domains' (1998: 160). The close relationship between personal histories and more 'abstract formulations', that seem appealing to the local actor precisely owing to their 'strong resonance with lived experience' (ibid.: 150, 158), provides a framework within which perceptions of terrorism – among other social phenomena – can be adequately analyzed and explained.

Focusing on local terrorism and the events of 11 September, I will look closely at the Athenian frameworks for interpreting political and historical causality (see Stewart and Strathern 2002: 16), collective responsibility (Amit and Rapport 2002; MacIntyre 2001; Sandel 1998) and the politics of vengeance. In my attempt to account for the indigenous meta-commentary in its historical, political, and cultural context, I propose that my informants are engaged in what Sutton calls 'analogical thinking as history' (1998; 2003). That is, they employ familiar metaphors in order to understand unfamiliar processes, as well as being inspired by large-scale events in forming their explanations of local crises (see Brown and Theodossopoulos 2000, 2003).

Perceptions of terrorism, justice, and responsibility in Athens often take the form of conspiracy scenarios supporting and being supported by profoundly anti-authoritarian holistic and collectivist discourses. Examining such narratives carefully, I will propose an argument that unfolds in two parallel directions. First, with reference to responsibility, which my informants understand as a collective attribute, I maintain that such a phenomenon is not only a characteristic of a society in transition from tradition to modernity, but also a feature encouraged by the very concepts that organize modern political thought and action (cf. Gledhill 2000: 14, 17; Rapport 2002: 145; Herzfeld 1993; Giddens 1985). Treating the nation-state as an imagined community (Anderson 1983: 15) and taking into account culturally specific idioms that mediate national identity, I will explore the possibility that, in Athenian consciousness, nations can be held collectively accountable for the actions of their members.

Notions of accountability and justice, however, are not sufficiently understood in the Athenian context separately from the lived tension between belonging to the Western world, and at the same time not necessarily feeling a citizen of it (see Argyrou 2002: 100–1; Herzfeld 1987). At the heart of Athenian perceptions of terrorism lies a strong anti-Americanism and the belief that terrorism is a multivalent trope manipulated by the US and presented as an excuse to intervene in local and worldwide politics. Choosing to explain these narratives against a larger, historically and politically informed framework, I will take a closer look at concepts such as consensus, citizenship, and civil society. I maintain that it is the perceived fragility of the 'social contract' as the first principle of Western post-enlightenment political organization that leads my informants to operate within a context of mistrust and a familiar ethos of retribution firmly established in history as the 'narrative of the interaction of narratives' (Stewart and Strathern 2002: 16).

The chapter is structured around two main themes: The first relates to 11 September and the Athenian explanations of, feelings and commentaries towards the events of 2001 in Manhattan. Perceptions of acts of terrorism beyond the confines of Greece and indeed Athens, are strategically examined first, although – as the general title of the section *in medias res* suggests – this is certainly not the historical moment that shapes Athenian political causality. My decision to structure the chapter on the basis of a time inversion serves to demonstrate that local histories affect the perceptions of large-scale events (see MacIntyre 2001: 258–9; Rapport: 2002: 83; Gray 1995: 5; Brown and Theodossopoulos 2003; Sutton 1998, 2003) understood in terms of familiar narratives of causality and accountability, and vice versa. Commenting upon 11 September, I will introduce the first part of my argument regarding collective responsibility and the liability of nations.

Athenian perceptions of the 17th of November provide the second main theme of the chapter. The narratives and exegesis of my informants on local terrorism present a striking similarity with the explanations they offer regarding the strikes on the World Trade Center and the Pentagon. The apparent discursive analogies in question further support the claim that there are historical and political arguments behind indigenous commentary on local and international terrorism. The second part of my case is based upon a consideration of the notions of 'social contract' and civil society and their perceived fragility. Local-level experience and large-scale events strengthen Athenian perceptions of Greece as the 'interior exclusion', or the exclusion within the new world order. Finally, the chapter concludes with the idea that local-level Athenian commentary and attempts at political aetiology are not only the means by which the actors make sense of history, but also the ways in which they participate in its making. Perceptions of terrorism, conspiracist or not, constitute one of the various discursive fields within which social actors understand, compose and negotiate agency, citizenship and their place and position in relation to other proximate and distant subjects. It is, then, precisely in these interpretative narratives that civil and political identities are formed, challenged, and crystallized.

IN MEDIAS RES – 11 SEPTEMBER

The fact that we had dreamt of this event, that everyone without exception has dreamt of it – because no one can avoid dreaming of the destruction of

any power that has become hegemonic to this degree – is unacceptable to
the Western moral conscience. Yet it is a fact, and one which indeed can be
measured by the emotive violence of all that has been said and written in
the effort to dispel it.

(Baudrillard 2002: 5)

[A]n idiosyncratic relationship connects us with an imaginary America, of
which we are simultaneously an image, a creation, an appendix, an ally and
an enemy; [the US is] the dark object of our passion, envy and hatred.[3]

(Pretenderis 2001: 16)

The events of 11 September were confronted in a different manner by
diverse segments of the Athenian public. First and foremost I ought to
document the 'official approach' adopted by the Greek government
and genuinely supported by a number of Athenians, according to
which the bombing of the WTC was clearly an unprovoked terrorist
act, an attack that cost the lives of many people and was probably
the result of blind Islamic fundamentalism. This line of commentary,
however, was by no means the most popular in Athens, the European
city which that particular September was beating to the rhythm of
a profound anti-Americanism[4] expressed in the conviction that
'America is paying the results of its own policies and decisions' (see
Dimitrakos 2001: 136, 137). The advocates of this view regarded
the attack as 'a justified response to the US's consistent cruelty and
barbarism', as an Athenian shopkeeper told me, or as a 40-year-old
woman commented: 'did they [the Americans] think they could
remain unpunished for ever? Well, gentlemen it's payback time.'[5]

Athenian perceptions of the events in Manhattan as the result of
the callous and arrogant foreign policy of an almighty nation-state
are theoretically explicated, so to speak, in the writings of authors
like Zizek (2002) and Chomsky (2002). In an attempt to account
for the existence of regimes and individual figures within them,
accused by the US of promoting or committing acts of terrorism,
Zizek claims that 'power generates its own excess' (2002: 27).[6] A direct
or indirect relationship between terrorism and 'state-action' is also
an argument put forward by Chomsky (2002: 57). His answer to the
European journalist's questions: 'did the US "ask for" these attacks?
Are they consequences of American politics?' was rather ambivalent:
'The attacks are not "consequences" of the US policies in any direct
sense. But indirectly, of course they are consequences; that is not
even controversial' (ibid.: 82).

Chomsky's ambivalence was a feeling that many of my Athenian
informants shared. A number of them maintained that the attacks
on the WTC were clearly crimes committed by fanatics, but by no
means 'unprovoked acts'.[7] 'The Americans have been exercising their
power all over the world in an indiscriminate fashion, designing and
promoting unwarranted interventions in the internal political affairs

of a number of sovereign states,' Athenian interlocutors emphasized, and added: 'The strike was an unavoidable reaction to the ever-present power of the US.'

More sophisticated commentators were also engaged in attempts to separate the 'atrocities' from 'their reasons', struggling to articulate a seemingly learned exegesis of the attack, but one that was nevertheless essentially the same as that of local-level interlocutors. Such is the case of Konstantinos Tsoukalas, a respected professor of sociology in Greece who, in one of his articles, launched a fiery assault on terrorism, claiming that 'terrorism is the *par excellence* primeval, superstitious and anti-rationalist form of action. It is not a rational means for the realisation of [political] goals, but exists only as a gleefully paranoid end in itself' (2001: 26). Despite his conviction about the irrationality of terrorism however, Tsoukalas still claims – similarly to Zizek I would argue – that terrorism is: the 'collateral damage of the society of knowledge ... the revenge of the lurking irrationalism to the dead ends of an unrestrained (*sic*) rationalism'[8] (Tsoukalas 2001: 27). For Tsoukalas – as for many non-academic Athenians – 'the pax americana is not and *could not be bloodless*. It exists and reproduces itself due to the flaming broadsword it brandishes against the innocent and the guilty alike ... no one is in a position to voice directly and forthrightly his own wish to the superpower' (2001: 25; my emphasis). Or, as a taxi driver emphatically told me: 'It was a shame that so many people died, but being a superpower has its costs I suppose. When as a nation you have caused so much bloodshed, it is unavoidable that one day you'll taste blood as well. Has the US ever distinguished the guilty from the innocent? Aren't we terrorized daily by the power of the superpower? They [the Americans] are ripping the fruit off the trees they have planted.'[9]

On 10 November 2001, just two months after the attacks in Manhattan, an opinion poll carried out on behalf of *Eleftherotypia* – an Athenian newspaper of wide circulation – showed that six out of ten Athenians did not believe that bin Laden was the perpetrator of the terrorist act against the WTC. Some 42 per cent believed that the attack was either carried out by the US secret services or by other cliques within the US, while 28 per cent were convinced that the CIA alone was behind the attacks. On 12 September (the day after the attack), *Rizospastis*, the newspaper of the Greek communist party, claimed that 'such a strike could not have been materialised by people "trained" in Palestinian backyards or in the hutments of the innocent people that the Americans like to call terrorists ... It is the CIA.'[10] A few days later, a rather right-wing but widely respected Athenian newspaper, *Kathimerini*, had an article titled: 'Global Junta enforced by the US'. In it, the journalist claimed that 'there is increasing evidence of a possible involvement of the Americans or the American secret services in the attacks against the Pentagon and the Twin Towers.'[11]

The scenarios involving the CIA and generally the US secret agencies were many and manifold among my informants who employed them in order to form their own idiosyncratic political aetiologies (see Brown and Theodossopoulos 2003). In the days immediately after the attack a number of Athenians were reluctant to believe that such a grandiose act of humiliation (see Baudrillard 2002: 26) was not actually the deed of a superpower. In the context of 'the war against terrorists and the states that support them', threatened by the US president, this line of explanation took two forms. First were the people who believed that either the CIA or extreme rightist groups launched the attack in order to provide the US government with an excuse to further intervene in world politics in an authoritarian, absolutist, and unilateral manner. 'They themselves did it'[12] was a comment that I was hearing almost too frequently in the streets and neighbourhoods of Athens, while according to the second version of this type of reasoning, the US might have not been *directly* involved, but it was nevertheless *responsible* for the existence of terrorist states and individuals. This latter view was epitomized in the short but powerful Athenian response to whoever conclusively pointed to bin Laden as the person behind the attacks: 'And who *made* [trained/ empowered] bin Laden?'[13]

It is perhaps no accident that Chomsky puts forward similar claims about the 'roots of the "Afghanis" such as Bin Laden' (2002: 32) or that Zizek argues that 'the war on terrorism is not our struggle, but a struggle internal to the capitalist universe ... *the very existence of Afghanistan is the result of the interplay of foreign powers*'[14] (2002: 55; original emphasis). With reference to the Greek case, however, and as I intend to show in the following sections, the power of such commentary lies in its historicity. As Stewart and Strathern have argued, narratives – despite their partiality – are impregnated with 'historical consciousness', thereby shaping and expressing 'intentions' and 'agency' (2002: 17).

'Does it matter who did it?' an Athenian female teacher told me emphatically and continued: 'As if we will ever find out! They [the Americans] will accuse whoever it is in their interest to accuse. It might have been the Arabs, or perhaps not. Who will ever prove beyond any doubt that it was bin Laden? And who made bin Laden anyway? It's probably the CIA, or the US military who crave for another war to have their salaries and power increased. But even if it is not their own deed, they will use it to instigate further wars, and to cause further pain. My God, what lies ahead of us!' Or, as Constantinos Vergopoulos, a Greek professor of economics at the University of Athens, put it: 'But the question remains. Has bin Laden any connection to all this? This strike was the deed of *agents provocateurs* and is used by America in order to continue the policies they have instigated a long time ago ... it might be the CIA, or even not [behind the attacks] ... but to US policy this was an unexpected gift.'[15]

A COMMENT ON HISTORICAL CAUSALITY, NOTIONS OF JUSTICE AND COLLECTIVE RESPONSIBILITY

In an attempt to explain anti-Americanism, Said argues that such a political stance is the result of 'a series of historical interventions and inhuman policies coldly exercised by the US' (2001: 45). With specific reference to Greece, the reactions to the terrorist attacks of September 2001 – which almost jeopardized the smooth relations with the Greek-American community[16] – were characterized by a profound, openly expressed, and diversely justified, holistic anti-Americanism. These anti-American feelings are potentially explained in the context of the historically formed collective consciousness of the Athenians as well as in the framework of political convenience and, as I am arguing, perhaps in the very concepts that organize modern political thought and action.

Baudrillard claims that 11 September was effectively the war of God against himself, the result of a system that effectively produces vengeance by 'seizing all the cards for itself', thus forcing the 'Other to change the rules' (2002: 9). Almost all of my Athenian informants would agree with both Baudrillard's statements. The belief that the attack was somehow the deed of *agents provocateurs*, exposes – if seen from a historical perspective – the Athenian conviction that no one else but the 'Great Power' could actually harm the 'Great Power'. The notion of the 'foreign finger', a metonym usually for the US – but also for Europe, depending on the circumstances – has been in Greece the key exegetical term for national and international political affairs, misfortunes and tragedies after the Second World War. Mouzelis (1993), anticipating Pipes (1996, 1997), criticizes the Greek 'fear of responsibility' evident in the popularity of conspiracy theories that promote 'outside intervention' as the pattern *par excellence* of political causality. Sutton, however, commenting upon both Pipes and Mouzelis, argues that foreign intervention constitutes 'the consistent pattern in Greece's relationship with the West which reflected Greece's relative lack of power and the realities of colonial and post-colonial world politics' (2003: 197). Had the strike on the WTC happened in Greece or any other 'peripheral' country, Greek political cosmologies would instinctively point to the US as the sole capable perpetrator of the crime. The fact that the attack took place in New York itself did not therefore prevent several commentators from applying the same line of reasoning, accusing the CIA and the US secret services for it. As irrational as a provocateur scenario might seem in the context of the great losses in human life, material resources, and prestige suffered by the US, it is still meaningful in Greek historical consciousness and cultural imagery.

An anthropological exploration of Athenian exegetical patterns in terms of indigenous historical consciousness and the conceptual background of significant institutions of modernity, such as the nation-state, could be perhaps challenged as ill-advised if I did not refer at this point to the role of the media and those specific historical events that synthesize the aetiological pattern of Athenian narratives. The importance of the media in analyzing terrorism has been already indicated by theorists in the field. Zulaika and Douglass comment extensively on the public attention that substantiates terrorist attacks and is guaranteed by extensive media coverage of those events (1996: 4–7), while Jenkins has claimed that '[t]errorism is violence aimed at people watching' (1975: 1). Much more important to the present argument, however, is the alleged influence the media exercise on the formation of public opinion. Discussing media events as the 'live broadcasting of history', Dayan and Katz claim that certain occasions are elevated into 'television ceremonies' (1992: 1, 5), 'integrat[ing] societies in a collective heartbeat and evok[ing] a renewal of loyalty to the society and its legitimate authority' (ibid.: 9). The two authors, very much in line with contemporary cultural theory on media, argue in favour of the creation of a kind of *communitas* between the viewers (1992: 196–7), and the ability of the media to effect institutional changes on politics, religion, collective memory, and symbolic interpretation of reality as the latter is presented and reworked in cultural tele-performances (ibid.: 189, 15).

It would be an ethnographic oversight not to admit that Athenian perceptions and explanations of events such as 11 September coincided with the stories and exegesis offered in television broadcasts, other popular media, as well as the World Wide Web. Brown and Theodossopoulos, assessing Greek and Macedonian commentaries on the war in Kosovo, were forced to deal with the same issue:

Globalisation operating through media conglomerates such as CNN or through the world-wide web, can engineer the production and distribution of news and information so that people in widely dispersed locations find themselves drawn into a single discursive space. (2003: 317)

Conspiracist scenarios and seemingly irrational explanations of the events of 11 September as a deed of the CIA and the US secret services are best explained not as 'systemic problems of an irrational periphery' reproducing uncritically populist stories offered by the media (Gledhill 2000: 167). Rather, a closer look is certainly worth taking at those historical moments that contributed – in Greece at least – to the formation of an image of the US as a powerful and all-mighty entity geared towards manipulating the course of international history in order to advance its own interests.

In an excellent overview of modern Greek history, Clogg (1992) offers abundant explanation for both Greece's ambivalence towards the West as well as the widely held belief that every significant historical moment is staged by the US and the Western powers in general. Just after the Second World War a bitter civil war broke in Greece, which ended in favour of government forces that were crucially empowered by British and American aid (Clogg 1992: 141–2). Real or sometimes alleged interference by the US[17] in post-civil war Greek political affairs culminated in the support – or better in the non-condemnation by the US government and the NATO allies – of the military junta that established itself in Greece in April 1967 (Clogg 1992: 165). The dramatic events on Cyprus in 1974 were also explained in terms of outside influence or the 'foreign finger', further strengthening negative perceptions of the US as the power that effectively steered local and international history (see Clogg 1992: 150–71; Sutton 2003: 201; Brown and Theodossopoulos 2003: 321–2).

Another feature of Greek political life that contributes to the perceived validity of conspiracist explanations for the existence and actions of local and international terrorist groups is closely related to the existence of a wider political network known as the *'parakratos'* (semi-legal state apparatus, para-governmental network, or 'parastate' as Clogg [1992: 157] translates it). The *parakratos* that surrounded Greek post-Second World War governments, at times imposing its wishes on them, was certainly thought as having a great influence in the course of political affairs until the early 1980s[18] (see Makrydimitris 2003: 98–9; Kassimeris 2002: 83–5). More often than not the *parakratos* has been associated with the most conservative forces within Greece, serving thus as a 'familiar' metaphor for the conceptualization of the 'unfamiliar' CIA and US secret agencies (see Sutton 1998; Herzfeld 1993). The 'lived experience' of my Athenian interlocutors alongside the standpoints of political parties and intellectuals (Papadakis 1998: 158) form the Athenian 'interpretative frameworks'[19] that collapse 'internalist' and 'externalist' perspectives onto each other (Stewart and Strathern 2002: 16).

Collective Athenian meta-commentaries are hence to be viewed neither as 'mystifications' (ibid.) nor as political aetiologies that have a *sensu stricto* claim to Historical Truth. They are rather the result of the dialectic interplay of a history lived and a history *felt, perceived,* and reworked by the social actors. They are, in other words, firmly situated within history as the 'narrative of the interaction of narratives' (Stewart and Strathern 2002: 16) by means of which original events were described and understood.

Anti-Americanism in Greece and the conspiracy scenarios it fuels, cannot be analytically understood outside these historically informed interpretative frameworks that have nevertheless – and it is indeed worth noting – been traditionally composed and cultivated in the context of a suffocating embrace with the rhetoric of political parties and individuals. The latter consistently utilized, reinforced, and resorted to local-level schemes of causality and accountability for reasons of political convenience. Political parties and intellectuals who shouldered the responsibility of legitimizing Greek *realpolitik* have been consistently capitalizing on such 'narratives of opposition' (see Stewart and Strathern 2002: 11; cf. Clogg 1992: 182). Politicians across the spectrum systematically transferred their own responsibilities and failures on to dark external forces, while simultaneously transforming cases of international crisis into internal political affairs in order to create the polarization necessary for their political survival.

All other particularities of local-level explanatory schemes of terrorism being equal, the overwhelming majority of my Athenian respondents had no difficulty understanding the 'politics of vengeance' in relation to 11 September. Almost no one refrained from admitting, and some even emphasized, that the people killed in the Twin Towers had – strictly speaking – done nothing wrong. Their 'objective innocence'[20] however, was always examined against my informants' perceptions of justice and collective responsibility informed by notions of kinship, blood, and national identity. I shall attempt to disentangle the aforementioned notions, showing that each of them and their *interrelation* forms a context for the articulation of the Athenian political cosmologies of justice that challenge and question the 'irrationality' of terrorism without – at the same time – endorsing its dreadful results. The latter are simply, and perhaps sadly, present in an exegesis that accounts for 11 September as a 'senseless', but nevertheless 'meaningful', event (Stewart and Strathern 2002: 164).

In an article on inter-communal fighting in Cyprus, Loizos notes that vengeance is 'conceptualised as a "natural" response founded in "blood"', constituting a dominant ethos for administering justice in the ethnographic context of Greece (1988: 648). If not always an idea practised nowadays, revenge is admittedly an ideology – once institutionalized in the form of *vendetta* killings – that informs Greek perceptions of social action. As Salamone and Stanton have argued, the Greek self is not conceptualized in terms of individuals but in terms of households (1986), or else kinship units, that collectively embody both blame and praise for the deeds of their individual members. In turn, a number of authors have attested that kinship is the metaphor *par excellence* that mediates the appreciation of ethnic and national identity in Greece (Loizos 1988; Just 1989; Sutton 1998; Hirschon 2000). This is, however, by no means a necessarily culturally specific analogy, and I claim that it should not be seen as an otherwise pre-modern phenomenon unrelated to the very structure of the nation-state as this has been constituted since the eighteenth century. Citizenship might be an unmediated form of belonging to the nation-state, as Gellner (1983) argues, but this does not preclude the importance of kinship and tribal analogies that mediate the understanding and experience of belonging.

Commenting upon the tendency of Athenian public opinion to regard 11 September as the almost 'natural' outcome of the US's cruel and arrogant foreign policies, Dimitrakos attempts to explain the claim supported by many Athenians that 'America is paying for her sins', in the context of a holistic view of the US as an abstract and mythical entity (2001: 137) or else as an 'imagined community' (see Anderson 1983: 15). As I have argued elsewhere, citizens of nation-states imagine the Other to be as much a member of a community as is the Self (Kirtsoglou n.d.). In the minds of a nation's inhabitants, the image of communion with their fellow members is strong and alive despite the fact that they will never know the vast majority of them (Anderson 1983: 15), while each citizen 'has complete confidence in the steady anonymous, simultaneous activity' of her fellow citizens (ibid.: 31). It is because of the latter conviction or 'sense of simultaneity' (Banks, 1996: 127) about the national Self that one perceives the national Other not simply as an individual or a group of individuals but as a member of an equally 'synchronized' and homogeneous community with common perceptions, aspirations, and desires for action (see Loizos 1988).

The sense of national Self is therefore constructed not only on the basis of the belief that one is part of an imagined community, but also and perhaps most importantly on the conviction that the national Other also belongs to a community, which is preferably homogeneous, *hitherto* essentialized and engaged in activity as 'steady, anonymous and simultaneous' as that of the Self (Anderson 1983: 31). In many ways the ability to imagine the Self and the Other as part of respective national communities rests on a vision of the nation as a metaphor for the 'family' constituting kinship as an idiom that mediates nationality, ethnicity, and notions of collectivity. In Greek consciousness, the American nation is therefore guilty in its abstraction for acts designed and committed by certain politicians. This derives from a 'totalizing doctrine of responsibility, a crude, disordered folk-legal doctrine … [that is] generalizing and collectivist and very hostile to both the idea of *individual* responsibility and to causal and contextual specificity' (Loizos 1988: 649–50; original emphasis). The 'totalizing doctrine' in question, however, which predicates that the imaginary community of the Other is responsible in its abstraction for real or assumed 'crimes' and therefore liable to their consequences (see Wilkins 1992: 134), might not be *just* a legal-folk doctrine as Loizos (ibid.) maintains, or 'a cultural survival of pre-modern societies', as Dimitrakos similarly claims (2001: 138). Rather, it could be seen as an element embedded in the very idea of nation-states as imagined communities[21] who continue to hold each other collectively accountable for the actions of their respective fictive kin-groups.[22]

Gledhill (2000: 14), in his discussion of 'tribalism' as a concept applied by Northern politicians and the media to account for non-modern political processes, claims that most features that characterize social conflict in different regions are thoroughly 'modern'. Herzfeld also points to the same direction in his work about the roots of Western bureaucracy and the social production of indifference by observing that the modern nation-states are built and depend upon symbolic motifs allegedly characteristic of older forms of social organization (1993). Seen in this light, revenge is 'therefore a vital element to study in any broad contemporary consideration of violence. Revenge does not enter as an "archaic" element ... It is itself reconstituted in the contemporary context' (Stewart and Strathern 2002: 13). When Athenian commentators talk about America they refer to a collective entity, with collective responsibilities, which suffers the consequences of what are perceived as unjust actions towards other collective entities.

Perhaps despite themselves, and certainly despite the honest attempts of some to point to another direction, my informants regard terrorism in this context as an act of retaliation, a form of vendetta, a cruel but thoroughly comprehensible act of *response*, a provoked and therefore a partly unavoidable crime. As a popular Greek saying goes: 'You can't pick a fight alone' (*monos kavgas den ginetai*).

17th OF NOVEMBER – THE SOCIAL CONTRACT AND THE EXCLUSIONS WITHIN

'The Revolutionary Organisation 17 November', or 17th of November, as most people call it in Greece, is an organization that from December 1975 until July 2002 committed various terrorist acts, mainly and largely successful assassination attacks against Greek and foreign political agents but also businessmen, judges, and journalists in Athens. The 17th of November chose to name itself after the anniversary of the three-day occupation of the School of Engineering in Athens by students and individuals who demanded the end of the military junta that had established itself in Greece after the *coup d'état* of April 1967. The occupation ended on the 17th of November 1973 with the intervention of military forces. The violent incidents in and around the University area[23] marked the beginning of the end of the dictatorial regime, which finally fell in 1974, after the events in Cyprus.

The 17th of November operated in Athens consistently for 27 years. Being probably Europe's last case of urban partisans or 'red terrorists' (Kassimeris 1997),[24] the organization promoted 'revolution' as the only political solution for post-dictatorial Greece. Most of its targets were carefully guarded, while 17th of November appeared to have inside information about Greek political and economic affairs which it disseminated by means of manifestos forwarded after each attack to the newspapers. The character of the targets in conjunction with the number of people actually assassinated – 23 – and the fact that none of the members involved had been injured or captured during its operations, contributed to the mystification of 17th of November.

The aforementioned reasons, combined with the would-be sophisticated rhetoric of the organization, led to the creation of a number of scenarios about its role and composition that were partly but not entirely disabused after the arrest of several individuals accused of being its core members in summer 2002.

A careful examination of the case of the 17th of November reveals that the popular explanations offered for the existence of the organization are similar to the exegeses and accounts of the events of 11 September. Four main discursive trends were promoted in Athens prior to the arrests in July 2002, which if compared to the commentary on the terrorist attack against the WTC and the Pentagon reveal a rather coherent line of political causality and justice. The action of the organization has certainly been 'senseless' but not necessarily meaningless (see Stewart and Strathern 2002: 164) to the Athenian public. It is worth noting that the different scenarios about the 17th of November enjoyed various degrees of popularity over the course of its 27 years of activity depending on the political context, the historical circumstances, and the targets chosen. The 17th of November began its activities in 1975 with the assassination of Richard Welch, the secretary of the US embassy in Athens and *chargé d'affaires* of the CIA in Greece.[25] At first nobody in Greece believed that a local revolutionary/terrorist organization could actually undertake such an operation,[26] and the newspapers kept referring to a 'face-off' between the CIA and the FBI (see Kassimeris 2002: 126–7). The 17th of November was established in the Greek consciousness a year later only after the second assassination of a police officer accused of being a junta collaborator, and the publication of a manifesto in the French newspaper *Libération*.

The first two targets, an agent of the CIA and an officer widely accused of being a junta collaborator, gave 17th of November a certain kudos and perhaps the sympathy of certain social segments in Greece (see Mpossi 1996: 120). Nevertheless, the suspicion that the organization was nothing but the extension of foreign secret services was never completely abandoned. As Kassimeris argues: 'in the seventies, a surprisingly wide range of outstanding politicians, academics and journalists preferred to promote poorly substantiated analyses and conspiracy theories which continued to appear well into the nineties' (2002: 316). Kassimeris is suggestively alluding to an interview that S. Papathemelis, the minister of public order at the time, gave to the British newspaper the *Guardian* in 1994 (ibid.). The minister supported the view that 17th of November was led and controlled by foreign secret agents whose 'specific interest is to harm Greece'.[27]

One of the most tragic attacks by the 17th November was the assassination of Steven Saunders, the British military attaché, in Athens in June 2000. Prior to this incident considerable pressure had been applied to the Greek government by the US State Department, and Congress reports on terrorism in Greece. In this context a number of journalists and politicians hinted – once again – that the assassination was the deed of *agents provocateurs* and the CIA who wanted to 'justify' the recent reports. The attack was seen by many as a 'curious coincidence'; political agents across the spectrum and the media were pointing towards the US[28] (see Vassilakis 2002: 441–50). It would be safe to argue that by the mid-1980s the 17th of November had lost the support of the Greek public while by the late 1990s the organization had completely forfeited ideological resonance. Condemnation of the organization's actions, however, did not prevent the Athenians from speculating about its role and composition, and the *reasons behind* the attacks. As already mentioned, during my fieldwork and prior to the arrests of several organization members, I could identify four main discursive trends in Athens.

First, there was the official stance, also adopted by the relatives of the victims, politicians, journalists, and a number of Athenians. According to this rhetoric – and similarly to what I called 'the official stance' in relation to 11 September – the 17th of November was a terrorist organization and as such it could not be said to have any 'ideology' or motive. Its unscrupulous attacks were regarded as blind strikes against democracy and society as a whole, and they were strongly condemned and denounced.

Those Athenians who expressed this point of view tended to treat the attacks as 'irrational, unprovoked crimes', not crediting them with any political character. The depoliticization and criminalization of the organization sought to deprive 17th of November of its very terrorist status. As Zulaika and Douglass argue, terrorism is a flexible category (1996: x, 12, 14, 26) and characterizing 17th of November as a group of urban partisans meant that their motives were political and therefore their acts potentially justified. Banishing the organization from the realm of discourse effectively cast out the relativism inherent in the political sphere about what can and cannot be deemed a valid form of political action.

The second approach, and one readily offered to the anthropologist, relates to the provoked/unprovoked aetiological scheme. Akin to the comment that the US was paying for her sins, the victims of 17th of November – since and perhaps because they were targets – must have done something wrong. The attacks, several Athenians maintained, were directed at people who were involved in one way or another in cases of financial and political misbehaviour. 'Somewhere along the line they must have had their hands dirty', a 50-year-old Athenian told me, and continued: 'they [17th of November] know who to target. Not that I agree, but they know.'[29] Interestingly, because the attacks were not seen as 'blind strikes', the majority of the Athenians did not feel threatened by the existence of a terrorist organization in their city. Suggestive is the comment of a 48-year-old civil servant: 'Why should I be scared? Am I a politician, a businessman or a journalist? The people who have power should be scared of 17th of November, not me!'[30] It is important to note that distinguishing between the cruelty of the act and the motives behind it does not necessarily mean that my Athenian respondents endorsed the attacks, or felt unsympathetically towards the victims and their families.[31] When compared to 11 September, many were readily commenting upon the sad character of the events. But as I have mentioned before, the tragedy is simply and indeed sadly present, rendering the event 'senseless' but not necessarily depriving it of its 'meaningful' status (see Stewart and Strathern 2002: 164).

Very much like the case of the strikes on the WTC, many Athenians insisted that 17th of November was part of the semi-legal state apparatus (*parakratos*). According to this explanation, the attacks had the sole purpose of either diverting the public attention from major events, such as matters of foreign and economic policy, or legitimizing governmental intentions and actions. '*They* [themselves] are the 17th of November,' several Athenians told me, emphatically pointing to a number of different individuals and agencies. By 'they' some meant the state and the politicians in general who, irrespective of their affiliation and circumstances, are regarded as having *hitherto* an interest in 'covering things up', of disorienting the public and of legitimizing unfair or harmful policies. 'Covering things up' refers in turn largely to financial policies, while disorienting the public is related to foreign affairs. Politicians are widely suspected in Athens for either 'stealing' people's money or – with reference to Greek foreign policy – 'submitting to the wishes of the West, which more often than not are distrusted for being anti-Hellenic' (*anthellinikes*). For other informants, however, 'they' refers to leftists and socialists. According to the latter perspective, 17th of November was the post-dictatorial (left-wing) semi-legal para-governmental network that succeeded the pre-dictatorial (right-wing) one. As such, its main purpose was to terrorize and threaten individuals who came from the conservative end of the political spectrum.[32]

Last but not least, a number of Athenians – and depending on the circumstances, of course, frequently the very same individuals who had offered a different explanation before – maintained that the 17th of November did not exist independently of the US. It was part of the US secret services (often referred to by the generic name 'foreign forces, or 'the foreign agent')[33] that used the premeditated strikes as an excuse to intervene in local politics and to gain access to local security services. 'They [the Americans] want to show that Greece is unsafe; and then they will say "we will come to help you find 17th of November". Can you think of a better excuse?' a 36-year-old businesswoman told me. US insistence upon the cooperation of states against terrorism further fuelled perceptions that effectively denied the existence of terrorism independently of the 'Great Power' and its intention to intervene and control local affairs on a worldwide scale.[34]

In July 2002 a bomb exploded in the hands of an individual called Savvas Ksiros leading to the arrest of 17 people, currently accused of being members of the revolutionary organisation 17th of November. Some of them confessed to having committed several of the attacks while others denied any involvement with terrorism. The profiles of the 17 defendants undoubtedly contributed to the demystification and disparagement of 17th of November. Three of them were brothers, the sons of a priest, while the entire captured network was composed of people related to each other by kinship or other ties. Best men, close friends, co-villagers, brothers, and a woman who was once the partner of one of the members but later the lover of another, were revealed to be the people behind the 'calculated' and 'professionally executed' attacks. The physique of the terrorists, their ordinariness, their low educational status and the fact that some of them admitted to a number of robberies, made them look more like a gang of bandits rather than a terrorist group of great consequence.

Immediately after the arrests and for months afterwards, the Athenians – and people in Greece generally – were expecting to see who was 'behind' these 'sorry fellows'. A great number of my informants still adhere to the theory that the organization was either part of the state or an extension of the 'foreign finger', simply because of their certainty that the particular individuals caught 'could not have been capable of conceiving of the attacks'; they were simply the 'executants'. Athens is continuing, to a certain extent, to wait for the *real* 17th of November, 'the masterminds', the ones who fit the profile of either the communist intellectual or the *agent provocateur* connected to the state, or the US secret services or both. 'This is simply eyewash,' many Athenians assert. 'We will never learn the truth,' others maintain, while yet others are desperately struggling to conceptualize 'how on earth these people succeeded in not getting caught all these years'. It is perhaps because there is no other, simpler and most self-evident truth, than the statement a member of the organization made during the trial: 'If it was not for the Americans there wouldn't be 17th of November.' It would be, I believe, safe to hypothesize that anti-Americanism as an emotion and as a discourse with historicity, depth, and cultural meaning played an important part in the political survival of parties and individuals employing it as well as in the organization's 27-year career.

TERRORISM AND THE PERCEIVED FRAGILITY OF THE 'SOCIAL CONTRACT'

The people who live and work in the Greek capital are possibly not alone in their conviction that terrorism is a 'shifty category' (Zulaika and Douglass 1996: x). The war against terrorism in Afghanistan, the Palestinian suicide bombers, even the recent war in Iraq, are for them simply 'excuses', examples of how to dismiss 'entire countries as "terrorists" or "terrorist sympathizers" ... by abolishing their long and rich histories', the most blatant reminder that a Great Power exists simply by being able to determine today's 'terrorist' who also happen to be yesterday's 'ally' and vice versa (ibid.: 23, 12, 81).[35] Suicide bombing, several Athenians maintain, 'is the last resort of people who are not supplied with arms and who are denied the chance to fight for their own country'. Most of my informants – engaging in political aetiology that, once again, attempts to separate the act from the motives – claim that 'it's a shame to be killed while shopping, drinking a coffee, or in the course of a meal, but the US, through forcing the international community to support her policies, denies the Palestinians the right to have a homeland. Their fight makes sense.' The strikes against Afghanistan and Iraq, on the other hand, make no sense at all to most local-level Athenian commentators, and the realization that 'Greece is forced to formally support' such actions further infuriates them. 'We are forced allies, bondservants, a conquered country,' they emphasize, and they add 'we are the serfs of the new world order'.

The idea that 'Greece belongs to the West' was undoubtedly the context of almost all political discussions and decisions that have taken place in Greece since the Second World War. Of equal importance, however, has been the feeling, the conviction that Greece is not part of the Great Western Powers (see Clogg 1992: 179, 181; Argyrou 2002: 100–1). The tension between *'belonging to but not necessarily feeling an equal member of'* is the core of Athenian political aetiologies and perceptions of terrorism as well as the organizing theme of Greek political cosmologies. Greece is not only oscillating between East and West, as Herzfeld pointedly claims, introducing the term *disemia* in order to analytically capture this phenomenon (1987), but also perceives itself as the West's 'interior exclusion' (Fuss 1991; cf. Tsing 2002: 334).

The role of religion and feelings of cultural intimacy between Greece and its Slavic neighbours ought to be discussed at this point as potentially significant factors towards understanding anti-Americanism and Greece's ambivalent relation to the West. Brown and Theodossopoulos (2003) discuss extensively the similarity between Macedonian and Greek views on the war in Kosovo in terms of certain cultural and historical patterns prevalent in the Balkan region. Although I do not deny the importance of common cultural patterns and the similar geopolitical and historical positionalities of the Balkan people, it must be said that Greece and its northern Slavic neighbours were never traditional allies in modern times (see Clogg 1992; Karakasidou 1997; Danforth 2003). It is nonetheless true that NATO military action against Serbia in Spring 1999 fuelled anti-American sentiments in Greece, manifested in frequent demonstrations, protests, and expressions of 'brotherhood' towards the Serbs. Adherence to the Eastern Orthodox tradition that binds a significant portion of the Balkan people could be a potential explanation for Greek feelings at the time (see Brown and Theodossopoulos 2000, 2003). The undeniable division between Catholic and Eastern Orthodox Christianity (Gledhill 2000: 45) – rooted in the reluctance of the Catholic West to stop the Ottoman expansion that led to the destruction of the Byzantine empire[36] (ibid.; Brown and Theodossopoulos 2003: 323) – cannot, however, be a sufficient explanation for Athenian and Greek attitudes towards the US and the Western Powers. As already mentioned, the role of the US in the Israeli–Palestinian conflict, the strikes against Afghanistan and later the war in Iraq triggered similar condemnation and extensive anti-American commentary in Athens,[37] although no cultural, political, or historical affiliation can be claimed to exist between Greece and the aforementioned states. As Brown and Theodossopoulos argue, such narratives of resistance can only be explained as 'conscious attempts [on behalf of the local interlocutors] to formulate coherent personal standpoints on causality, accountability and the moral order and attempts to explain justice, injustice and human suffering in the political arena' (2003: 24). I would like to further claim at this point that the study on perceptions of terrorism in Athens, with its unavoidable emphasis on scenarios permeated by anti-Americanism and claims relating to 'foreign intervention', reveals certain weaknesses inherent in the political vision and reality of the modern era. It is these weaknesses that ultimately constitute terrorism in the discourses of Athenian individuals, a *context*, an *excuse*, an *occasion*, or a *pretext* for the expression and negotiation of a more general system of accountability and political and historical causality.

My aim has not been to discuss the moral and political dimension of terrorist acts *per se*. By concentrating on perceptions of terrorism in Athens, my intention has been to explore the framework of asymmetrical relations of power within which Athenian social actors strive to decipher the motives and logic behind actions they cannot otherwise control. The complexity of indigenous forms of political causality inherent in my ethnographic material has, I believe, its roots in an otherwise straightforward conviction that the 'social contract' as a principle of Western post-enlightenment political organization has been and is being constantly violated. As Gellner argues: 'social contract theories are indeed a *kind* of foundation myth' (1995: 62), and it could be argued that, as exemplified in the writings of theorists like Rawls, the social contract is nothing more than a hypothetical imaginary concept (Sandel 1998: 105) that underpins the modern *principles* of social organization rather than *realpolitik*. Nonetheless, 'consensus' *is* deemed to be the ultimate criterion of legitimacy in modern Western societies (see Scruton 2002: 8), and in this context, Athenian subjects feel excluded because the obligations arising from their 'citizenship' appear to be not freely undertaken but imposed.

Perceptions of terrorism in Athens re-enact the debate between retribution and restitution, retributive and restorative justice (Govier 2002: 66). The most fundamental difficulty the majority of Athenians face, however, arises from what they regard as a paradoxical lack of consensus upon the basic principles of justice (see Rawls 1971) combined with what is seen as a call on behalf of the US for worldwide consensus upon acts of collective and unilateral retribution. My informants are thus treating 'terrorism' as an 'excuse' employed by the 'Great Power' in her effort to dissolve the 'constraints of justice that binds us', and to thereby cast certain nations 'outside the protection of the rules of justice' (Frey and Morris 1991: 9, 10). What is then left to people but the ethic of retribution that the Athenian subjects – also perhaps founded on culturally specific reasons (see Loizos 1988) – understand and trust?[38]

In a discussion of the concept of 'civil society'[39] Dimitrakos debates the notion of 'trust', arguing that in 'traditional' societies trust is 'ensured through hierarchical relations of obedience and reciprocal obligation inscribed in custom' (2003: 29). Conversely, within the context of the 'civil society', trust is ensured through freedom and a sense of 'self chosen obligation' (Scruton 2002: 8) to commit oneself 'to sanctioning mechanisms in the event that the contract is broken. [Civil society] presupposes the equality of the signatories' (Dimitrakos 2003: 30). Defining civil society in terms of the 'plurality of institutions that are both opposing and balancing the state', Gellner (1994: 1) claims that the civil society ensures the 'impossibility of ideological monopoly' (ibid.: 3–4; 211). The Athenian historical and political experience, however, is somewhat dissonant with that contractual promise. The relations of Greek people to the state have certainly been generally hierarchical (see Theodossopoulos 2003), guided by an ethos of patronage and clientelism (see Campbell 1964; Mouzelis 1978; Clogg 1992), impeded by the indifference of bureaucracy (Herzfeld 1993) and organized around the 'importance of political "connections" for getting things done' (Sutton 2003: 200). The geopolitical importance of Greece in the Cold War years constituted 'foreign intervention', 'not an exception but a consistent pattern in Greece's relationship with the West' (ibid.: 197; see Nachmani 1990; Samatas 1986: 15; Papadopoulos 1989: 49; Clogg 1992: 146–71). And last but not least, the power of the *parakratos* (semi-legal state apparatus) proved important in shaping the political developments within Greece (Kassimeris 2002: 83–5; Papahellas 1997; Makrydimitris 2003: 98–9; Clogg 1992: 157). Further confronted with the US's documented 'political unilateralism' (Chomsky 2002: 111) and the partiality with which human rights are dealt with (Zizek 2002: 150), the Athenians find it difficult to accept that the 'Great Power' of the new world order is concerned with humanitarianism and restorative justice rather than simply with 'its own interests' (see Chomsky 1988; 2002: 14–15; Sutton 2003).

The conspiracy theories that empty terrorism of its political meaning, diverting Athenian attention from the consequences of acts of terror – ultimately executed by individuals – are an example of what Sutton calls 'analogic thinking as history' (1998; 2003). Trust that arises from consensus, contract, and an 'equal commitment to sanctioning mechanisms' was never established in the Athenian consciousness: neither in relation to citizenship within the nation, nor with reference to participation in the global community. The experience of familiar local-level Greek history fed the collective imagery of the unfamiliar, large-scale international politics and vice versa, for years, constituting the 'open society of contract and freedom', a promised fantasy but as yet unseen reality. Terrorism and violence have become in this context features of a still hegemonic *realpolitik*, and are interpreted by the Athenians in the framework of anti-authoritarianism, a discursive practice that finds its best representation in anti-Americanism. The latter has indeed been elevated into a kind of 'national dogma which offers security in an uneasy and confused nation' (Kassimeris 2002: 75; cf. Legg and Roberts 1997).

Perceptions of local-level and international terrorism reveal an Athenian political cosmology of mistrust that aims to account for the disappointments and inconsistencies of the contractarian land of promise. It is to this land that the Greeks, by committing themselves to the West (see Clogg 1992: 179, 181; Argyrou 2002: 100–1), have started a long journey that never seems to end. This is not to say, of course, that such a place does not exist, but the political scene of Cold War and post-Cold War politics has not been entirely directed by either the principles of the 'social contract' or those of social trust based on such a contract. This realization leads my Athenian informants to speak of terrorism as a response to 'the other' terrorism (see Chomsky 1988; Gilsenan 2002; Gledhill 2000: 153; Honderich 1976), which is seen as guilty of constantly and brutally committing 'unspeakable crimes in the name of justice'.[40]

AFTERWORD – BY WAY OF CONCLUSION

Violent acts, terrorist or not, are hardly easy to legitimize. Especially when these acts are retributive, inspired by and organized around notions of collective responsibility while simultaneously circumventing collective consensus, they can be seen as a direct threat to both the ideas of the social contract and the civil society. It is perhaps unfortunate that Athenians and Greek subjects in general, irrespective of their particular political affiliations, largely confront modernity and modernization as a venerated condition of existence. I say that it is unfortunate because so far on a number of occasions these very same subjects have felt betrayed by their own vision, having to deal not only with the ambiguities of terrorism and violence but also with the inconsistencies of a harsh and not always straightforward political reality. They do so under the weight of their own historical narrative and in anticipation of a future that at times is envisaged as being no different from the past. Local perceptions of terrorism reveal a culturally and historically rich set of political cosmologies filled with anxiety and mistrust.

I have argued and ethnographically substantiated two main points in this chapter. First that notions of collective responsibility and retributive justice are not simply 'archaic element[s]', but 'reconstituted in the contemporary context' (Stewart and Strathern

2002: 13; cf. Gledhill 2000: 14, 17), reinforced by the idea of the nation-state as an imagined community that 'stands as the fullest institutional expression of human solidarity we have to date' (Wilkins 1992: 26). My second point relates to the majority of my informants' perception that terrorism is mainly an 'excuse', and their insistence upon treating terrorist acts as largely senseless events with sad consequences but not as meaningless actions. The Athenians show tremendous perseverance in constructing provocateur scenarios of political causality. This tendency alongside their view of terrorism as a multivalent trope easily manipulated in favour of the powerful, ought not to be treated as a case of irrationality, mystification, and lagging modernization. Such perceptions of terrorism, I have argued, are expressive instances of the perceived circumvention of consensus and fragility of the social contract that undermine in Athenian consciousness the very notion and experience of the civil society. The selective application of 'sanctioning mechanisms' and what is seen as a flagrant exhibition of power on behalf of the US promote further mistrust in Athens. As a result, social actors view themselves as the 'interior exclusion' or the 'exclusion within' a world order that ought to be composed of equal citizens but appears instead as consisting of distinguished citizens, bondservants, and subjects.

Indigenous commentary on terrorism – and politics in general – is the very discursive field where political identity is constituted, not simply against abstract ideologies, but in the context of relations between persons and between collectivities. Political cosmologies, then, are not only 'systems of accountability', or the means by which actors make sense of history. They are also symbolic spaces where the actors participate in making history and as such they deserve a sophisticated theorization, for they can also become contexts for intricate discussions of individuality, agency, cultural, and political membership.

NOTES

1. *'Tromokratia sou leei! Poios t'agorazei auta? Edo ftynoume aima na kanoume ekato metra stin Kiffisias kai prospathoun na mas peisoun oti dyo typoi skotosane enan allon kai fygane kyrioi. Oxi tipota kommantos, dyo tromokrates leei. Kai pou kserane autoi gia ton Saunders mou les? A, re amoire lae, enas Theos kserei ti paihnidia paizoyne piso ap'tin plati mas ki auti ti fora.'*
2. The locus of my fieldwork has mainly been the 'municipality of Athens', although other areas have by no means been excluded. Most of my informants belong to the typification of the 'ordinary' Athenian, who is – more often than not – born in a provincial village or town and has migrated to Athens in search of better work opportunities, recently or decades ago. The socio-economic and educational profiles of my informants vary greatly, reflecting the multiplicity of the city. However, they are in their totality Greek-identified subjects.

3. The author is referring here to the US's position in the collective Greek imagery.

4. Throughout the chapter I document mixed, contradictory, and even self-contradictory Athenian perceptions about local and international terrorism. Owing to these apparent contradictions I was unable to typify Athenian views into self-contained categories that explicitly indicate class and political affiliation. An attempt to do so would have simply violated the qualitative complexity and fluidity of the accounts I recorded and the intentions of their authors.

5. '*kyrioi, irthe i ora na plirosete to logariasmo*'.

6. Paralleling terrorism with cases of sexual scandals involving priests, the author finds the Catholic Church's insistence on treating such incidents as 'internal' matters justified: 'abuse of children is the Church's internal problem; that is to say, an inherent product of its very institutional symbolic organisation, not just a series of particular criminal cases concerning individuals who happen to be priests' (Zizek 2002: 29–30).

7. '*den itan aproklites energeies*'.

8. It is perhaps not very clear what Tsoukalas means here by 'unrestrained' rationalism. I take 'rationalism' to stand as a culturally specific metonym for a number of notions like capitalism, liberalism, positivism, and globalization that are frequently grouped together in Greece by academics and non-academics alike.

9. '*oti spernoun therizoun*'.

10. It is probably important to note at this point that when the Greek media employed the term 'terrorists' to refer to those officially accused of terrorism – be it bin Laden or the Al-Qaeda network – the word most frequently appeared in inverted commas to denote the questionable validity of the accusations.

11. Indicative of a context of intolerance to pro-US attitudes in Athens at the time is perhaps the dismissal of Athanasios Ellis, the US correspondent of *Kathimerini*, allegedly owing to his pro-US stance and the fact that in his articles he highlighted the irrationality of conspiracy scenarios involving the CIA, urging the Greeks to 'prove in practice that they belong to the West' (7/10/2001; cf. Vassilakis 2002: 204).

12. '*Autoi to kanane.*'

13. '*Kai ton bin Laden poios ton eftiakse?*'

14. Gledhill also puts forward a similar claim in relation to Saddam Hussein's survival in power for reasons related to the economic and geopolitical interests of the NATO alliance (2000: 158). Similarly, Western intervention in Iraq provoked in Athens a line of commentary analogous to that on the strikes in Afghanistan. US political interests were seen by my Athenian informants as the only rationale behind US's initial support of the Hussein regime and its subsequent destruction.

15. Extracts from interview in the Athenian newspaper *Ethnos*.

16. For more information on the Greek-American community and its importance, see Clogg 1992: 4–5.

17. While in certain occasions US interference is well-documented, in some others it is not (see, e.g., particular instances discussed by Clogg 1992: 147, 155). What is perhaps more important for the argument of this chapter is that allegations of that type illustrate the long-run Greek historical consciousness and Greek attitudes towards the US and the Western powers in general (see Loizos 1981; Herzfeld 1993).

18. The *parakratos* has been widely considered as responsible for a number of events that were seen as having led to the establishment of the seven-year-long dictatorship in Greece. As a term, it was coined in 1963 after the assassination of the MP G. Lamprakis by para-governmental agents. According to some, the *parakratos*, in one way or another exists even today. The role of the *parakratos* becomes especially important in the case of local terrorism in Greece, accounted for in the following section.

19. Schröder and Schmidt (2001: 12), quoted in Stewart and Strathern (2002: 163).

20. As a 30-year-old public servant told me: 'objectively speaking, the 3,000 were innocent' (*antikeimenika oi treis hiliades itane athooi*).

21. As Wilkins has argued: 'the political community or nation state stands as the fullest institutional expression of human solidarity we have to date' (1992: 26).

22. A similar observation is made by Stewart and Strathern (2002: 12–13), echoing Ferguson and Whitehead.

23. During these episodes 34 students were killed and 800 individuals were injured.

24. For a detailed account of the 17th of November, see Kassimeris 1997, 2002.

25. See Kassimeris 2002: 13; Papahellas and Telloglou 2003: 74, 75. An interesting discussion on political violence as rational and compatible with democracy can be found in Honderich (1976), while Lodge's volume contains an anthology of case-studies on terrorism in Europe (1981). According to Lodge's typification '17 of November' is – as Kassimeris 2002 claims – a revolutionary terrorist organization since it aimed at 'effecting a complete revolutionary change within the political system' (1981: 3).

26. The first track-manifesto of 17th of November was sent to all the Athenian newspapers but it was never published. The organization had to send a second one, two days later, insisting upon the 'authenticity', so to speak, of the attack, which was equally ignored. Noteworthy is the extreme anti-American content of the first manifesto, which revolved around the idea that 'American imperialism is the number one enemy of our people, the chief responsible [force] along with the local fascists, for the numerous inflictions, tragedies and crimes against our people in the last decades. Wherever we cast our eyes on, we see the CIA's finger' (24 December 1975).

27. *Guardian* (30 September 1994): see Kassimeris 2002: 317.

28. This is not to say that there were no exceptions. The ease with which CIA scenarios are revived, however, is indicative of the strength or rather the depth that the belief in 'foreign intervention' still has in Greece.

29. '*Kapou ehoun ki autoi leromeni ti folia tous. Kseroun poion htypane. Ohi oti symfono, alla kseroun.*'

30. '*Giati na fovitho? Ti eimai ego? Politikos eimai, ergostasiarhis, i dimosiografos? Autoi pou ehoun eksousia na fovithoun ti 17 Noembri ohi ego!*'

31. 'What a pity!' (*krima*) was a frequent remark that a number of Athenians made. Especially in the case of Steven Saunders the attack was also seen by many as a violation of hospitality. The British – unlike the Americans – are hardly ever accused of intervening in Greek internal affairs. It is perhaps because Saunders was British that he was considered a 'guest'

and not an imposition on Athens. As a 35-year-old woman told me, 'if it was us, it's a shame; like killing a guest in your own house...What a pity for his poor lady too! Imagine what they will think of Greece now!' (*An to kaname emeis einai ntropi. San na skotoneis ton mousafiri sto spiti sou ... kai i kaimeni i gynaika tou krima ... Fantasou ti tha skeftontai gia tin Ellada tora!*) Still, it is interesting to note the doubt – '*if it was us*' – which directly refers to the involvement of foreign agents, as well as the assumption of collective responsibility.

32. The only difference of this latter perception with its 11 September counterpart is that in the US case the attack was credited to *agents provocateurs* with conservative interests.

33. *Ksenes dynameis, ksenos paragontas.*

34. Another interesting extract from my fieldnotes is the following: 'The Americans are behind all this. They want once again to come and sit in their high chairs in the middle of Athens and survey us. Not even a fly can go by without their approval, but they won't have it their way!' (*Oi amerikanoi einai piso apo ola auta. Theloun na erthoun stin kardia tis Athinas, na piasoun tis karekles kai na mas epitiroun. Oute myga den petaei ama den poun autoi to ok, alla den tha tous perasei.*)

35. Leach advances an argument on this issue in his book *Custom, Law and Terrorist Violence*, where he points out the similar characteristics of the terrorist and the hero and discusses extensively the issue of legitimacy and power. According to Leach, the terrorist can be seen as an inverted ruler who exercises power not on the grounds of a legitimate authority 'delegated from society', but 'by virtue of an illegitimate authority delegated by a factional group of revolutionaries' (1977: 18). Legitimacy is for Leach what distinguishes criminality from lawfulness since 'legitimate actions of the ruler become the criminal acts of the ex-ruler' (ibid.: 16).

36. The rift between Catholicism and Eastern Orthodoxy dates back to the schism between the two churches in the eleventh century. The unwillingness – or inability – of the Orthodox West to halt the Ottoman expansion that culminated with the destruction of the Byzantine empire in 1453 led to a further deterioration of the relationship between the two churches.

37. The spirit of anti-war demonstrations during the war in Iraq could further support my claim here. A number of the demonstrators were holding Iraqi flags, and the statement '*We are all Iraqis*' was written on one of the largest banners held by the protestors. The picture was of course very similar to all previous demonstrations against the strikes on Yugoslavia and Afghanistan. The American Embassy has traditionally been the final destination of various demonstrations in the last two decades.

38. As Wilkins argues, 'to the extent that we have recourse to violence we have lost faith in the justice of society's basic institutions or in society's willingness to rectify an unjust state of affairs' (1992: 6–7).

39. Dimitrakos exemplifies the notion of civil society as 'the sphere [of social action] between the state and the citizen...which counterbalances political society. Civil society operates in a complementary fashion to the state, insofar as the latter is based upon a consensus formed within the former' (2003: 19). For further discussion of the notion of 'civil society' see suggestively Gellner 1995; Hann and Dunn 1996; Gray 1995.

40. '*Aneipota eglimata sto onoma tis dikaiosynis.*'

REFERENCES

Amit, V. and Rapport, N. (2002) *The Trouble with Community: Anthropological reflections on movement, identity and collectivity.* London: Pluto Press.

Anderson, B. (1983) *Imagined Communities: Reflections on the origins and spread of nationalism.* London: Verso.

Argyrou, V. (2002) *Anthropology and the Will to Meaning: A post-colonial critique.* London: Pluto Press.

Banks, M. (1996) *Ethnicity: Anthropological constructions.* London: Routledge.

Baudrillard, J. (2002) *The Spirit of Terrorism.* London and New York: Verso.

Brown, K. and Theodossopoulos, D. (2000) 'The Performance of Anxiety: Greek narratives of the war at Kosovo'. *Anthropology Today*, 16(1): 3–8.

—— (2003) 'Rearranging Solidarity: Conspiracy and World Order in Greek and Macedonian Commentaries of Kosovo'. *Journal of Southern Europe and the Balkans*, 4(3): 315–35.

Campbell, J.K. (1964) *Honour, Family and Patronage; A study of institutions and moral values in a Greek mountain community.* New York and Oxford: Oxford University Press.

Chomsky, N. (1988) *Culture of Terrorism.* Cambridge, MA: South End Press.

—— (2002) *9–11.* New York: Seven Stories Press.

Clogg, R. (1992) *A Concise History of Greece.* Cambridge: Cambridge University Press.

Danforth, L. (2003) 'Afterword'. In *The Usable Past: Greek metahistories*, ed. K.S. Brown and Y. Hamilakis. Lanham: Lexington Books.

Dayan, D. and Katz, E. (1992) *Media Events: The live broadcasting of history.* Cambridge, MA: Harvard University Press.

Dimitrakos, D. (2001) 'The Socialism of the Idiots'. In *The New World Disorder*, ed. G. Pretenderis. Athens: To Vima–Nees Epoxes.

—— (2003) 'A Discussion on the Civil Society'. Introduction, in *State and Civil Society*, ed. A. Makrydimitris. Athens: Metamesonykties ekdoseis.

Frey, R.G and Morris, C.W. (1991) 'Violence, Terrorism and Justice'. Introduction, in *Violence, Terrorism and Justice*, ed. R.G. Frey and C.W. Morris. Cambridge: Cambridge University Press.

Fuss, D. (1991) Introduction. *Inside/Out: Lesbian Theories/Gay Theories*, ed. D. Fuss. London: Routledge.

Gellner, E. (1983) *Nations and Nationalism.* Oxford: Basil Blackwell.

—— (1994) *Conditions of Liberty: Civil society and its rivals.* London: Hamish Hamilton.

—— (1995) *Anthropology and Politics: Revolutions in the Sacred Grove.* Oxford: Blackwell.

Giddens, A. (1985) *The Nation-State and Violence.* Cambridge: Polity Press.

Gilsenan, M. (2002) 'On Conflict and Violence'. In *Exotic No More*, ed. J. MacClancy. Chicago and London: University of Chicago Press.

Gledhill, J. (2000) *Power and its Disguises: Anthropological perspectives on politics.* London: Pluto Press.

Govier, T. (2002) *Delicate Balance: What philosophy can tell us about terrorism.* Boulder: Westview Press.

Gray, J. (1995) *Enlightenment's Wake: Politics and culture at the close of the modern age.* London: Routledge.

Hann, C. and Dunn, E. (1996) *Civil Society: Challenging Western models.* London: Routledge.

Herzfeld, M. (1987) *Anthropology Through the Looking-Glass: Critical ethnography in the margins of Europe.* Cambridge: Cambridge University Press.

—— (1993) *The Social Production of Indifference: Exploring the symbolic views of Western bureaucracy.* Chicago: University of Chicago Press.

Hirschon, R. (2000) 'Identity and the Greek State: Some Conceptual Issues and Paradoxes'. In *The Greek Diaspora in the Twentieth Century*, ed. R. Clogg, London: Macmillan, pp. 158–80.

Honderich, T. (1976) *Three Essays on Political Violence.* Oxford: Basil Blackwell.

Jenkins, B. (1975) *International Terrorism: A new mode of conflict.* Los Angeles: Crescent.

Just, R. (1989) 'Triumph of the Ethnos'. In *History and Ethnicity*, ed. E. Tonkin, M. McDonald and M. Chapman. London: Routledge, pp. 71–88.

Karakasidou, A. (1997) *Fields of Wheat, Hills of Blood: Passages to nationhood in Greek Macedonia.* Chicago: University of Chicago Press.

Kassimeris, G. (1997) *Europe's Last Red Terrorists. The Revolutionary Organisation 17 November.* London: C. Hurst and Co.

—— (2002) *The Revolutionary Organisation 17 November.* Athens: Kastaniotis.

Kirtsoglou, E. (n.d.) 'Phantom Menace: What Low Rank Greek Army Officers Have to Say about Turks and Turkey'. In *When Greeks Think about Turks: The View from Anthropology*, ed. D. Theodossopoulos. London: Frank Cass.

Leach, E. (1977) *Custom, Law and Terrorist Violence.* Edinburgh: Edinburgh University Press.

Legg, K. and Roberts, J. (1997) *Politics in Modern Greece.* Stanford: Stanford University Press.

Lodge, J. (1981) Introduction. In *Terrorism: A challenge to the state*, ed. J. Lodge. Oxford: Martin Robertson.

Loizos, P. (1981) *The Heart Grown Bitter: A chronicle of war refugees.* Cambridge: Cambridge University Press.

—— (1988) 'Intercommunal killing in Cyprus'. *Man* (N.S.), 23: 639–53.

MacIntyre, A. (2001) 'The Virtues, the Unity of a Human Life and the Concept of a Tradition'. In *Memory, Identity, Community: The idea of narrative in the human sciences*, ed. L. Hinchman and S. Hinchman. Albany: State University of New York Press.

Makrydimitris, A. (2003) *State and Civil Society.* Athens: Metamesonykties ekdoseis.

Mouzelis, N. (1978) *Modern Greece: Facets of underdevelopment.* New York: Holmes & Meier.

—— (1993) 'Nationalism', Part 1. *To Vima*, 16 May.

Mpossi, M. (1996) *Greece and Terrorism: National and international aspects.* Athens: Sakkoulas.

Nachmani, A. (1990) 'Civil War and Foreign Intervention in Greece 1946–9'. *Journal of Contemporary History*, 25: 489–522.

Papadakis, Y. (1998) 'Greek Cypriot Narratives of History and Collective Identity: Nationalism as a Contested Process'. *American Ethnologist*, 25 (2): 149–65.

Papadopoulos, Y. (1989) 'Parties, the State and Society in Greece: Continuity within Change'. *West European Politics*, 12/2: 55–71.

Papahellas, A. (1997) *The Violation of Greek Democracy: The American intervention, 1947–1967.* Athens: Estia.

Papahellas, A. and Telloglou, A. (2003) *17 November.* Athens: Estia.

Pipes, D. (1996) *The Hidden Hand: Middle East fears of conspiracy*. New York: St Martin's Press.

—— (1997) *Conspiracy: How the paranoid style flourishes and where it comes from*. New York: Free Press.

Pretenderis, G. (2001) 'The New World Disorder'. In *The New World Disorder*, ed. G. Pretenderis. Athens: To Vima–Nees Epoxes.

Rapport, N. (2002) 'The Truth of Movement, the Truth as Movement: Post-cultural Anthropology and Narrational Identity'. In *The Trouble with Community: Anthropological reflections on movement, identity and collectivity*, ed. N. Rapport and V. Amit. London: Pluto Press.

Rawls, J. (1971) *A Theory of Justice*. Cambridge, MA: Harvard University Press.

Said, E. (2001) 'A War without Fronts'. In *The New World Disorder*, ed. G. Pretenderis. Athens: To Vima–Nees Epoxes.

Salamone, S.D. and Stanton, J.B. (1986) 'Introducing the *Noikokyra*: Ideality and Reality in Social Process'. In *Gender and Power in Rural Greece*, ed. J. Dubisch. Princeton: Princeton University Press.

Samatas, M. (1986) 'Greek McCarthyism: A comparative assessment of Greek Post Civil War Repressive Anticommunism and the US Truman/McCarthy era'. *Journal of Hellenic Diaspora*, 13/3–4: 5–75.

Sandel, M. (1998) *Liberalism and the Limits of Justice*. Cambridge: Cambridge University Press.

Schröder, I. and Schmidt, B. (2001) 'Violent Imaginaries and Violent Practices'. Introduction, in *Anthropology of Violence and Conflict*, ed. I. Schroder and B. Schmidt. London: Routledge.

Scruton, R. (2002) *The West and the Rest: Globalisation and the terrorist threat*. London and New York: Continuum.

Stewart, P.J. and Strathern, A. (2002) *Violence; Theory and Ethnography*. London and New York: Continuum.

Sutton, D. (1998) *Memories Cast in Stone; The relevance of the past in everyday life*. Oxford: Berg.

—— (2003) 'Poked by the "foreign finger" in Greece: Conspiracy Theory or the Hermeneutics of Suspicion?' In *The Usable Past: Greek metahistories*, ed. K.S. Brown and Y. Hamilakis. Lanham: Lexington Books.

Theodossopoulos, D. (2003) *Troubles with Turtles; Cultural understandings of the environment in a Greek island*. Oxford: Berghahn.

—— (n.d.) Introduction, in *When Greeks Think about Turks: The View from Anthropology*, ed. D. Theodossopoulos. London: Frank Cass.

Tsing, A.L. (2002) 'Politics on the Periphery'. In *The Anthropology of Politics; A reader in ethnography, theory and critique*, ed. J. Vincent. Oxford: Blackwell.

Tsoukalas, K. (2001) 'The Globalisation of Insecurity'. In *The New World Disorder*, ed. G. Pretenderis. Athens: To Vima–Nees Epoxes.

Vassilakis, M. (2002) *It Served Them Well*. Athens: Gnoseis.

Wilkins, B.T. (1992) *Points of Conflict: Terrorism and collective responsibility*. London: Routledge.

Zizek, S. (2002) *Welcome to the Desert of the Real*. London and New York: Verso.

Zulaika, J. and Douglass, W. (1996) *Terror and Taboo: The follies, fables and faces of terrorism*. London: Routledge.

3 THE INDIAN STATE, ITS SIKH CITIZENS, AND TERROR

Joyce Pettigrew

THE POLITICAL SETTING TO THE BRUTALITIES IN PUNJAB'S VILLAGES

The Sikhs of the Indian Punjab sit astride the Islamic and Hindu worlds of South Asia. They are connected to both by the land, language, and culture of the Punjab. Borders in this region are recent, minority nationalities, such as the Sikhs, showing little interest in them until recent times. Also, in the north-western part of the Indian subcontinent, in which the Punjab with its Sikh population is situated, small-scale social worlds – social units such as household and kinship groups and groupings whose members were bound to each other by mutual interest – had traditionally enjoyed a large measure of freedom. Hence for both these reasons the centralizing and interventionist policies of the central government of India on the Punjab were to become a particular source of discord. Additionally, secularism, the doctrine that India had so fervently espoused at birth, was increasingly being challenged by Hindu interests.

The creation of the two states of India and Pakistan in 1947 sets the scene for what Valentine Daniel has called the 'historicization of place by its transformation into space' (Daniel 1996: 58). The reconstitution of South Asia in terms of communal majorities led the Sikhs in turn to make a plea for recognition on a similar basis. Until the partition of Punjab in 1947 Sikhs had always lived amidst other peoples. One of India's smaller nationalities, they had protected themselves in the past through loose alliances, military defence, and political ententes. As a people they had lived scattered across the entire Punjab and were indeed a people of the Punjab. But in the partition of the province in 1947 they received no territories because of their lack of numerical dominance in any one of its districts. The significance of their belief system as an identity marker came about as a result of having lost their position in the wider Punjab. Until 1947 nothing had chained them to particular pieces of territorial space. Indeed, it was not until

89

the events of 1984 that the consequences of these boundary changes were to take their full effect.

The events of that year followed a decade of peaceful protest concerning economic issues over the right of the state to control the productive process, through controlling water distribution, water rights, and the wheat procurement price. These brought it into conflict with the province's dominant farming population (Jats), who were also prominent in India's ruling elite as army and police officers and civil servants. They demanded financial autonomy from Delhi but this was deemed secessionist. That such a claim for home rule could have been seen as such was essentially because the old idea of India as a cultural entity was being replaced by the actuality of India as a centralized state. It was subsequent to the demand for financial autonomy that political interference in the province's affairs increased. The state was not comfortable when Punjab's elected governments were not dominated by the Congress Party and it proceeded to topple them.[1] Additionally the state felt uneasy with the value system of the Sikhs, which emphasized equality. At the heart of the centralization of the economy, the manipulation of the outcome of the democratic process and the efforts to undermine the Sikh ethic, was an attitude that felt threatened by difference and distinction, seeing these as the forerunners of independence. Three features of Sikh life – that they farmed rich agricultural land, were adjacent to the border, and were prominent in Indian institutions, especially the army – made the process of consolidation of state power in this region essential. And, as Verdery (1994: 39) has noted, 'aspects of the state making process tend to make identities more rather than less imperative, as identity categories become mandatory elements of peoples' existence within the state'.

As non-violent protest for financial autonomy within conventional political channels went unheeded, there came to the fore a charismatic figure named Sant Jarnail Singh Bhindranwale, of small farmer background and with great popularity as a preacher in all sections of Sikh society. He acted as a catalyst for a multitude of accumulated grievances, reframing agrarian protests and rechannelling the people's anger over army recruitment policy, using historical and religious imagery. The grassroots problems of the rural areas turned into Sikh national problems when Sikh institutions in the Golden Temple complex, the Darbar Sahib, were attacked in June 1984. Then, not surprisingly, the affairs of farmers became the concerns of Sikhs as a nation. As Vandana Shiva puts it, 'the Sikhs as a farming community were forgotten, only Sikhs as a religious community remain in the national consciousness' (1991: 184). Collective terror on the part of the state preceded the many acts of individual terror visited on families by the various police agencies. It was well planned and well co-ordinated. First the Golden Temple complex (the Darbar Sahib), symbol of the Sikh community's separate cultural, religious and political existence, was attacked (Operation Bluestar). Sovereignty over the Darbar Sahib complex had never been ceded to any government, and hence the state's action was regarded as an invasive assault. Moreover the Golden Temple, symbol of the Sikh nation as it was, was regarded with great fondness in rural Sikh households. It was called Babaji da ghar (old, respected person's house). Families went there on outings and would often casually wander in after work to meet their friends. When the Indian army invaded, it was on the martyrdom day of one of the gurus and whole families were there. Countless civilians were killed. There are no reliable figures as to how many, but they were in their thousands.[2] Then, secondly, Sikh young men and thereby the Sikh future were attacked in Operation Woodrose. In every village in the three months following the invasion, the army hunted down the followers of Bhindranwale. Sikh youth in the 15–25 age group were taken away from their homes in large numbers and remained in army custody for significant lengths of time. Thirdly, in the first days of November 1984 Sikh communities outside Punjab were attacked. Those killed in Delhi alone numbered 3,750.

Many young people who survived the experiences of 1984 became involved in the fight against the terror of the state with the death of close relatives and friends. It was the behaviour of security forces in the Darbar Sahib and during Operation Woodrose that drew them into the struggle. Also, when friends and family members were arrested and tortured, resistance to terror in the name of honour and justice began.[3] Those who fought, unlike ordinary civilians, felt no terror. They fought to overturn unjust rule. The harassment, torture,[4] and killing of ordinary families brought many recruits in to the movement. Particularly the attacks on *amritdharis*,[5] simply because they were *amritdharis*, caused outrage throughout the entire population and in the early years of the insurgency villagers gave willing assistance to young people on the run. Attempting to avoid surveillance and repression, and in an effort to reorganize the movement, many young people, as well as the leaders of the insurgency, went to Pakistan. From then onwards the Punjab of the Sikhs was to become a centre of intrigue for both states.

The events of 1984 gave Sikhs themselves more reason to make the boundaries of state and nation commensurate with Sikh values as the basis for reorganizing their socio-economic order. Moreover the existence of certain political boundaries meant that identity could only be defined in relation to religion, morality, and culture as they had no sovereignty over any territorial space, only a claim to such space based on their numerical majority in the East Punjab. The

Declaration of Khalistan, an independent Sikh state, established that claim in April 1986.[6]

The above account has presented a specific set of historical and political events in which the key players are an interventionist state and the Sikh status as an incorporated nationality. Together they formed the social fabric through which terror was interwoven. The structures that accommodated terror and to a certain extent sustained it were the more permanent features of Punjab rural life: the service employment of large numbers of the population in the army, civil and police administration; the nature of village society; and the physical environment of the province. All played a significant role in the spread of actual terror as well as in its imagining. To these must be added the changes in legal structure and practice following the events of 1984. The latter sanctioned police and paramilitary action in a wide range of circumstances, allowing certain practices to occur that engendered terror. However, it was the counterinsurgency practices of the state that were of primary significance in the creation of terror, all the more so for being adapted to the social structure of the villages. The dynamics of militant organizations also contributed to terror in the countryside. Actual terror will be discussed by looking at individual cases. It will be contended that although much of the terror was state-directed and state-controlled, nonetheless rural social structure enabled terror to spread significantly. There was an intimate connection between weak neighbourhood ties and the spread of terror.

SMALLHOLDING PATTERNS AND MILITARY RECRUITMENT

After the annexation of what had been the Sikh kingdom of the Punjab in 1849, the Sikh forces were disbanded and formed into new regiments. The British quelled the Indian mutiny with the help of Sikh units and subsequently heavily recruited from them in Punjab, giving many of them distinguished military careers. Men enlisted in the army to supplement their income from smallholdings and indeed to be eligible after long years of loyal service to a fertile plot of land.[7] Through time, army service came to be as much a part of the rural Sikh tradition as farming. Additionally it was thought of as an honourable occupation and a source of honour, prestige, and status for individual families. Because of land being divided equally among all sons, the income from it needed to be supplemented by other forms of activity. Besides the army, government jobs were favoured, and securing them was something to boast about.

Since the independence of India the Sikh percentage of the armed forces has declined under a central government policy that connects recruitment policy to the population sizes of the different Indian provinces. This change in recruitment policy has coincided with the effects of the Green Revolution on Punjabi farmers. Although characterized by an agriculture that exports cereals to the rest of India, Punjab has very few large landholdings. The farming population consists mainly of medium-sized proprietors some of whom, since the Green Revolution, manage their holdings using labour from other parts of India. Although these medium-sized proprietors are the most important economic category, since the Green Revolution a large number of them have fallen into the category of small and marginal farmers. This was because so much had to be acquired for the process of production: special types of seed, which needed more water (and hence more electricity) and more fertilizer and pesticide. Holdings under five acres were no longer viable owing to the cost of inputs and a low wheat procurement price, and the rural economy was under stress, with production costs being higher than returns in the shape of procurement prices. Holdings that were once profitable were no longer so because of the cost of production and there was hence an even greater reliance on other traditional sources of income such as the army and the police.

Collaboration with conquerors had become a visible trend from the time of British rule. On this point a former Inspector General of Police, Bhagwan Singh Danewalia, had a pertinent remark to make regarding the recurring dream of Sikh sovereignty (interview September 1992): 'One has to consider how one comes to lose things. After all, the opportunity for independence came as long ago as the Indian Mutiny. But then reliance set in.' It set in to the extent that Sikh generals were involved in the attack against the Darbar Sahib. Not all Sikhs favoured independence. The wider system offered more opportunity and indeed framed their aspirations. Although their religion, culture, and shared historical experience were quite distinct, their commitment to preserving their own separate identity has been affected by Indian government policies of assimilation. Indeed, what most influenced the outcome of events during and after 1984 were the twin allegiances of the Sikhs themselves to the state and to their own tradition. In contemporary times nowhere could this have been better expressed than by Sant Jarnail Singh Bhindranwale in a speech on 16 July 1983 entitled 'Sikhs in Government Service are being used to destroy Sikhs' (quoted in Sandhu 1999: 188–9). The relevant parts of his speech are as follows:

It is our misfortune that if a person comes to spy on us he is from those who wear turbans. ... Why don't you ask some cleanshaven person to do the espionage? Our misfortune is that when they attack and someone on this [our] side is killed, it is a Sikh. And when something is done from this side and someone on their side dies, it is again a Sikh. What do these cap wearers [Hindus] lose? In the army it is the Sikh who dies; in the police it is the Sikh who gets killed; in the PAP (Punjab Armed Police) it is the Sikh who gets killed; in the CRPF (Central Reserve Police Force) it is the Sikh who gets killed, but when it comes to [army] recruitment, 98.5% is for them and 1.5% for you. Are you suffering from a certain itch that you must fight among yourselves? Being a Sikh myself and considering their Sikh appearance, I should like to say this to those Sikhs who are in the police and in the military: It is correct that you are serving the government; do so, the country must be defended. But ... the Hindus and the government should give us a clarification. Do they want to keep us with them or not? If they want to keep us with them they should treat us as equal citizens. All of you should work in cooperation and be alert to the discrimination that is being practised against us in various places.

Sikh officers serving the majority Hindu state in New Delhi had no concept of the Sikhs as a separate nationality and consequently, in the absence of this spiritual, moral and cultural boundary, they did not conceive of that state as an enemy. That state in turn with respect to the Sikhs adopted General Wolfe's position on the Scottish Highland regiments at the siege of Quebec, namely 'they are hardy, intrepid, accustomed to a rough country, and no great mischief if they fall' (Cran and Robertson 1996). Since the time of my first fieldwork in Punjab in 1965 I had been accustomed to hearing from parents that their sons were always sent to danger spots when a war was on, for example, to the Chinese border and to Kargil in Kashmir. Their prejudicial treatment was a recurring topic in Sikh conversation. Yet parents could never have conceived of what would happen to their children in Operation Woodrose nor of the savage tortures or callous killings that would be visited on their families. It was worse than their imagining. In their imaginings too (as the two appendices to this chapter show) they thought they could achieve redress for any wrong done. They failed to see that this could not happen because a policy devised by one's enemy would not take into account the innocence of the children of particular families nor the army service of their parents. Most Sikhs had not considered the state as an enemy, as they had been and continued to be employed by it. That the state which they had served could visit such savagery upon them was unimaginable to them. They were, after all, its citizens and the state itself still claimed democratic credentials.

FAMILY, VILLAGE, AND ONE'S NEIGHBOUR

The village environment was not one of mutual reliance, trust, and security. One's neighbour could not be relied upon because they might have police, army, or intelligence connections. For example, in 1993 there was a heavy recruitment of young people of both sexes from villages in the border areas into the intelligence services in an attempt to finish off the insurgency once and for all. Punjab had stable villages but the people in them were not attached to them or to each other. Its villages were spatial units that existed only in the revenue records. There were no forms of cooperation or protective association based on local contiguity. In fact villages were divided by factional alliances and by family feuds. In general, farmers had more ties outside the village than within it. This was due, firstly, to employment patterns. Family members had a variety of occupations other than landowning: in the army, the police, and the administration; in transporting, working for the central body controlling the Sikh temples, and in the regional assembly as politicians; as teachers, nurses, smugglers, and professional persons. Many had also moved to the urban areas where they were small businessmen, restaurateurs, and hotel owners. Secondly, it was due to exogamy. Jats married out of the clan of their father and mother and out of the village of both. Many important political leaders, administrative officers occupying senior government positions and innumerable army officers may have come from the villages, but the institutions in which they served had no connection to these small units and frequently had an India-wide reference. This gave a family protection and some advantages in the situation under discussion, yet others in the village, seeing a family's connections, would be worried in case these connections were used against them. Thus the village atmosphere was characterized by tension and provided few social supports in the post-1984 situation.

Rural political practices such as factionalism and feuding also resulted in divided local communities, and state involvement in these added another dimension to what would have been merely problems between families in a village or groupings within a village. Rural political patterns in all village localities are certainly implicated in the spread of counterinsurgency and hence in the spread of terror. Terror develops as the state gains control over local structures, using the enmities in them for its own purposes. Even in societies where there are more linkages within the village, social intercourse is totally paralyzed by those conflicts in which the state involves the civilian population. For example, Patricia Lawrence, reporting on the villages of eastern Sri Lanka (2000: 177) quotes one woman as saying 'when there is crying and shouting next door in the night people in this village can't go over and ask "why are you crying" because we don't know if the LTTE (Liberation Tigers of Tamil Eelam) or the army is there.'

In the traditional political system the main organizing unit in political life had been the *paarti* or faction. This consisted of a combination of persons at different levels of the political system who shared loyalty to each other's interests; different goods and services were also exchanged within this rubric. Given to these informal structures, village quarrels and local disputes frequently involved state politicians. Under present conditions this set of relationships could be disrupted at any time. Although police officials and politicians are still involved in village alliances, the nature of this involvement has altered totally. The police monopoly of the use of superior force has changed the nature of these alignments as has the official attitude to them, which is to exploit and control them in order to win what they call their anti-terrorist war. Terror is about having no redress. In normal political times redress would have been achieved through a lawyer favourable to one's faction or through persons of importance in the village – larger landlords and military personnel. But from the beginning of the insurgency, the normal court system did not operate. Also people of integrity and honour in a village, for example, large landowners of good reputation and military officers were intimidated into leaving the village. Hence families who were already isolated from each other were further isolated through the intimidation of respected families. It was into these disunited villages that the state came, targeting particular people for arrest and certain death.

COMMUNICATIONS ACROSS THE PLAINS

When those who were committed to an independent Sikh state (Khalistan) and those who sought safety went to Pakistan, the ordinary civilian population was left on an open plain without defences. Their ability to see what was happening in their province and to their people was facilitated by the transport system, and by the fact that this transport system was used because relatives and friends resided in other places. The state's terrorist apparatus was before Sikh eyes as they travelled whether by private car or on the state-owned bus service: there were machine guns mounted on jeeps, bullet-proof tractors, and CRPF patrols on the main GT road. Sikhs would be exposed to such sights as they made trips to see friends and relatives, going in to the city or town, to and from work, to Chandigarh on some legal or political business. The physical and social infrastructures that allowed and enabled easy movement also enabled people to see the nature of the state presence in the Punjab. People were talking to each other on the buses about what was going on and the talk, if not engendering terror, certainly gave it substance. In this small, compact province, where villages were interconnected by roads, family links, friendships and ties of reciprocity, imaginings and fact were one and the same. The province-wide network of social links was mirrored in the physical connectedness that made all areas penetrable. The accessibility of the rural areas, criss-crossed by a network of roads, enabled attacks to be easily mounted on villages and also for them to be known about. Newspaper reports kept people apprised of what was happening[8] and reinforced what people saw and heard. Irrespective of what was seen and read in newspapers, people were also aware of terror because of what they heard through their own family networks and through strangers on the bus en route to seeing a relative, friend, lawyer, or state minister.

CHANGES IN LEGAL STRUCTURE AND PRACTICE

Subsequent to the events of 1984 the state set up a corpus of law intended to deal with the secessionist tendencies of the Sikhs and all those individuals who would destroy the territorial integrity of India. These laws were the National Security Act (NSA), the Terrorist and Disruptive Activities (Prevention) Act (TADA), and the Special Courts Act and the Disturbed Areas Act. The National Security Act provided for detention without trial for a period of two years and continued detention for further periods on the production of fresh evidence. One did not need to engage in subversive activities to be so detained. The Act allowed for the detention of those with certain views and who were promoting these views not only by speeches but also through song, writing and in social gatherings or who were rumoured to be doing this. Under TADA, confessions extracted under torture were admissible as evidence and the onus was on the accused to prove his innocence. No arrest warrant was ever issued. The Special Courts Act allowed only for trial before a designated judge, of which there was one for each district. The trials were *in camera* and without legal representation, and unnamed witnesses could be called. All of these Acts provided immunity to the police and paramilitary forces, who got away with torture, murder and many other crimes in the course of carrying out their designated duty. Likewise the Armed Forces (Punjab and Chandigarh) Special Powers Act, introduced in October 1983 and still in force, gave immunity from prosecution to members of the military. In the spring of 1988 the 59th amendment to the Constitution was passed allowing the suspension of all rights, including the right to life. Not only could one be detained at will, one could be shot at will. In 1993 India set up a National Human Rights Commission (NHRC) under pressure from the international community. However, the NHRC had no power to prosecute violators or to compensate victims. Also there is a one-year statute of limitation based on when the crime was committed, and a consideration of killings could only happen within one year of that killing. Thus the vast majority of Sikh killings and disappearances could not be brought before the Commission. In 1997 proceedings were initiated against 5,000 policemen for taking part in extrajudicial killing and torture, but so far no police officer has been disciplined for violations committed.

COUNTERINSURGENCY

The purpose of the Indian state's counterinsurgency in the Punjab was to defeat the Sikh campaign for a sovereign state. An independent Sikh state would threaten the unity and integrity of India, a state, which, at the time the Sikh insurgency began, was barely 50 years old. It also aimed to defeat any notion that would allow scope for a federal India to flourish. Thus, in the 1970s, the idea that Sikh economic success in the Punjab could be used as a basis for financial autonomy likewise had been deemed separatist. It was subsequent to this that a political movement demanding not just autonomy but political sovereignty for the Sikhs arose. There were three elements necessitating the counterinsurgency operations from the state's point of view. First was the involvement in the insurgency of a foreign power (Pakistan) interested in weakening India. Second was the support the young fighters had from local populations in the early years in an area bordering on the territory of that foreign power. And third was the declaration of an independent state by the Sikhs in 1986.

In the first four years of the insurgency, the young men who fought the state found warm support for their struggle from the civilian population. The head of the civil administration in the most terrorist-affected area told me that there was considerable sympathy for the insurgents so long as their killings were targeted. They lost that sympathy only when they attacked innocent families and engaged in indiscriminate killings. It was because of such civilian support that counterinsurgency operations that did engage in arbitrary killings were initiated. And it was in the course of these that terror of the sort described in the following pages occurred. Sudden killings, abductions, and abrupt disappearance were part of a policy to subdue the local areas. Terror generated by the threat of disappearance, happening in the most ordinary places and during the most ordinary activities, was different from the violence of family and factional feuds. For one thing the activities of those engaged in abduction could impinge on those who had no direct political involvement. It was also hidden, furtive activity in which private gain, spurred on by animosities inside the villages, coincided with intelligence policy.

Through counterinsurgency practices, the state planned and controlled the social disorder in the rural areas firstly through ridding them of respected and prominent persons to whom ordinary people could turn in times of difficulty. The state disabled this section of the population by making them the subjects of kidnapping and extortion and forcing them to flee to the towns. The state interfered in family feuds, which became a primary source of disorder. To the violence caused by old enmities between families was now added terror as the greedy, the ambitious, the needy, or those with personal grudges made alignments with local police officials to satisfy their ends. Case 4 (below) illustrates that (though I think the case material has limitations and cannot be used to illustrate other than this point). To a certain extent this process made all who were party to it participants in terror. There was obvious political advantage to the state in involving the population in criminality as it sapped the independence movement of its ideological fervour and kept young people occupied with other than the political goal of a separate and free Sikh state. Those in authority turned a blind eye to what was going on. They thought that if they allowed certain elements to profit,[9] it would create a great deal of local social dissension in which people would be absorbed. And they, meanwhile, would also benefit financially. Involving the population in criminality, as in feuding, became state policy. As the police chief for one of the border areas told me, 'they would fight the bad, using the bad'.

A second source of disorder were the various police agencies, some controlled from the Punjab and others from Delhi,[10] which provided a shield for special units operating in plain clothes and from cars without number plates – death squads, so to speak.[11] The third were the breakaway militant units. Of the second of these a US Congress report of 19 January 1993 states that

In Punjab there were credible reports that police in particular continued to engage in faked encounter killings. In the typical scenario, police take into custody suspected militants or militant supporters without filing an arrest report. If the detainee dies during interrogation, or is executed, officials deny that he was ever in custody and claim he died during an armed encounter with the police or security forces. Afterwards the bodies reportedly are sometimes moved to distant police districts for disposal, making identification and investigation more difficult.

Regarding breakaway units, it may be said that maximum pressure was placed on militant organizations by the police to encourage defections. Warren (2002: 385) has commented on the effort the state invests in counterinsurgency.[12] Certainly the Indian state had a huge budget to spend on creating rifts within militant organizations by exploiting personal ambitions and by offering arms to encourage breakaway groups. Creating such groups, then controlling them and getting them to fulfil government policy, formed a large part of counterinsurgency operations. According to highly placed sources, the central government had made available a huge amount of money to a former Governor of Punjab, Surendra Nath, who was also a member of the Indian Police Service, to prop up terrorism in Punjab (and Kashmir) in a bid to discredit the Punjab and Kashmir militants (report in *Hitavada*, 6 November 1994). The state itself aided the proliferation of militant units by protecting those who wanted to set up on their own and supporting them by giving them arms. As a ruse such militants would be declared dead. In exchange for police protection, judicial immunity they would provide information on other militants. Many were used to create divisions in militant organizations. The police allowed them, in the name of militancy, to create terror, for it was all the easier then to separate them from the people. That achieved, they would subsequently be killed.

MILITANT GROUPINGS AND TERROR

The disunity and lack of amity that plagued the Sikh secessionist movement were in large measure responsive to local rural social structure. What had been a popular movement for independence became affected by traditional models of political organization. This progressively became the case as the charismatic leaders of the movement and most of its renowned fighters were slowly eliminated, leaving the movement to carry on, obstructed in its ideals by innumerable divisions, and by groups that had degenerated into gangs with little direction and certainly without money or ideology. It was all the easier for rifts to develop in the absence of direct control as the political leadership of most militant groups was in Pakistan. Political friction within small localities, the ongoing politics of patronage in securing jobs, and disputes between families over land were the continuing structural bases for conflict. These interplayed with the contemporary political conflict between those favouring secession and those collaborating with the ruling elite of India in stamping it out.

The head of the civil administration in the area most affected by the insurgency acknowledged that the government was engaged in a war. The police point of view was similar and its reviews of operations, placed at the disposal of the author, indicate that its target was society at large. These reviews identify university professors, human rights activists, smugglers, criminals, transport companies, army men, religious functionaries, the sons of farmers in certain border areas, especially if they had some education, and some police, naming them as 'terrorists'. Because of this view, which targeted nearly all of rural society, Indian atrocities were far more widespread and arbitrary than the more precisely targeted reprisals of the Khalistani insurgents, and their need to create division within the militant ranks was an absolute condition of their success. Because of the nature of militant groupings, this was relatively easy.

Militant groupings were person-centred linkages often with little durability. Their leadership rested on consent and allegiance was conditional, marked by trading and bargaining especially over arms and areas of influence. When personnel within a group secured the protection of someone more powerful they would secede. This obviously gave the security forces some leverage in creating divisions. Members of militant organizations also broke with one another for their own fame and fortune and because they held themselves in high esteem. Allegiances were frail. The ambition, egoism, and search for individual glory that resulted in groups disintegrating also allowed the security forces to pursue their policy of encouraging opposing gangs to neutralize each other. In the process, civilian casualties were high. Area commanders who were popular and well-armed would desert the parent guerrilla organisation. However, once their arms supply dried up, these small groups operating on their own used local structures of power as a temporary shield. The latter might include police informers and the predominant faction in the village of which they were part. When villagers found that they had links with the police they would request them to harass their opponents. Militants were drawn thereby in to local power structures. The dynamics of militant organizations contributed to terror in the villages, for militants had multiple roles.[13] Some were employed as hit men by political leaders, or by feuding families. Also, in order to survive they eventually had to engage in extortion, or find work with the police, and the intelligence services, infiltrating and informing on their former comrades in return for payment. Those who were paid by the state to infiltrate and inform managed to build small economic empires for themselves.

THE ACTUALITY OF TERROR

The substance of terror is contained in various reports, especially the Amnesty International report of 1992 and a US State Department Document of 1993. People themselves characterized their state as being one of *zulm* or *dakashahi*, terms that refer to the cruel and barbarous treatment directed against an entire category of people, in this case Punjabi villagers. *Zulm* covers a whole range of behaviour on the part of the police and made possible by the new laws: abduction; detention without trial; no records kept of arrest or detention; torture and extrajudicial execution, the latter covering both deaths in custody and killings in false encounter. All branches of the police and paramilitary forces were involved in arrests and interrogations as the security forces operated jointly under the command of the state's director general of police. In the court cases and interviews mentioned below as well as in the account and letter in the appendices, terror is portrayed as a condition in which people lived, a tangible part of the day-to-day fabric of their lives and not a product of their imagining. These cases show that terror was essentially about having no redress either through the courts or through persons occupying positions

Figure 3.1   A village home, destroyed in a battle between police and militants

Figure 3.2   Interior view of the destruction of a neighbouring house

of influence. Its implementation required considerable thought, planning and organization with the entire state machinery devoted to rupturing the society they believed had spawned separatism. As the case studies show, terror was an event in the lives of families that destroyed the innocent. It was testimony to the presence of evil. State terror was not just directed against armed groupings favouring

Figure 3.3 A village house deserted through fear of the police

independent rule. It was also against civilians among whom these armed individuals moved or were alleged to move, in other words, the entire population of the rural areas. Its victims were ordinary civilians, uninvolved in armed or even political conflict.

Mostly terror affected the young. As civilians were arrested on mere suspicion that they were linked to the militants or had information about them, young people fled their homes out of fear. When their parents approached the various officials and endeavoured to find out the whereabouts of their children often they themselves were detained and tortured in order to procure information about their sons as well as their surrender. Family members who gave affidavits were always arrested. In a civil writ petition of 15 June 1995 in the High Court one Gurdev Kaur relates events in December 1993 and early 1994 when police of District Ropar picked up her elderly husband, and severely tortured him in order to discover the whereabouts of their sons. Her husband was released but the sons' whereabouts have never been discovered. No case has ever been registered against them. So families do not know if their missing members are dead or illegally detained. This is the case with all who have been taken into police custody. They are not shown as alive or dead and no one knows where their remains lie. Bodies are often cremated to hide the injuries they have suffered in police custody. In the case of one Piara Singh from a village near Barnala (case brought under the civil writ jurisdiction in July 1995) his widow procured the post mortem report, which showed that her husband had fifteen injuries. Because he died in police custody, his body had been cremated. In some cases families

Figure 3.4   The marble surrounds of the Golden Temple precinct
damaged by tanks during the army offensive in 1984

manage to see the body of their relative and then they also see the
injuries that the police have inflicted. In such circumstances the
police pressure the family into signing a statement allowing the body
to be cremated, thus avoiding any investigation into alleged torture.
More commonly, families wait years to find out information about
the whereabouts of family members. In the absence of any such
information, the terror of the past blights the future. In some cases
a parent, after failing to get justice, commits suicide (see report in
The Tribune, 9 July 1997: 'Frustrated father ends life').

Entire families become the object of police interest if they have
even one militant member in their midst, and even after that militant
has been killed the police continue to harass the family and in some

cases kill them (see report: 'Unending wait for loved ones', in *The Tribune*, 19 December 1994). Those in any way associated with militant families also suffered. For example, in one household, a servant to a known militant family blamed the fact that she worked in their house for the loss of her son and grandson in police encounters.

Frequently an entire family was wiped out owing to a militant being suspected of hiding somewhere on the property. Such a case was reported in civil writ petition 12330 of 1995 referring to events in the third week of May 1991, in a village in District Ludhiana. The family concerned were poor and under threat allowed the militant to stay at their *dera* or outhouse. They themselves were living in the village. But sometimes they visited the *dera*, which was a very beautiful place framed by eucalyptus trees with the River Sutlej flowing on both sides. It was where both their children had been born. However, it was a deserted spot. Whether the militant was killed or not on their property, the police suffered casualties and because of this wiped out the innocent: one brother, his wife, 3-year-old daughter and 2-month-old son as well as his 62-year-old mother. The dead body of the brother was declared as unidentified and the rest of the bodies were disposed of in a clandestine manner. The one surviving brother made a complaint against the police. They responded by registering a false case against him, saying he had joined the militants.

A more general and everyday feature of living in terror was that movement became problematic. Careful behaviour in this regard in fact gave families little protection because one could be abducted or gunned down doing the most ordinary, innocent activities that were essential for daily living: travelling to work; doing one's job; going out to one's fields; visiting relatives; helping a friend. The following cases show this.

1. *Case of Bharpur Singh Brar, son of Gurdip Singh (the father's documents are attached as Appendices 1 and 2).*
   On the night of 27/28 December 1990 three young Sikhs were travelling home after visiting a relative of one of them in a nearby city. On the outskirts of a town not far from their home they were ordered to slow down and stop by the police. As was customary procedure in such instances, the driver switched on his interior light so that the police could see the occupants. The car was allowed to proceed and reached the next checkpoint where the same exercise was repeated. However, this time, despite having seen that its occupants were unarmed, the police began firing at the car at close range. Bharpur Singh was killed on the spot. His companion bled to death in the car. The driver of the car was ordered to crawl towards the police.
   Bharpur Singh's father reacted to his murder by reassuring himself he could get justice. In other words, as Appendix 2 shows, he turned to the perpetrators of the terror for aid. It might be thought that these boys were travelling home late at night when prudence should have dictated otherwise. Their parents and they themselves must have been aware that in the same year, in the month of November alone, 364 civilians had been killed. Yet returning

home at a late hour was not the cause of their death. For one was not safe staying at home either. Moreover, this was not unexpected violence. It was planned terror. As the policeman admitted to the driver of the vehicle, 'our DSP (Deputy Superintendent of Police) was killed yesterday'. Not only was all movement dangerous, existence itself was.

2. *Case of a hospital compounder working for a Hindu doctor at a hospital in the town of Moga.*

He had worked there for six years and was 25 years old. His widowed mother told me that someone had written a letter to the doctor demanding a ransom payment. The doctor had then telephoned the police. When the other registered medical practitioners who were working alongside him heard of this, they left. Her son remained there on his own. According to his mother, his colleagues gave false information about him on the basis of which he was taken into police custody. She said her other son and a cousin went in search of him and also went to see the doctor, who told them he would secure his release. But when nothing happened and they saw him a second time the doctor said he was helpless. They then telegrammed and went in person to different police stations within the district and got a prominent local politician to intervene. The latter went to see the DC (Deputy Commissioner) Faridkot. The police line was that he had escaped and while doing so had sustained injury. According to the family, the then SSP (Senior Superintendent of Police) Faridkot, at that time Swaran Singh, said that the hospital compounder had neither been tortured nor beaten. He said that the officer in charge of the case had gone on leave and he, Swaran Singh, could tell them nothing else. According to the grandmother they begged the police to be told the truth about what had happened for the sake of his young wife, saying 'what shall we to do with this young girl if he is not found?' According to them, Swaran Singh answered 'So you do the last rites.' However, they searched for the son for one year more. They never found him, and his young wife is now married to his younger brother. The only explanation they received from the police was that when they were taking him from Jaito to Moga one night, they encountered some fire and in their words 'from there his friends took him from us'.[14]

Yet if there was no freedom to quietly do one's job, equally there was no freedom to remain safely at home either. Militants would visit the houses demanding shelter. The fear was then that the police, on information provided, would attack the houses. Families did not want either the militants or the police visiting their houses when they had young girls still at home. If they were rich enough, as was the case with Mohinder Singh, they would move to a nearby town.

3. *Case of Mohinder Singh, a rich farmer from a village near Dehlon, District Ludhiana.*

Mohinder Singh felt unable to remain at home and left because of a terror he could foresee rather than a terror practised. The area in which his farm was located was within the boundaries of the five police stations of Payal, Raikot, Ahmedgarh, Dehlon, and Malerkotla. It had been controlled by a militant called Jagrup Kalak, who, when he was killed, had a bigger funeral procession, despite the police blockade, than one held for a famous local Saint. According to the farmer, after the militant leader's death the area was destabilized, as 'he was a good-charactered person'. He said he had felt safe when the leader was alive and had received protection from him. He said that the first time armed persons came to his house they asked him for weapons. As he was unsure of their identity he declined, saying they were with the police. As proof of this they asked for a receipt. When he showed them the receipt they said they would be back some time in the future so he should keep his weapons in the house. They came back again three weeks later scaling a wall at 2 to 3 am and demanding to be allowed to stay, to take food and rest. They carried Chinese revolvers and assault weapons. They said to him, 'Before you would not give us your weapons. Now you can have as many as you want from us.' They came a third time when his wife was in the house alone and again asked to stay. She said she was going in to the town for medicine. They said 'go, we'll rest here meantime'. She hastened to nearby Khanna to inform her husband not to take their younger daughter back to the village. It was not long after this that they left their farm. Their house was deserted for ten years and their land rented out – 80 acres of some of the best land in Punjab, rich because of the subsoil water.

Some of the court cases that have come before the High Court in Chandigarh, the state capital, show how in a situation where the police had vast powers any conflict between families over land and any neighbourhood enmities were liable to be exploited by them. The wider conflict between the militants and the police provided a perfect setting for the enactment of family and neighbourhood enmities and demonstrated that there was an intimate connection between weak neighbourhood ties, family enmities, and the spread of terror. The following case illustrates this further.

4. *Case of Jaspal Kaur.*

In an undated civil writ petition under article 226 of the Indian constitution, Jaspal Kaur requested an independent investigation, preferably by the CBI (Central Bureau of Intelligence), into her illegal detention, torture, and rape. Charged were the state of Punjab and eight police officers. According to Jaspal Kaur, she was picked up from her village on the 17 June 1994 by ten police who had come in two vans even though she had been granted anticipatory bail. On the 18th at 12 pm she was beaten to the ground twice by two female police officers. She was given a further beating in the middle of the night by a male constable and in the course of this beating she was told to reach an agreement with one Ravinder Singh, a neighbour and father of a woman known to her who was deceased, by paying him 3 lakh rupees [300,000 rupees] and placing 21½ acres of land in his name. The police also demanded she should pay 20,000 rupees to them. On the 18th Jaspal Kaur's husband sent a telegram to the High Court that despite anticipatory bail orders passed his wife had been picked up. A habeas corpus petition was filed on 24 June and again on 7 July for her release from illegal custody. A warrant officer was then appointed by the court and charged with raiding the police station concerned and recovering the prisoner. The police came to know about the raid before the warrant officer's visit. She was taken to the house of the SHO (police officer in charge) and there she was tortured with electric currents attached to her nose ring and earrings, made to lift a heavy roller and denied sleep. She was told she must reach an agreement with Ravinder Singh, otherwise she would never be let out of prison. On 8 July she was taken to the civilian house of a relative of one of the policemen and on the 9th to yet another house where she was kept for ten days. On the 23rd at night she was brought back to the police station, and there she was raped by three policemen in the quarters behind the police station. She was eventually released on bail on 23 November 1994 after having been confined in Central Jail Patiala. Throughout her imprisonment she was asked to reach an agreement with Ravinder Singh concerning the land.

5. *A case in which all the features of terror already described are evident is contained in the following criminal petition of 19 August 1996*, Modan Singh *vs* State of Punjab.

On 27 July 1996 at about 7.30 am two men, father and son, were cycling from their village to Nabha (District Patiala) for their daily work. En route a small truck came alongside and a policeman in charge of the main CIA (Central Investigative Agency, see notes 8 and 10) station in Nabha town got down along with five or six police personnel. They dragged the petitioner's son, Balbir Singh, aged 24 years, into the truck. The petitioner returned to his village and told its *sarpanc* (head of the village council), who was also chairman of the Block (a development unit covering up to one hundred villages), about the abduction. The *sarpanc* accompanied the petitioner to the CIA staff headquarters in Nabha. When they went inside they saw the said policeman (the CIA officer) in charge torturing his son, Balbir Singh, along with four to five of his men. They were pushed out of the room and told to return the next day. The torture of this young man continued throughout the day and was witnessed by several local officials, who had come to the police station on other business. They queried why this was occurring and were told to mind their own business. The following day at about 4.30 pm two *sarpancs* from neighbouring villages were standing near the bridge of the Sirhind canal. They saw the said policeman and two others get down from their vehicle and dump the body of a young man in the canal. They recognized it as being that of Balbir Singh. People from the surrounding villages gathered to search for the body. It was found the next day, the 29th, at 9 am by the villagers. Photographs were taken and the body was put into a tractor trolley and taken to Nabha in a procession.The whole town of Nabha remained closed in protest against the murder. Some persons went to Patiala to see the SSP and the DC and to inform them of the incident. The SSP told them he was deputing a senior officer to look into the whole matter and the DC said he was ordering a magisterial inquiry. Meanwhile the procession was blocking the traffic. And so at about 1.30 pm the superintendent of police, Patiala and the district magistrate Nabha assured the agitated villagers that they had formed a panel of three doctors to do a post mortem on the body and that an inquiry would begin. The dead body was then taken to the civil hospital and the magistrate started recording villagers' statements. However, a year later, action had still not been taken against the police officers involved.

The court case records a similar situation to that of the Bharpur Singh case (see above, and the father's testimony as noted in the appendices), namely: 'that the petitioner is an old man and his son was his ray of light for his old age'. Compensation was demanded for the loss of his son not only because he was in the prime of his life but because the old man thought that the policemen involved should be given exemplary punishment for their crime and also for abusing the power and faith vested in them. He requested the court that they be punished, according to law, for murder.

The post mortem revealed that there were multiple injuries over Balbir Singh's hips, back and groin and that his backbone had been fractured. In the course of the trial it was also revealed that owing to multiple injuries the condition of Balbir Singh became precarious and the inspector of police took him to a private nursing home. He was refused admittance as his chances for survival were nil. The police party then, according to court documents, took him to the civil hospital, where doctors advised them not to get Balbir Singh admitted in order to avoid proof of injuries. The doctors at Nabha civil hospital did not like to offend the police inspector lest he let loose terror on them. He had a reputation for this – indeed, those who instigated the inquiry and who appeared as witnesses in the inquiry against the police had false cases registered against them and subsequently feared elimination.

CONCLUSION

My intention has been to convey the omnipresence of terror by presenting a variety of cases. I have suggested that politics between families and within small localities entangled the militants and that the state was successful in controlling local conflicts for its own ends. I have also suggested that, paradoxically, terror of the nature described here occurred because of the extent of Sikh incorporation into Indian institutions. Such incorporation caused the state to imagine conspiracies and fear uprisings. Hence in the words of Taussig (1984), writing of a similar situation in a different continent: 'in order to save themselves from these fancied perils ... they killed and killed without compassion'. Thus, although the Sikh presence in the ruling class of India was a prominent one, that incorporation was to work against them as large sectors of the community did the state's bidding, while other sections fought the state. Truly, 'what happens in tragedy is the coming to life of our background', as Freya Stark has remarked (1963: 100).

Most of the individual experiences of terror, whether described in interviews or taken from court records, are those of ordinary people.[15] They are a documentation of evil. 'Stories about evil are ... stories in need of being retold; while re-experiencing them we aim not only at understanding but also at weaving a moral understanding of the past' (Lara 2001: 248). Sikh moral law that there should be no attack on the vulnerable or on non-combatants, has been transgressed. Social and religious practices of respect for the elderly have been reversed.

Crude violence achieves the destruction of physical life. Terror lies in a realm beyond that, where terrible things are done to the body of the victim because terrible things are meant to be done, in the process, to his honour, dignity, and pride, indeed to his entire being. In this way, those belonging to the counterinsurgency apparatus in the Punjab and Delhi have, with their terror, appropriated the future of entire families through killing their children.[16] This is why it becomes important for parents to tell the unencumbered witness like myself, or a court, about the fate of their children. They hope it will give them the means to reclaim the future, restore their own power and their control over the past. So far the court cases have been unavailing; not restorative of justice but of humiliation. And the effects of the terror have lingered on because there has been no public acknowledgment of evil, no redress, no official admission that their experiences actually came to pass. Their suffering, and the evil accompanying it, have gone unrecognized. Such public admission is important because terror was conducted in secret.

Terror is organized political crime. This is shown by the way the state treated the civilian population. That it was seen as such by these civilians is evidenced by the statements in court documents. For example, in one of the court cases the following is mentioned: 'That it is submitted that those who kill for promotions or ranks and rewards are "hostes humani generis" i.e. enemies of mankind, who should be dealt with accordingly' (civil writ petition 12330 of 1995, in the High Court of Punjab at Chandigarh, p.6. *Swaran Singh petitioner* vs *State of Punjab*).

The experience of evil, lack of redress for wrong, and criminality, shared by an entire civilian population, creates a potential public space for retelling. If a community agrees that such traumatic events occurred 'and weaves this fact into its identity, then collective memory survives and individual memory can find a place within that landscape' (Kirmayer 1996: 190). In the case of the Sikhs, this has happened only with respect to the collective terror to which the community as a whole was subject. It has not occurred with respect to the experience of individual families.

The songs of the *dhadhis* (eulogists) during the early stages of the insurgency had been sung so that families would not succumb to feelings of terror. They were a challenge to the defeat that had been collectively and individually experienced. As the court cases from which I have quoted show, the strong sense of personal worth and inner strength of fathers, brothers, wives, and mothers enabled them to seek justice through the courts and through world attention to their plight. Their demands for redress suggest that they were not disabled by the terror of the state. When their cases were not taken up by the appropriate authorities the innocent felt the necessity to tell and tell again their experiences because they believed their act of witness had gone unheeded. They were obsessed with this witnessing rather than with the terror to which they had been or would be subject. For how long this can continue is an open question. For a principal feature of their imagining was hope. And for so many families such hope has been extinguished. They now face a situation similar to that depicted by Spencer (2000: 134), for the inhabitants of southern Sri Lankan villages, of 'living with torturers'.

APPENDICES

Appendix 1. A statement of Gurdip Singh Brar's hearing with Mr Swaran Singh, Senior Superintendent of Police, Faridkot, on 21 September 1991 at the Durbar Gunj Guest House, Faridkot in the presence of the Deputy Commissioner

The meeting begins, according to Gurdip Singh's records, with the SSP asserting the following:

SSP: They [Gurdip Singh's son, Bharpur Singh and his companions] did not stop the car.

Parent: The car in which the innocent boys were travelling was stopped and checked by the police at the *naka* (police post) on the outskirts of Moga, near the Nestlé factory. They were asked to show a receipt for some cassettes in the car, which they did, and the car was allowed to travel on. Further on the car stopped immediately when signalled to do so by the police at the Khukhrana police post. Hence the police version is false.

SSP: They stopped the car after crossing the *naka* (in other words, giving the police a reason to fire).

Parent: That is not correct. They stopped when told to.

[The SSP then calls in the police inspector for Moga.]

Police Inspector: They had taken the car ahead.

Parent: That is wrong. According to the driver's affidavit he stopped the car just short of the *naka* in front of the shops where the police were positioned and when signalled to do so by the police torch light. All the shots of the police are on the left side of the car and very few are from the temporary sentry defence post. There is not a single mark in the rear of the car (which would indicate the car had gone beyond the police post). The car slowed down, stopped, and an interior car light was put on after switching off the headlights, to facilitate the police to check the car.

[The SSP gives no answer.]

Parent: They started shooting into the car when it had come to a stop. The boys cried out that they were innocent shopkeepers returning home and were carrying nothing objectionable. But the police continued shooting at them for about 10 minutes from a distance of 10–15 yards. The driver came out of the car, raising his hands and lay on the ground, pleading with them to stop firing, but they continued.

SSP: Who says so?

Parent: Nearby villagers told us.

SSP: People tell lies.

Parent: The car driver's affidavit and the bullet marks are the proof.

SSP: Your son had two shots.

Parent: Post mortem reports show 10 shot wounds.

SSP: [Silent.]

Parent: The DC and the SSP are supposed to be the custodians of the people of the district. I received no condolences from either.

DC: I have come to know only now.

SSP: We are too busy in other matters.

DC: Why do you think the boys were killed?

Parent: When I reached Moga hospital to collect the dead body of my son, a police inspector retorted 'Our DSP was also killed yesterday.' I heard another police officer on the SSP's personal staff saying outside this room that all the relations of the militants should be killed.

SSP: They are fools.

Parent: The killers should be punished. They are the takers of innocent lives, our lovely children. The law must take its course.

DC: They get acquitted for want of evidence in the law courts.

Parent: Sir, the SSP could have taken action. The SSP has got vast powers.

DC: A magisterial inquiry can be ordered. They can be tried for murder.

DC and SSP: You can take the compensation of Rs. 50,000 being offered.

[This compensation was on account of the police having registered a first information report that these two boys, Gurdip Singh's son and his friend, were killed by militants during crossfire with the police. Compensation was not accepted.]

Appendix 2. Gurdip Singh's letter presented to myself in September 1992

Dear Madam,

It is a relief to see that God has sent you to our land to hear our gagged voice. I am a retired ex-soldier with 25 years' service to the Indian army. My innocent son Bharpur Singh (21) was killed by 'Indian Protection Forces', mercilessly, in cold blood, on the Grand Trunk road by police, shooting from a distance of 10–15 yards continuously despite his pleas of innocence until his voice was silenced. He was a popular, lovely boy of Faridkot town. I hereby attach the full case in correspondence to members of Parliament, Chief Justices of the Supreme Court and Judges. None save two MPs from the minority communities acknowledged my letters. Even their letters to the Home Minister of India have fallen on deaf ears. Madam, there are huge killings going on by Indian mercenary forces. Besides my son Bharpur, and his friend Bobby these are some of the other cases I know about:

Darshan Singh (25) and Jagtar Singh (20) sons of Pritam Singh, village Bodhiwala, *tehsil* Muktsar, District, Faridkot, killed on 29/8/91 near their farmhouse, the plea by the police inspector of Fazilka was one of mistaken identity.

A youth killed by Sgt Gurjant Singh on 20/21 January inside Sadar Faridkot police station at midnight reported by a villager from village Chahel who was inside the police station at the time.

Gurmeet Singh (20) son of Sgt Major Grewal, Harindra Nagar Faridkot – killed in police custody. Tortured to death by Bagha Purana police, District Faridkot.

Gurmeet Singh (20) of village Machaki Kalan. Killed in police custody. Tortured by the inspector police station Muktsar.

Malkiat Singh known as Meeta. A tall, young, handsome boy brought into police station Bagha Purana, hale and hearty and immediately shot dead at 1.30 pm in the presence of the Superintendent police operations. People seeing him dying in a pool of blood were rushed out of the station by the police. My source is a sewing machine mechanic from Faridkot who was present on the spot along with an advocate from Bathinda. A fake encounter was declared the following night.

There have been innumerable false encounters in the preserved forest areas around the town but who knew who was being killed? It was an endless spree of killings but who would dare to speak a word? The present ministry in Punjab and its forces are all mercenary killers of the Sikhs, especially of its youth.

You will kindly notice that there has been an enormous weapon proliferation as if there are more forces than ordinary public and there are more vehicles and jeeps with plain clothes police on the roads than there are private cars or public transport.

Please help and save our people. It is horrible the number of killings going on unheeded and unaccounted.

NOTES

I wish to record my thanks to the Harry Frank Guggenheim Foundation, New York, for their invaluable support during my fieldwork trips to the Punjab in 1992 and 1993.

1. The recent account of Sarab Jit Singh (2002), who was deputy commissioner Amritsar 1987–92, demonstrates the extent of interference from the central government of India.
2. The bodies were taken to Amritsar mortuary by police in municipal refuse lorries. Doctors were rounded up by the army from towns across the province to do post mortems. One doctor alone (see report in *The Tribune*, 14 June 1984, 'Sikhs were shot with "hands tied"') dealt with 400 cases. The late Prime Minister Rajiv Gandhi estimated that 700 Indian soldiers and 3,000 civilians died in the attack.
3. An account of the resistance struggle is given in my own book *The Sikhs of the Punjab* (1995a).
4. The types of torture used were first documented in the Tiwana Commission's report, which was not published. Full details as well as illustrations can be found in the second edition of a report by the Medical Foundation for the Care of Victims of Torture, 1999.
5. An *amritdhari* Sikh is a baptized Sikh. Under the influence of Sant Bhindranwale many young Sikhs were baptized and so *amritdhari* came to mean a certain loyalty to one's separate cultural and political identity.
6. Part of the text of the Declaration of Khalistan can be found in Gopal Singh (ed.) 1987.
7. For a full description, see Omissi 1994.
8. For example, people would be reading about how one Kulwant Singh, a lawyer at Ropar District Courts, had gone to the police station on 25 January 1993 accompanied by his wife and small child to seek the release of a woman and her son belonging to his ancestral village. He had done so on the request of the village council (report in *Indian Express*, 6 February 1993). However, neither he, his wife nor his child ever emerged from the police station. People talked a great deal about this case to me and to each other, as also about the newspaper report (*The Pioneer*, 26 March 1992) that numerous bodies of murdered young men were regularly dumped into the canals of Punjab. They would read about the activities of the different special police units as in the following case in the *Indian Express*, 19 January 1988: 'An official but lawless agency called the Central Investigative Agency has been spreading terror, torturing and killing young men for the past many months ... Part of the CIA's modus operandi is to move around in Maruti Gypsy vehicles and Matador Vans without number plates, containing crews armed with AK-47 rifles, not in uniform

... They kept no records of persons arrested or detained for purposes of interrogation, irrespective of the duration of their detention.' Various sections of the press daily reported the numbers of militants, security personnel and civilians killed in clashes. The death toll was intimidating, as were accounts of false encounters. There were innumerable killings in trains, buses, and in the market places. Ordinary Sikhs felt bemused by these and talked a lot about them.

9. I cite one small example of this that I came across while staying in Sarhali village, in the Tarn Taran area of Amritsar. One small farmer had been collecting money in the name of a militant leader but keeping some of it for himself. Hence, although he had only 2 acres of land, yet he had trucks and his own generator. As the insurgency was brought under control the police asked for the profits from his theft to the tune of 2 lakh rupees. They then asked him to get out of the district. His opportunism had served its purpose, namely branding the militant cause as disreputable.

10. The paramilitary police units were controlled from New Delhi. These were the Central Reserve Police Force (CRPF) and the Border Security Force (BSF). A newspaper report (*Hitavada*, 6 November 1994) alleged that the late Governor of the Punjab, Surendra Nath, had used men from the Central Industrial Security Force to kill innocent persons as well as teachers, doctors, engineers, media men, and political personalities. Within the Punjab, aside from the police controlled by the district police chiefs, of whom there were 70,000, there was, additionally a body known as the Central Investigative Agency (CIA) whose role was to gather information for intelligence purposes and who conducted many interrogations.

11. Material on death squads from a comparative perspective is contained in *Death Squad. The Anthropology of State Terror*, edited by Jeffrey Sluka. Further information on the Punjab situation is contained in my own chapter in that book (2000: 204–25). Note should also be taken of a journalistic comment that 'In Punjab it is an accepted view that at least some of the death squads have been unleashed by the government' (Manoj Joshi, 'An Explosive Secret', *Frontline* 14–27 May 1988).

12. She says: 'In order to divide civilians from the organized resistance, states have invested a great deal of energy in undermining the bond of trust between citizens, community members and close family relatives – the very people upon whom individuals were dependent for survival – by forcing people to spy on each other or encouraging people to settle old scores by secretly reporting their enemies to the state.'

13. For the mixed nature of militant groupings, see my article in the *International Journal of Punjab Studies*, 1995b: 94.

14. This is what was termed crossfire by the police, namely, when they take a suspect out of the police station and they come under fire from militants. In the 'crossfire' everyone escapes except the detainee.

15. I have chosen the cases of ordinary families, for it seemed to me that the terror they experienced would otherwise not feature at all in reports. Wilson (1996: 139) comments on the process by which some events become recorded as human rights violations and are given more attention than others.

16. Brian Axel (2001: 136) writes: 'Often the first act during an arrest is to cast off the detainee's turban, effectively enforcing a surrender by deploying the symbolics of Sikh history against the victim. After this surrender, the genitals and anus become the foci of taunts ... and violation'. Because these practices cause impotence, 'they interrupt the community in the sense of not allowing its procreation'.

REFERENCES

Amnesty International (1992) *India: Torture, Rape and Deaths in Custody.* London: Amnesty International.

Axel, Brian (2001) *The Nation's Tortured Body.* Durham, NC and London: Duke University Press.

Cran, Angela and James Robertson (1996) 'On Highland Soldiers in the British Army'. Letter to a fellow officer in Canada in June 1751, in *Dictionary of Scottish Quotations*. Edinburgh: Mainstream Publishing Company.

Daniel, E. Valentine (1996) *Charred Lullabies.* Princeton: Princeton University Press.

Kirmayer, Laurence J. (1996) 'Landscapes of Memory'. In *Tense Past*, ed. Paul Antze and Michael Lambek. New York and London: Routledge, pp. 173–98.

Lara, Maria Pia (2001) *Rethinking Evil.* Berkeley and Los Angeles: University of California Press.

Lawrence, Patricia (2000) 'Violence, Suffering, Amman. The work of oracles in Sri Lanka's eastern war zone'. In *Violence and Subjectivity*, ed. V. Das, A. Kleinman et al. Berkeley and Los Angeles: University of California Press, pp. 171–204.

Medical Foundation for the Care of Victims of Torture (1999) *Lives under Threat: A study of Sikhs coming to the UK from the Punjab*, 2nd edn. London.

Omissi, David (1994) *The Sepoy and the Raj.* London: Palgrave Macmillan.

Pettigrew, Joyce J.M. (1995a) *The Sikhs of the Punjab. Unheard Voices of State and Guerrilla Violence.* London and New Jersey: Zed Books.

—— (1995b) 'Achieving a New Frontier: Rural Political Patterns and their Impact on the Sikh Independence Movement', *International Journal of Punjab Studies*, 2(1): 89–101.

—— (2000) 'Parents and their Children in Situations of Terror'. *Death Squad. The Anthropology of State Terror*, ed. Jeffrey Sluka. Philadelphia: University of Pennsylvania Press, pp. 204–25.

Sandhu, Ranbir Singh (1999) *Struggle for Justice.* Ohio: Sikh Educational and Religious Foundation.

Shiva, Vandana (1991) *The Violence of the Green Revolution.* London and New Jersey: Zed Books.

Singh, Gopal, ed. (1987) Document of the Declaration of Khalistan, *Punjab Today*. New Delhi: International Publishing House, pp. 387–94.

Singh, Sarab Jit (2002) *Operation Black Thunder. An Eyewitness Account of Terrorism in Punjab.* New Delhi: Sage Publications.

Spencer, Jonathan (2000) 'On Not Becoming a Terrorist: Problems of Memory, Agency and Community in the Sri Lankan Conflict'. In *Violence and Subjectivity*, ed. V. Das and A. Kleinman. Berkeley and Los Angeles: University of California Press, pp. 120–40.

Stark, Freya (1963) *Journey's Echo.* London: John Murray.

Taussig, Michael (1984) 'Culture of Terror, Space of Death: Roger Casement's Putumayo Report and the Explanation of Torture'. *Comparative Studies in Society and History*, 26: 467–97.

US State Department (1993) *India. Country Report on Human Rights*. Unclassified State Department Document 018642/17.

Verdery, Katherine (1994) 'Ethnicity, Nationalism and State Making'. In *The Anthropology of Ethnicity*, ed. H. Vermeulen and C. Govers. Amsterdam: Het Spinhuis, pp. 33–57.

Warren, Kay B. (2002) 'Toward an Anthropology of Fragments. Instabilities and Incomplete Transition'. In *Ethnography in Unstable Places*, ed. C.J. Greenhouse, E. Mertz and K.B. Warren. Durham: Duke University Press, pp. 379–92.

Wilson, Richard (1996) 'Representing Human Rights Violations: Social Contexts and Subjectivities'. In *Human Rights. Culture and Context. Anthropological Perspectives*, ed. Richard A. Wilson. London and Chicago: Pluto Press, pp. 134–60.

4 BETWEEN VICTIMS AND ASSAILANTS, VICTIMS AND FRIENDS: SOCIALITY AND THE IMAGINATION IN INDO-FIJIAN NARRATIVES OF RURAL VIOLENCE DURING THE MAY 2000 FIJI COUP[1]

Susanna Trnka

In May 2000, the nation of Fiji suffered its third political coup. This time the violence was set off by George Speight, a Fijian businessman with links to Fiji's mahogany industry. Due in court later that week on charges of fraud, Speight strode into Parliament on 19 May 2000 and took Prime Minister Mahendra Chaudhry and 43 MPs hostage.[2] Unlike the previous coups in 1987, which soon resulted in the establishment of a newly recognized central political authority, Speight's overthrow sent Fiji spiralling into months of political, economic, and social chaos with at least three factions (the military, Speight's proposed cabinet, and the former coalition government) vying for the reins of leadership. The turbulence played out across the country. Urban areas became the staging grounds of the mass lootings of shops and businesses, and in rural areas, disaffected Fijians physically attacked Indo-Fijians in settlements and villages.

Violence targeting Indo-Fijians was not a new phenomenon, but galvanized by the anti-foreigner and anti-Indian rhetoric of *Taukei* or Fijian nationalists, its intensity in the months immediately following the 2000 coup reached unseen heights (at least since the end of Indian indenture in 1920). Battery, rape, and the burning of Indo-Fijian homes occurred throughout Fiji's largest island, Viti Levu, and in parts of the second major island, Vanua Levu. The violence was most prevalent in Speight's stronghold of Naitasiri Province where police proved generally ineffective in curbing the activities of bands of local Fijian youths. Lack of manpower as well as shortages of arms may in part explain the inability of the police to curb the violence (Maci 2000). Eyewitness accounts as well as media stories suggest, however, that in some cases, the police and the military ignored or participated in acts of violence. Fiji's TV One news reported in June 2000, for example, that police were assisting in the thefts of cattle taken from Indian farmers and transported to the Parliament grounds to feed rebels and Speight supporters. Given the overall climate of violence and hostility, a number of Indian families fled from the interior and settled in Fiji's first refugee camp in Lautoka or moved in with kinsfolk in other rural areas, including the village of Upahār Gaon, where I was conducting fieldwork at the time of the coup. As these people travelled, so too did their stories.

During the months of upheaval,[3] Indo-Fijians' efforts to give order and ascribe meaning to the tumultuous events in which they found themselves involved the telling and retelling of accounts of violence. My focus here is on narratives and fragmentary accounts of rural violence as they were told by victims, their kin and other interested parties. The accounts I collected circulated among victims who fled from the interior, the relatives who took them in, and their neighbours in a village community that lay outside of the areas of severest violence. My interest is in how these narratives of rural violence were recounted in ways that evoked not only images of ethnic difference but also the importance of inter-ethnic friendships. In their portrayals of Fijians as both friends and foes, these accounts reflect an ambivalence toward the perception, widely voiced among Indo-Fijians during the coup, that Fijians are dangerous 'junglis' or primitives who endanger the safety of Indo-Fijians, and at the same time emphasized personal relations of neighbourliness, cooperation, and amicability between Indo-Fijians and Fijians. Through their criticisms of the police, these narratives furthermore suggested that the state promoted circumstances conducive to violence and was thus in part responsible for these events. The telling of these narratives thus simultaneously undermined, supported, and added new fodder to pre-existing racial imaginaries of irreconcilable Indian and Fijian difference.[4]

The paradigm of local identities transformed by violence into nationalist and/or ethnic ones has been broadly documented (e.g. Daniel 1996; Brass 1997; Williams 1989; Mehta and Chatterji 2001). Here, however, I suggest that rather than being indicative of a transformation of local identities into ethnic ones, Indo-Fijian narratives of rural violence demonstrate the multiple kinds of knowledges of 'the other' that Indians used as they endeavoured to make meaning out of a society transformed by violence.[5] The seemingly conflicting claims of the ethnic 'other' as both possible assailant and ally can be better understood if we note how narrators deployed these accounts as part of their struggle to make sense of events that were radically altering social spaces into sites of chaos and fear.

This sense of struggle is perhaps best seen in how these stories were circulated. Often what was passed along were fragments of narratives or lists of violent events, which I have called 'inventories of violence'. Mirroring short news broadcasts, these accounts were exchanged through avenues of gossip and material goods exchange and in the process were amended by multiple narrators. By paying attention not only to the content of such narratives and inventories of violence but also to how these narratives were pieced together, we can see how ambiguities and conflicting explanations came into play in the ways that not only violence, but sociality, was narrated in a time of intense upheaval.

THE MAKINGS OF INTER-ETHNIC DIVISIONS AND SOLIDARITIES

According to the most recent census of 1996, Indo-Fijians currently make up 44% of the population of Fiji. Their numbers following the May 2000 coup have diminished, as in the first two years over 8,500 departed for Australia, New Zealand, Canada, and the US ('Social Inequalities the Key', 4 March 2003).

The first settlement of ethnic Indians in Fiji occurred in 1879, five years after Fiji became a British colony. Provided with five-year contracts or 'agreements' on the basis of which they named themselves *girmitiyas* or the people of the agreement, indentured labourers were brought from across India to work on Fiji's sugar plantations. Initiated by the colony's first Governor, Sir Arthur Gordon, indenture was seen as a means of providing labour without 'endangering' the traditional cultures and lifeways of indigenous Fijians. Between 1879 and 1916, approximately 60,000 Indians were brought to Fiji and subjected to the extremely harsh conditions of plantation life (many of the *girmitiyas* later referred to this period as *'narak"* or hell (Ali 1979; Lal 2000)). Most of the *girmitiyas* were cut off from their relations in India, and the majority of them stayed and settled down after the expiration of their labour contracts. The experiences of indenture as well as the loss of caste, the intermixing of families from the North and the South of India, and the development of a unique dialect of Hindi (locally called 'Fiji *bāt*' or 'Fiji language') served to differentiate Indians in Fiji from those of their homeland. Today, many families in Fiji do not know their forefathers' and foremothers' home provinces in India. None of the residents I knew in Upahār Gaon had ever been to India and few had any desire to go. In fact, it was a common joke during the coup that while the British, American, Australian, and New Zealand embassies in Fiji were not issuing travel visas, you could still apply to go to India though no one would dream of doing so.

During the era of British rule, political power and rights to representation were delineated along ethnic lines with the category of 'Indians' constituting one of the three primary ethnic groups, the other two being indigenous Fijian and European (Lal 1995). When Fiji achieved its independence in 1970, its constitution continued the tri-partite racial division through the allocation of parliamentary seats along communal (ethnic) lines. Political power remained primarily in the hands of a Fijian elite until in 1987 Timoci Bavadra, the Fijian Labor Party leader, was elected Prime Minister, drawing the support of voters from a number of ethnic constituencies (Lawson 1991). Bavadra was a Western indigenous Fijian from a chiefly line but his cabinet included a number of Indo-Fijian MPs and was widely criticized as being an 'Indian government' by members of the Taukei or Fijian Nationalist movement. It was purportedly to return Fiji into the hands of an indigenous Fijian government that Lieutenant-Colonel Sitiveni Rabuka forcibly took over the government during the coups of 1987. In many ways, both the anti-Indian violence and the rhetoric of returning Fijian political power to indigenous Fijians that were employed by Speight and his supporters were echoes of the political and social climate during Rabuka's initial bid for power. Rabuka's final (at least for the moment) dismissal from political office[6] took place in 1999 when Mahendra Chaudhry was elected Prime Minister. Like Bavadra, Chaudhry was elected on the Fiji Labor Party ticket, and his success has been attributed to an ethnically diverse coalition of voters (Norton 2000). Chaudhry lasted only one year in office before Fiji found itself in the midst of another coup and another round of violence.

SITES OF VIOLENCE, SITES OF NARRATION

During the 2000 coup, attacks directed against Indo-Fijians were the most acute in the interior of Viti Levu, particularly in the areas in or near Speight's stronghold of Naitasiri Province. Indo-Fijians living in the rural farming areas of Muaniweni and Vunidawa were forced to flee from their homes, many of them taking refuge with relatives in nearby areas or in the refugee camp set up for them on the western side of Viti Levu. While it is difficult to get an accurate account of the violence, as much of it was not reported, Amnesty International estimates that 'hundreds of Indo-Fijian homes and businesses were burned down or looted' and that 'at least 1,000 Indo-Fijians were internally displaced or made homeless as a result of the violence and thousands were forced to leave leased properties' (Amnesty Internal Report 2001).

Upahār Gaon, the peri-urban neighbourhood where I conducted fieldwork before and during the coup, is situated on the outskirts of

Nausori town, about 20 km outside the Fiji capital Suva.[7] When the weather is dry and the road is easily passable, the village is about one and a half hour's drive from Vunidawa. Many of the settlement's Indo-Fijian residents had previously lived in interior areas such as Vunidawa and Muaniweni and had close relatives there. Numerous families living in the interior were thus able to make extended visits or to move in with their kin in Upahār Gaon as the violence in their home villages escalated.

Upahār Gaon itself is a relatively new multi-ethnic neighbourhood consisting of approximately 56 Fijian and Indian households. According to local residents, the land had previously been part of a European sugar plantation. The first Indo-Fijian families moved into the area in the 1940s but a large part of the settlement was not developed until the mid-1980s. Currently Indians are the majority ethnic group and make up approximately 73% of the households in the village. Most of the families in the village are middle to lower middle class. They are employed in a range of professions including teaching, clerical work, and the running of small home businesses such as residential construction, plumbing, car repair, or tailoring. A number of families rely on homegrown produce and, in some cases, livestock such as poultry and cattle. Many residents either work or are pursuing tertiary education in Suva.

For most of the Indo-Fijian residents, much of the social life in the village is organized along religious lines, with three Hindu *mandalis* or prayer groups providing their members with religious services as well as avenues for gossip, the exchange of news, and entertainment. Many of the Indo-Fijian families also exchange labour and material goods with one another.[8]

In contrast to Indo-Fijian evocations of inter-ethnic friendship and exchange that were commonly made about more rural areas, my impression was that there was very little communication or material exchange between Upahār Gaon's Indo-Fijian and indigenous Fijian residents. Given that the land in the village was freehold, there were no rental agreements between Indian tenants and indigenous Fijian leaseholders (as is common in Fiji). In some cases, Indo-Fijian residents were unaware of information such as the genders or the names of the children in the indigenous Fijian families who lived next door to them – information that it would have been socially impossible for them not to know about other Indo-Fijian families in the area.

During the coup there was some evidence that Indo-Fijian families were attempting to increase their ties with their indigenous Fijian neighbours. A number of Indo-Fijian residents discussed the possibility of visiting Fijian residents with whom they had previously little social contact in order to open up new pathways of acquiring news of the coup. I was also told that Indo-Fijian and Fijian men were taking part together in a neighbourhood patrol whose duty was to police the area and frighten away the bands of youths who occasionally tried to attack the local school or private homes.

Figure 4.1 One of the many Indian-run establishments that were attacked in the hours following George Speight's coup attempt, this local primary school was still smouldering the next morning. (Photo by John Correll)

Throughout the coup, Upahār Gaon witnessed sporadic incidents of violence. Almost immediately after the hostage taking on 19 May, an Indian-administered school in the village had some of its classrooms burnt down. An arson attack reduced a local temple to ashes. In late July 2000, on the night of a rebel shoot-out at the nearby Nausori Bridge, residents feared that Upahār Gaon might be the next neighbourhood overtaken by rebels. Villagers frantically phoned one another (and me) with the news that it was time to flee our homes as the rebels were advancing towards the village and would soon be camped out on the local school grounds. The village was not, however, subjected to attack and there was no sign of the rebels until another shoot-out occurred in a neighbouring community two weeks later.

While not under nearly the same level of attack as Indian settlements in the interior, Upahār Gaon was in a constant state of uncertainty should the violence in the village and the nearby vicinity intensify. Residents' constant state of alert and vigilance over any news of violence, as well as the influx of peoples fleeing from areas of more severe upheaval, made Upahār Gaon one of the sites where anti-Indian attacks were given meaning.

THE UBIQUITY OF VIOLENCE NARRATIVES

In the initial weeks of the coup, most of villagers' talk focused on the looting of commercial shops as well as on the overall political situation. Many people expressed disbelief and confusion about what was happening. Everyone was struggling to keep up with the latest political events. All the families I knew kept a radio or the TV, and sometimes both simultaneously, continually running in order to monitor the situation.

Once it became clear the hostage-taking would last more than a few days, there was growing concern over the country's leadership crisis. Speight's inability to take control of the government was met with fear and some mockery, and both Indo-Fijian and Fijian villagers expressed the desire for a strong leader or set of leaders to emerge and restore the country to economic, political, and social stability (see Trnka 2002). Hopes were alternatively pinned on the Great Council of Chiefs, the military, and in later months, former Prime Minister Rabuka. There was little suggestion that Chaudhry would be able to return to power.

As rural violence escalated and the numbers of people leaving violent areas grew, their stories increasingly began to circulate in public space. Within a matter of weeks, talk of rural violence became a new form of everyday discourse that one could hear while visiting friends or waiting at the bus stop. It also permeated conversations that were not focused on the violence *per se* so that all manner of community conversations came to be punctuated with stories of violence. I felt this most profoundly during my fieldwork when I found myself unable to escape talk of violence even during the birth of my daughter in mid-August in a maternity clinic in Suva. An hour after I gave birth, a nurse just coming on duty introduced herself as hailing from Labasa, and then entirely unprompted began to tell me about the violence residents in her village had experienced when the police came in to arrest rebel sympathizers. Later, in the corridors of the maternity ward of the main hospital, I overheard visitors in the midst of discussing the health of a newborn baby, relating how they had begun to flee from their homes into the surrounding bush each night in case they were attacked.

Feldman has noted that violence is not so much a disrupter of an established cultural order but, as culture is itself processual, a part of the making and remaking of society (1991).[9] In Fiji this insight was manifested not only in the ways that talk of events that had previously been 'extraordinary' became a part of everyday life and discourse, but also in the ways in which the 'ordinary' events of daily living became implicated as sites of communication and understanding of political conflict. It was as if there could be no event that was not in some way narrated as a part of the political situation.

Talk of Violence as a Community Discourse

In mid-July 2000, after a morning spent learning how to cook jackfruit curry with my Indo-Fijian neighbour Devi, we'd just settled down at her kitchen table for a cup of tea, when Devi related the following story of an attack against her *Bhābhī* or brother's wife that took place a few years back:

'About four or five years ago in Vunidawa, during rugby time, my brother was going out to milk the cows. *Bhābhī* was doing the dishes, when she heard someone in the house. She heard his footsteps and thought it was Brother coming back. But it was a Fijian who knew them, who was Brother's friend. He was wearing something on his head [so that] you could see only his eyes and nose. He came up behind *Bhābhī* and when she turned he hit her with a piece of firewood, cutting her hand. She cried out and Brother heard her. When Brother came into the house and saw the man, they began to fight and the stocking on his face was pushed up [she gestures]. He hit Brother and Brother fell to the floor. An uncle heard the commotion and came in. The Fijian ran off into the bush.'

'But they knew him, he was their friend?' I asked.

Devi nodded. 'They used to exchange dalo and cassava,' she said. 'They did not pay him money. He was their friend.' She continues, 'They called the police but they [the police] did not do anything. He [the attacker] ran off into the bush. *Bhābhī* could have been raped, her hand was cut so. It was about five years ago.'

'Why during rugby time?' I asked.

Devi looked at me as if this should be obvious. 'Because they [i.e. Fijians] need ticket money, and money to buy things at the game, not just dalo and cassava,' she said.

Devi's narrative encapsulates many of the explanations for violence that were offered by Indo-Fijians during the 2000 coup. As I've discussed elsewhere (Trnka 2002), Devi depicts *Bhābhī*'s indigenous Fijian attacker as motivated by his desire for certain material goods. This suggestion was part of a widely voiced attitude among Indo-Fijians that when Fijians needed commercial goods unavailable beyond the market economy, they resorted to theft rather than to labour. Lower-, middle- and upper-class Indo-Fijians were the targets of such assaults not only because of their actual material wealth but also because of what they represented through their historical association with wage-labour and the production of market-based goods. But Devi's narrative also complexifies the motivations of 'the Fijian' by invoking the possible threat of sexual assault. At the same time, she highlights a connection between *Bhābhī* and her attacker, referring to an exchange relationship between *Bhābhī*'s husband and 'the Fijian' that we are told made them 'friends'. Finally, Devi also implicates the police by suggesting the futility of their involvement in investigating the crime. In these ways, the story of *Bhābhī*'s attack exhibits a tension between attributing violence to widely perceived notions of ethnic difference and the need to recount incidents of violence as contextually specific and shaped by factors other than ethnic antagonism.

These themes – of radical ethnic difference, sexual violence, cross-ethnic friendship and collaboration, and the lack of appropriate protection by the police – surfaced throughout narratives of rural violence that I collected in 2000. The diversity of circumstances and relationships these accounts consider strikingly contrasts with the same Indo-Fijians' responses to urban violence, which explain the violence as based on an imagined irreconcilable ethnic dichotomy between Indians and Fijians, attributing Fijian violence to perceptions of Fijians as primitive 'junglis' (or people of the jungle) motivated towards crime solely by a desire for material goods.

The differences between accounts of rural and urban violence were due in part to the nature of the violence. Unlike the mob violence of looting or the attack of an unknown urban mugger, rural attacks often involved victims, assailants and involved third parties such as neighbours and friends who were known to each other. The complexities of their interrelationships were clearly reflected in the ways that narrators struggled to account for how and why the violence had happened or – as was more often the case – it was happening.

A second difference lay in their modes of transmission. Most residents were initially informed of incidents of nearby urban looting from the local news media.[10] Many narratives of rural violence did not make it into the local media, and when they did, they were usually reported long after accounts of the incident had been circulated by villagers. It was much more common for stories of rural violence to be exchanged word-of-mouth from one resident to the next. Such narratives reflected the efforts of multiple narrators to pull together some sort of account of an event that was still unfolding, a process that required continual interpretation and reinterpretation as narrators attempted both to make sense of the relationships of those involved in the incident as well as to piece together the events that constituted it.

FRAGMENTARY EXCHANGES

While some accounts of rural violence were initially told as narratives, most emerged as fragmentary accounts circulated by multiple authors. Narrators of these stories frequently consulted each other to collect additional information about the people and events in their tales. A lot of effort was put into getting this information as close to correct as possible and to slowly piece together, from various sources and accounts, narratives of the incident in question.

Often, these stories were told in the very matter-of-fact manner of a news report. Thus one day when I stopped by Devi's home, the conversation began with her listing off an inventory of the latest violence she had heard: 'In Tailevu, a girl was brutally raped and has killed herself; an old woman, 70 or maybe 60 years old, was beaten up in Tailevu and now lives here in the village; it's going to be very bad now, a lot of people are losing their jobs,' she said. ['*Tailevu me, ek larkī ke kharāb se rape karis aur āpan āpan suicide kiya* …(Hindi unavailable) … *ab bahut kharāb hoga – sab naukrī se nikal gaya*']. The community news that Devi had always been on top of and that had once consisted primarily of births, deaths, wedding invitations, and *pūjās* (Hindu prayers), was now devoted to violence and its repercussions.

The main avenue by which news and stories of violence travelled was through kin relationships and through geographic proximity. Not surprisingly, the stories that people knew the most about, and that most impacted their lives, were those that directly involved themselves or their own relatives. When these stories were disseminated in the village, the avenues by which they were circulated were also highly localized. Men would tell stories of violence when they visited one another at home or outside the corner shop, usually when they congregated there to drink grog (yagona or kava) and discuss community events, an activity that was increasingly on the rise during the coup when many men were unable to leave the village to go to work (because of the curfew in place as well as out of fear of attack). Women's circulations of stories were more constricted as some of their primary sites of news and gossip such as the village *kirtan* club (women's devotional song group) were suspended during the coup. Women passed stories along on the phone, over the fence with their direct neighbours, and, when the situation was stable enough, by visiting nearby friends' homes. What people knew about each other varied according to the sites of news and gossip circulation that they shared in common. When I moved from one side of the village to the other, the stories I heard 'over the fence' involved a different set of families and events than those I was previously party to.

Some of the incidents of rural violence, both past and present, were recounted as narratives, such as the story of *Bhābhī*'s attack. But others were circulated piecemeal. Through the efforts of multiple narrators exchanging stories, fragments were collected, embellished with the addition of further details, and, when possible, assembled into more-or-less coherent narratives.

One such account involved a woman named Shanti. Shanti had been living in Vunidawa, in the interior of Viti Levu, but her husband Ram was related to a number of residents in Upahār Gaon. I first heard of the attack against Shanti when my husband and I stopped by the local corner shop and an Indian friend began to tell us how he had heard from a new resident in the village that in Vunidawa an Indian man had come back from a hunting expedition to find his wife being physically attacked by some Fijian youths. Our narrator was however quickly interrupted by a second man. It was not the husband who was out hunting, he told us, but it was their son who then gave the father the gun. Corrected, the first narrator resumed the story, 'the man then shot one of the Fijians in the leg, but there were so many Fijians that they overpowered him and beat him up. Some houses were broken into and set on fire there too.'

It was a few days later that I happened to meet Shanti who was seeking refuge in Upahār Gaon and had come into the village accompanied by her daughters and her maternal relatives, while her husband stayed behind minding their shop in Vunidawa. It was clear that Shanti was still in shock as she described how a group of Fijian youths had filled drums with kerosene, surrounded her husband's shop and threatened to burn it down. I told her that we'd heard about a shooting in that area, and Shanti replied that it had been her uncle who had brought in the gun and tried to shoot one of the youths. She did not mention whom her uncle was trying to protect. Later, as she grew more upset, she told us that the youths out there might rape her daughters if they did not get out of Vunidawa and then suddenly, she excitedly exclaimed 'there was a knife at the throat!' at which point her relatives hastened to quiet her down.

Shanti's words about the knife made very little sense to me until some time later when her husband Ram telephoned from Vunidawa. I mentioned Shanti's agitation to him and Ram explained that she had been attacked by a Fijian youth who had held a knife at her throat. A few weeks after that, Ram's maternal cousin, who also lived in Upahār Gaon, along with Ram's maternal aunt who was visiting, asked me if I knew what had happened to Shanti and recounted a version of the incident in which a group of Fijian youths were playing pool in the shop when they turned on Shanti. 'It's terrible where they are and what happened,' the aunt said, grimacing and gesturing with her hands back and forth in a slashing motion along her own throat. Both women then questioned me about my own conversations with Shanti and her husband, asking about the details of what they had said and Shanti's state of mind when I'd spoken to her.

The story of Shanti's attack was assembled and reassembled as it was circulated among village residents. It appeared to me that the multiple narrators did not hope to produce a definitive account but were attempting to get as close as possible to reconstituting at least some of the events that had driven Shanti out of Vunidawa. For even Shanti could not, at least at that time, coherently relate what had happened to her. In her own words, she distanced the weapon that had been used against her, referring to it as 'a knife at the throat' rather than admitting it had been held against her own body. The trauma that Shanti had undergone had made her desirous of telling her story of the attack but unable to represent herself as the victim.[11]

The circulation of Shanti's story was exemplary of the fragmentary nature of news of violence as it came into the village and the attention that residents paid to sorting out and refining each other's accounts. I had a similar experience with another woman when we thought we were discussing the same story of a woman being sexually assaulted. One morning in early August, when I was visiting her home, Meena commented that the situation in the country was increasingly desperate. I asked her if she thought that things might soon get better. She shook her head and shrugged.

'Do you know a 60-year-old woman got attacked', she said, '... raped.'
I nodded, thinking I knew the incident she was referring to. I said, 'In Tailevu?'
She said, 'Yes.'
I said, 'And she lives here, now.'
'In Nausori?' Meena replied. 'No.'
'I thought she has relatives here,' I said. 'I thought she was actually 70 and they broke her ribs.'
'No,' said Meena, 'this woman is 60 and they [she gestured at her ear].'
'Cut her ear?' I asked.
She nodded. 'Can you imagine, at 60?' she said.

As is evident in the above dialogue, in many cases confusion existed due to the overwhelming number of reports of violence, several of which were little more than fragments devoid of any context. Villagers, however, considered it extremely important to try to sort out who were the victims of these incidents so that they could respond to relatives and friends in distress as well as to assess their own safety both in Upahār Gaon and should they need to travel into the interior. They thus engaged themselves in concentrated efforts to guess where, when, and how such violence might occur again.

If there was uncertainty over the events that were happening in the interior, there was similarly ambiguity expressed over what precipitated these attacks. In addition to factors of sexual violence and the acquisition of material goods, there were also suggestions, though these were less frequent, that rural attacks were occurring out of political motivation, because of alcohol use, or because of the 'hotness' of youths whose impulsiveness had been allowed free rein.

BEYOND ETHNICITY: IMAGINING SOCIALITY IN TIMES OF VIOLENCE

While Indian villagers in Upahār Gaon were quick to paint a portrait of 'the Fijian' as a predator, there also, however, circulated throughout the village numerous stories of rural violence that demonstrated cooperative cross-ethnic endeavours and agreements. In fact, throughout narratives of rural violence, the images of the 'good' Fijian were not an extraordinary occurrence but were frequently referred to, often by the same people, and in some cases in the same narratives, as those that depicted caricatured images of 'the Fijians' as dangerous thieves.

This phenomenon of the 'ethnic other' as both an aggressor and a saviour is not unusual. Other studies of inter-ethnic violence have also frequently remarked upon this dual presence. Some scholars have gone no further than to note its occurrence (e.g., Das on Hindus who assisted Sikhs in fleeing the riots (1996)), while others have ascribed to the informant who tells such a tale the 'remarkable' capacity to overcome prevailing anti-ethnic sentiment by recalling the help they received from a member of the 'enemy' group (Kanapathipillai 1990: 327). One of the most extended commentaries of the ethnic other as protector appears in Liisa Malkki's analysis of narratives told by victims of Hutu–Tutsi violence. Throughout the text, Malkki paints a highly stylized portrait of Hutu conceptions of the '"the Tutsi" as a homogenous category' (1995: 93). While her focus is firmly on Hutu assumptions of Tutsi's 'otherness,' at one point she acknowledges that Hutu narratives of violence often diverted away from these stereotypes by invoking images of Tutsi individuals who assisted in their escapes from violent areas. Malkki explains that

the position of these accounts of individual Tutsi saviors in the mythico-history is not clearly articulated, but they could be interpreted as a way of accounting for one's good fortune in being spared from death. ... They did not seem to attenuate in the least the categorical distinction otherwise drawn between good and evil, Hutu and Tutsi – if anything, these exceptions seemed to strengthen the categories. (1995: 94)

Unfortunately Malkki does not go far enough to explain *how* the exceptions proved the rule, nor does she take up the opportunity to use such exceptions to reflect further upon the possible complexities of the otherwise 'categorical' distinctions her interlocutors used.

My concern here is with what might happen if rather than relegating these images of the ethnic other as protector to the sidelines, we instead attempt to integrate an understanding of the 'good Fijian' with the abundance of negative ethnic stereotyping. In the rural areas in the interior that were hardest hit by incidents of violence, the protective nature of affiliations between Fijians and Indo-Fijians was put stringently to the test. Friendships between Fijians and Indo-Fijians were often highlighted as the reasons why people were able to escape violence. Newspaper reports of the violence in these areas made a point of describing how Indo-Fijian victims of house burnings often fled into the homes of Fijians in surrounding *koros* (Fijian villages). Likewise, in some of Devi's repeated remarks regarding the safety of her elderly mother in Vunidawa, she commented that it was some of her mother's Fijian neighbours who forewarned her that other Fijians from a neighbouring village were planning to burn down her house. Both before and during the coup, a number of Indo-Fijians similarly asserted that in rural areas their relationships with Fijians were 'good' because they exchanged food with them. Repeatedly I was told that people who trade together and who are thus 'friends' would not resort to violence against one another.

But just as many of the narratives pivoted on the theme of inter-ethnic friendships gone awry. These narratives point to a breakdown of friendly relations both between residential groups (an Indo-Fijian settlement and a neighbouring *koro*, for example) as well as between individuals who once considered themselves to be friends. In attempting to understand which factors made for good and bad relationships, people often noted that the histories and length of their residence influenced their relations with neighbours, as well as the specificities of their land lease arrangements. But sometimes there was no telling how strong or weak a friendship might be.

In late June, following one of the rare *pūjās* to be held in the village, Rajesh's family invited my family and the pandit who had conducted the ceremony to share a meal with them. Given the tense climate, the men chose not to eat separately on the veranda as was usual, but to eat inside with the women. As the food was served, the family waited respectfully to see how the pandit would open the conversation. The pandit began by repeating a story that had been told to him by one of Rajesh's wife's relatives, a farmer who had fled the violence in Muaniweni. The farmer had had a visit from one of his Fijian neighbours, he told us. As they often did, on this occasion they drank grog (kava) together, an act usually taken as a sign of cooperation and amiability. They then ate together a big meal prepared by the Indian family. The pandit gestured towards our table of food to imply that it was the same as us sharing food together now. Then as the Fijian was leaving he saw a bull outside. He turned to his host and said, 'We used to be (good friends) but not now.' He then violently slapped the man and took the bull away.

The pandit's story dramatically articulated the perception that rural violence between Fijians and Indians was highly unpredictable. Even close friends, those who sit and drink grog and eat together, could turn into enemies. The question of how and when friendships might give way to enmities made for not only a poignant narrative account, but was an issue of serious reflection as many Indo-Fijians, including the pandit and those seated around the table with him, had to judge the odds of their own safety.

Taking Risks – Uses of Ethnic Stereotypes and Local Knowledges

For many Indo-Fijians during the coup, one of the most difficult judgments they had to make was to assess the likelihood of whether they too might become victims of violence. Weighing who might be potential attackers and who might constitute a potential victim were serious issues for those who lived in especially violent areas, those who feared the spread of violence into their own residential areas, and those who travelled into violent areas in order to assist their family members.

The uncertain and confusing process by which such assessments of safety were made is well demonstrated by an account from Rajesh who told me how, at the height of the violence, he enlisted the aid of a Fijian friend to drive up to Muaniweni to rescue his wife's relatives whose house was being stoned by Fijian youths. Like the pandit's story of the stolen bull, this narrative revolves around the question of the reliability of inter-ethnic friendship in the face of escalating levels of inter-ethnic violence. As a first-person account, Rajesh's narrative goes further in evoking some of the possible stakes involved in making these assessments.

'Yesterday, the Nausori police rang me. The police in Muaniweni had radioed them. Some Fijians were throwing stones at the house (of my wife's relatives) so they asked if I could go up there in my van and get them, I rang them back, half an hour later and asked if it was safe for *ME* to drive up there and they said no. They said they'd give me one boy from the police but.... But then a Fijian I know, a *Ratu* (chief) from Muaniweni came into the shop (that I own.) He said he would go up with me, but how would I get back? So we hired one carrier and drove up. I hid in the back.'

He gestured that he covered himself with a blanket or rug. 'At the roadblocks (which were set up and manned by Fijian villagers) they saw the driver – a

Figure 4.2 Military checkpoints, such as this one, were erected throughout the Suva–Nausori corridor to monitor residents and enforce the curfew. (Photo by John Correll)

Fijian – and the *Ratu*. I hid in the back. The *Ratu* is well known there but I didn't know even with him if I'd be safe.'

He went on to say how he brought the relatives back to his house in Nausori along with some of the Fijian relatives of the *Ratu* whom he invited over for the day. 'When we got home, the Fijians went to the back room. You've seen the backroom?'

I shook my head.

'Oh, there is another settee there, so my wife came home and said, who are all those people in the back? So we spread out a mat and had them down here (in the front room), drinking grog (kava) and telling their stories, yarning, I don't know about what...'. He gestured vaguely.

'But you know (how to speak) Fijian?' I asked.

'Yes, a lot, but I don't understand everything. ...'. He paused. 'Up there (in the interior) it is very bad. Here – (he names off some Fijian villages) are safe, safe for *me*. Not *everyone* can go there. But up there, it is very bad.'

Rajesh's narrative demonstrates his perception of the complex role that race might play in rural conflict. On the one hand, he depicts the violence in the interior as racially motivated. A *Ratu*, a Fijian driver, a Fijian 'boy' from the police station can all travel up there, but they all agree that Rajesh by virtue of being Indian would not be safe. And yet Rajesh was also acutely aware of the ways in which individualized relationships intersect with racial stereotypes. He noted that his friendship with the *Ratu* grants him protection. There are furthermore other places, he asserted, in which he by virtue of his knowledge of Fijian and his local connections to Fijian villagers, could travel unharmed. The multitude of Rajesh's responses to violence demonstrated his ability, and it was an ability widely shared by many of Upahār Gaon's residents, to draw upon *both* prevalent ethnic stereotypes and their personalized knowledges of Fijian individuals and particular local situations to interpret interpersonal violence.

ETHNICITY AS AN EXPLANATION FOR URBAN VIOLENCE

In contrast, accounts of urban violence and of the general circumstances leading up to the coup were most often couched solely in ethnic stereotypes. There was much less ambiguity expressed over motivation as almost without exception urban attacks were explained as a fulfilment of indigenous Fijians' desires for material goods. In their discussions of the possible reasons for the overthrow of Prime Minister Chaudhry, the motivations of the Taukei movement, and the actions of the looters, the Indian villagers I talked with had very similar responses: the troubles arose from differing attitudes to work between Indians and Fijians. They described Fijians as 'lazy' and unmotivated to work, preferring to have an 'easy life' by living off of Indian labour. Desiring commodities and mass-produced goods they could not afford to buy, Fijians were characterized as resorting to small-scale violence and theft (such as muggings or burglary), widespread looting, or the implementation of government-sponsored 'affirmative action' programmes that channel resources to indigenous Fijians (see Trnka 2002).

Numerous Indo-Fijians also told me that, unlike indigenous Fijians, Indians are very hard working. As John Kelly has pointed out, labour has religious connotations for many Sanatan Hindus as it is perceived as a necessary aspect of one's relationship to God (Kelly 1992). In the months following the coup, the notion of work as service to God was explicitly stated by Hindus, often with not only religious but ethnic implications as well. A popular description of national development as characterized by the clearing away of the 'jungle' or bush through human cultivation utilized the religious terminology of the transformation of the 'dirty' into the 'clean' and was depicted as a highly ethnically segregated endeavour. Frequently I was told that it was the *girmitiyas* and their descendants who through their sweat and blood had propelled Fiji out of its 'jungli' past and toward modernity. One Indo-Fijian woman said to me, 'When Fijians were here, it [the village] was only jungle. Then Indians came and cleaned it.' When, on a mass scale, some Fijians looted shops, smashed down businesses, and frightened away foreign investment, this was interpreted as further evidence of not only their lack of participation in the development of Fiji as a 'modern', capitalist nation but also of their essentially uncivilized nature.

It is important to note that these terms of ethnic differentiation were drawn not only from Sanatan notions of labour but also from the language of the debates on Fijian and Indian rights that were and still are widely employed in public discourses. These stereotypes furthermore have deep roots, arising out of the colonial codification of racial identity that posited Indians as plantation labourers or 'coolies', indigenous Fijians as the providers of land, and the colonial elite as the economic and political leadership of Fiji (Lal 1995; Scarr 1983; Kelly 1992).

The Police and the Politics of Violence

Rajesh's narrative, like many accounts of rural violence, also suggests that in addition to relationships between aggressors and victims, another factor in Indo-Fijians' understandings of rural violence was that the violence was being played out in a context in which the police and the military, both of which are made up of predominantly indigenous Fijians, were either not present or not responding to the needs of local residents. Frequent references to the incapability of the police to halt the violence attested to the widely held sentiment that events of explosive violence could not have happened outside a political atmosphere conducive to them. Unlike in other situations where narratives of police involvement evoke specific members of the police involved and their local relationships (see, e.g., Das 1996; Brass 1997), Indo-Fijian narratives depicted the police and the military not as individuals with personal interests at stake but as state officials who joined in a widespread campaign to destabilize the country and terrorize Indian citizens. By not specifying the actual individual police or police stations involved, Indians thus continued to hold 'the police' and by extension the state responsible for their protection and as negligent in their duties.

These narratives of police and military involvement took a few weeks to emerge in Upahār Gaon. Initially, in the first few weeks following the coup, many villagers contrasted the violence of 2000, which they attributed to the behaviour of Fijian civilians, with that of 1987, which they stated was conducted predominantly by the military. Stories were told of harassment, rape, and theft conducted by the military against Indo-Fijians during 1987, in contrast to the present situation. But in later weeks, as stories from rural areas started to circulate through Upahār Gaon, Indo-Fijians began to comment upon the complicity of the military and police in the violence of 2000. Many stated that local police were taking part in the intimidation in the interior. For example, when I asked one woman why the police or army were not protecting the safety of Indians in the interior, she replied, 'because they are mixed ... The police and the people doing it, they are mixed together, they are the same.' On another occasion, my husband and I met an elderly man who was among the relatives that Rajesh and the *Ratu* had brought back from the interior. My husband asked him what the situation in Muaniweni was like. 'It's very bad,' he said. 'When do you think you can go back?' my husband asked. The man shook his head and replied, 'There is no government [there].' A few others asserted that the police and military were doing a good job of keeping the peace but complained about how much money local Indo-Fijians were spending on food and beverages for the police in order to ensure that they received protection.

Given the general environment of intimidation, most of those who were victimized did not feel secure in publicly voicing their criticisms of the police. The images of police and military complicity that narratives of rural violence depicted were an alternative way of giving expression to these sentiments in that they acted as a non-threatening form of protest, allowing villagers to assign blame to the authorities without forcing them to further put their lives on the line.

Circumstances Conducive to Violence

Narratives and fragmentary accounts of rural violence were distinct from explanations of urban violence in the attention that they paid to specifying the circumstances in which violence was likely to occur. Rather than portraying an essentialized struggle between 'the Fijians' and 'the Indo-Fijians', these narratives reveal that some Indo-Fijians (particularly middle-aged women and young girls by virtue of their perceived sexual vulnerability) were considered more likely to be victimized. Other people, owing to their personalities, friendships, local histories, and knowledge of Fijian culture – *'me,* not *everyone'* – were depicted as less likely to be victimized even in areas of the country that might be dangerous to others. Thus even when racial antagonisms were considered by Indo-Fijians as a primary factor for motivating attacks against them, the specific relationships between victims and potential assailants were also seen as crucial to assessing whether inter-ethnic attacks would take place. Only some Fijians were considered likely assailants while others were depicted as protecting potential victims and actively averting further violence. Trust was most often placed in those with whom Indo-Fijians had personal histories and therefore considered to be their friends. Often these friendships were explained in terms of longevity, referring to people who had lived together in the same area for a long time, or through their involvement in exchange relationships. There was, however, an ever-present awareness that one had to be ready to make judgments regarding which relationships – such as that of Rajesh and the *Ratu* – could be relied upon in potentially very violent situations and which ones – such as between the farmer in Muaniweni and the Fijian who stole his bull – were likely to fall by the wayside. In such situations, it was up to the individuals involved to make these decisions since the police and other state authorities were often unable or unwilling to ensure one's safety.

Making Meanings

In his introduction to *The Anthropology of Violence* (1986) David Riches writes that one of the essential characteristics of violence is that its legitimacy is questionable. Unless an action involving physical harm entails a struggle over legitimacy, he argues, it would not be deemed 'violent'. But violence also, he contends, acquires its potency from its ease of recognition. Regarding communal or ethnic violence in particular, he states that 'images of violence are among the few social images which are likely to be well understood across major ethnic divisions....' (1986: 13). He considers violence 'an excellent communicative vehicle' because of its visibility as well as 'the probability that all involved – however different their cultural backgrounds – are likely to draw, at the very least, some basic common understanding from the acts and images concerned' (1986: 12).

While I agree that 'some basic common understanding' of violence as a struggle for power might be drawn by the various parties involved, what Riches fails to explore are the gaps in understanding and the struggles for meaning that characterize many violent situations.[12] Indians in Fiji did not apply to rural violence the straightforward meanings that Riches might imagine for them. Rather, their accounts of violence reveal the muddled, sometimes frantic, often contradictory, struggle to make sense of the violence that occurred. Narrators of rural narratives neither embraced nor disassociated from racial stereotypes but wrestled with a racial imaginary that attributed violence as stemming from Fijian 'jungliness' and the need to assess carefully the trustworthiness of each individual relationship in a social climate that promoted anti-Indian violence.

WHO DEFINES THE 'ETHNIC' IN 'ETHNIC VIOLENCE'?

What then is to be made of the suggestion proposed by so many case studies of 'inter-ethnic violence' that violence between members of different ethnic groups precipitates a shift from local identities and relations to stereotyped ethnic identities?

Analysis of violence narratives in Upahār Gaon suggests that in a time of intense violence and social crisis, the perceptions and meanings of ethnicity were variously configured as stories of violent events, which became part of social discourses of identity and community. Stories of urban violence and political upheaval tended to elicit a common set of reactions as urban looting, the hostage-taking, and the coup itself were generally blamed on Fijian cultural practices that were perceived to place Fijians beyond capitalist exchange and its attendant modernizing capabilities. Narratives of rural violence, however, reflected a tendency to depict specific relationships between the parties involved. This emphasis on describing the context of the violence reflects some of the differences in interpreting the faceless violence of an urban mob and that of attackers in rural areas who (even when they were masked, as in *Bhābhī*'s attack) were often known by their victims. Where the police and other government authorities could not be counted upon, local social bonds created through networks of exchange and residential histories were evoked as stabilizing forces that would hopefully – in most cases, if not in all – ensure trust and cooperation between those who otherwise might be separated by political and/or ethnic loyalties.

What occurred was not so much a transformation of identities from local to ethnic, but a struggle to find and make meanings within a context of a transformed social space. Narratives of inter-personal violence that occurred in rural areas did not dismiss the factor of ethnicity in rural violence but complicated it by employing ethnic stereotypes alongside motivations that stemmed from the particularities of personalities, relationships, and histories that existed between victims and assailants, between victims and friends.

NOTES

1. Acknowledgments: John Correll kept my spirits and sanity intact during the coup for which I cannot thank him enough. Many thanks to Rena Lederman who engaged with earlier versions of this essay and encouraged me to develop it in its current form. Pamela Stewart and Andrew Strathern also provided much-needed feedback on an earlier draft. Lisa Guenther

kindly gave comments on the final draft. Joao Biehl and Emily Martin were instrumental in helping me develop the larger project of which this is a part. Thanks also to Sarah Pinto, Kavita Misra, and Mark Rowe who have provided invaluable critical engagement during the writing process. Stephen Jackson offered his own exchange of violence narratives and kept me focused when I needed it most. I'd also like to thank the Social Science Research Council for the pre-dissertation grant that got me to Fiji, Princeton University for funding part of my time there, and the Government of Fiji, Ministries of Health and Education for enabling this research.

2. It was widely noted that Speight was most likely a frontman for various other parties who may have masterminded and/or funded the coup. Trials for those involved and suspected of involvement in the coup have been underway in Fiji.

3. These accounts were collected during the months of May–August 2000 when coup-related violence was at its height in Viti Levu. There was a decrease in violent episodes from late August to October 2000, so much so that many Fijians and Indo-Fijians told me that the worst of the coup was behind them when I left the field at the end of October 2000. In November 2000 the shooting at the Queen Elizabeth Barracks (QEB) disrupted any such notions.

4. My focus here is on how victims and members of victimized communities narrated the violence, and in particular how they represented the motivations behind such violence. I do not want to make claims about the actual motivations behind violence against Indo-Fijians as I was not privy to the perspectives of assailants.

5. Das offers an example of this approach in her work on the anti-Sikh riots in Delhi by demonstrating how the Delhi attacks must be understood as motivated by the intertwining of specific local grievances with nationalist rhetorics. In her analysis of the spatial mapping of violence and of the language used by assailants and victims, Das describes how assailants, who in many cases were partly motivated by tensions between particular local relationships among households, castes, and alliance groups around local underworld leaders, used nationalist language during their attacks (1996: 195). She concludes that the rioters 'were literally embodying [both] local and national narratives in their somatic actions and in their speech' (1996: 194). I am attempting a similar strategy here, looking however at the perspectives of victims of violence, rather than those of the perpetrators.

6. In 2003 there was some speculation that Rabuka might be considering running in the next Fiji elections. *The New Zealand Herald* reported in June 2003 that Rabuka 'is looking a strong prospect for re-election amid uncertainty over the fate of the [Fiji] Government' ('Rabuka Sways Some with His New Pitch for Power', 20 June 2003).

7. At first I considered the neighbourhood to be an extension of the urban centre of Suva. Residents, however, were quick to inform me that they did not live in an urban area 'where people are strangers to one another' but had all the sociality of a village. Indeed, they always referred to the neighbourhood as a *gaon* or village. Residents of Suva concurred but on different grounds, telling me that Upahār Gaon must be a village as the residents keep cows there. The name of the village as well as the names of all of my interlocutors are pseudonyms.

8. Politically, prior to the coup, the Indo-Fijians in the area were a mix of supporters of the National Federation Party (which dramatically lost the 1999 elections) and Chaudhry's Fiji Labor Party. I do not know the political affiliations of the indigenous Fijians living in the area.

9. Das and Deborah Poole also make compelling arguments for this notion of violence as part of the 'making' of culture in their respective work on communal riots in Delhi (Das 1996) and on the violence in the Peruvian Highlands (Poole 1994).

10. While the internet was a widely used source of information for relatives, friends, and academics observing events from overseas, it was not noted as a significant source of news for those in Fiji. In part this might be related to the practical difficulties of accessing the internet during times of curfew and especially during the power cuts that followed the rebel take-over of Monasavu Dam. The exception was the initial news of the coup. Some village residents told me they first found out about the crisis from phone calls they received from overseas relatives who had read of the hostage-taking on the internet. Foreign newspapers were difficult to obtain and the BBC television world news programme, which was being shown nightly during this period, offered only scant coverage.

11. A similar situation is seen in Das's work on survivors of communal riots, where she highlights how victims of violence must overcome the numerous difficulties in remembering and understanding not only the events themselves but also their own place in them (Das 1990).

12. In their recent assessment of Riches' work, Stewart and Strathern (2002) point out another shortcoming of Riches' approach as stemming from the exclusivity of the three participants in his 'triangle of violence' – the performer, the victim, and the witness. Stewart and Strathern suggest that some forms of violence, such as warfare or revenge killings, muddy the distinctions between performer and victim and, in many cases, require something other than purely rationalist explanations of motivation. Interestingly, Indo-Fijian narratives and eyewitness accounts very rarely mention physical resistance much less revenge attacks as a response to violence. I collected only two such accounts. One was the incident involving Shanti's uncle that is told above. The other was a story of Indian youths who burnt down indigenous Fijian homes in the interior following the 1987 violence – and the Indo-Fijian narrator of this story forcefully denounced their actions. Overwhelmingly such accounts were downplayed in favour of portraying Indo-Fijians as, on a national level, promoters of development, and on local levels, as desirous of peaceful relations between neighbours.

REFERENCES

Ali, Ahmed (ed.) (1979) *Girmit: The Indenture Experience in Fiji*. Suva: Fiji Museum.

Amnesty Internal Report (2001) Fiji. Online version available at: http://web.amnesty.org/web/ar2001.nsf/webasacountries/FIJI?OpenDocument

Anon. (2003a) 'Rabuka Sways Some with His New Pitch for Power'. *The New Zealand Herald*. 20 June, B3.

Anon. (2003b) 'Social Inequalities the Key: Report'. *The Daily Post*. From fijilive.com. 4 March.

Brass, Paul R. (1997) *Theft of an Idol: Text and Context in the Representation of Collective Violence*. Princeton: Princeton University Press.

Daniel, E. Valentine (1996) *Charred Lullabies: Chapters in an Anthropography of Violence*. Princeton: Princeton University Press.

Das, Veena (1990) 'Our Work to Cry: Your Work to Listen'. In *Mirrors of Violence: Communities, Riots and Survivors in South Asia*, ed. Veena Das. Delhi: Oxford University Press, pp. 345–98.

—— (1996) 'The Spatialization of Violence: Case Study of a "Communal Riot"'. In *Unravelling the Nation: Sectarian Conflict and India's Secular Identity*, ed. Kaushik Basu and Sanjay Subrahmanyam. Harmondsworth: Penguin Books, pp. 157–203.

Das, Veena, and Arthur Kleinman (2001) 'Introduction'. In *Remaking a World: Violence, Social Suffering, and Recovery*, ed. Veena Das, Arthur Kleinman, Margaret Lock, Mamphela Ramphele and Pamela Reynolds. Berkeley: University of California Press, pp. 1–30.

Feldman, Allen (1991) *Formations of Violence: The Narrative of the Body and Political Terror in Northern Ireland*. Chicago: University of Chicago Press.

Kanapathipillai, Vali (1990) 'July 1983: The Survivor's Experience'. In *Mirrors of Violence: Communities, Riots and Survivors in South Asia*, ed. Veena Das. Delhi: Oxford University Press, pp. 321–44.

Kelly, John D. (1992) 'Fiji Indians and "Commoditization of Labor"'. *American Ethnologist* 19(1): 97–120.

Lal, Brij V. (1995) 'Managing Ethnicity in Colonial and Post-colonial Fiji'. In *Lines Across the Sea: Colonial Inheritance in the Post-colonial Pacific*, ed. Brij V. Lal and Hank Nelson. Brisbane: Pacific History Association.

—— (2000) *Chalo Jahaji: On A Journey Through Indenture in Fiji*. Suva: The Fiji Museum.

Lawson, Stephanie (1991) *The Failure of Democratic Politics in Fiji*. Oxford: Clarendon Press.

Maci, Ruci (2000) 'Rebels Seize Rural Group'. *Fiji Times*, 31 July, page 1.

Malkki, Liisa (1995) *Purity and Exile; Violence, Memory, and National Cosmology among Hutu Refugees in Tanzania*. Chicago: University of Chicago Press.

Mehta, Deepak, and Roma Chatterji (2001) 'Boundaries, Names, Alterities: A Case Study of a "Communal Riot" in Dharavi, Bombay'. In *Remaking a World: Violence, Social Suffering, and Recovery*, ed. Veena Das, Arthur Kleinman, Margaret Lock, Mamphela Ramphele and Pamela Reynolds. Berkeley: University of California Press, pp. 201–49.

Norton, Robert (2000) 'Understanding the Results of the 1999 Fiji Elections'. In *Fiji Before the Storm: Elections and the Politics of Development*, ed. Brij V. Lal. Canberra: Australia National University, Asia Pacific Press, pp. 49–72.

Poole, Deborah (1994) 'Peasant Culture and Political Violence in the Peruvian Andes: Sendero Luminoso and the State'. In *Unruly Order: Violence, Power, and Cultural Identity in the High Provinces of Southern Peru*, ed. Deborah Poole. Westview Press: Boulder, pp. 247–81.

Riches, David (ed.) (1986) *The Anthropology of Violence*. Oxford: Basil Blackwell.

Scarr, Deryck (ed.) (1983) *Fiji: The Three-Legged Stool. Selected Writings of Ratu Sir Lala Sukuna*. London: Macmillan Education.

Singh, Shailendra (2001) 'After Beating Govt. in Court, Fiji Farmer Seeks to Flee'. *Indiaabroaddaily.com* (online journal). 4 March.

Stewart, Pamela J. and Andrew Strathern (2002) *Violence: Theory and Ethnography.* London: Continuum.

Trnka, Susanna (2002) 'Foreigners at Home: Discourses of Difference, Fiji Indians and the Looting of May 19th'. In *Communities in Crisis: Ethnographies of the May 2000 Fiji Coup*, ed. Susanna Trnka. Special issue of *Pacific Studies*, (December).

Williams, Brackette F. (1989) 'A Class Act: Anthropology and the Race to Nation Across Ethnic Terrain'. *Annual Review of Anthropology*, 18: 401–44.

5 NARRATIVES OF VIOLENCE AND PERILS OF PEACE-MAKING IN NORTH–SOUTH CROSS-BORDER CONTEXTS, IRELAND

Andrew Strathern and Pamela J. Stewart

The argument of this chapter is that the historical creation and recreation of borders between political zones pervasively engenders ambiguities and tensions regarding identities that provide a fertile ground for ongoing conflict and struggles for power as well as a challenge to peace-making. Our case study relates to the border areas between Northern Ireland, which belongs to the United Kingdom, and the Republic or Ireland, a polity brought into being through a struggle for independence from the United Kingdom. Much of our materials presented in this chapter is from our work in the County Donegal area of the Republic of Ireland over the last five years. The original struggle for independence was carried out in the name of the island of Ireland as a whole, and the partition of Ireland that emerged was a compromise between the opposing forces favouring continued incorporation into the British state as a part of the United Kingdom (known as unionists) and those favouring a complete break from that union (known as nationalists, or republicans). The specific ironies, ambiguities, and awkwardnesses created by the partition, beginning in 1920–1 with the inception of the Irish Free State, have much to do with the fact that the wider entity of Ulster was split into two by this division: six counties of the ancient province of Ulster (Antrim, Armagh, Down, Fermanagh, Londonderry, and Tyrone) were included in Northern Ireland, while three (Cavan, Donegal, and Monaghan) were assigned to the Republic. The partition of Ireland was therefore most poignantly the partition of Ulster, and it is for this reason that unionists in Northern Ireland often make their claims in the name of Ulster rather than Northern Ireland as such. 'Ulster' for these political activists represents a historical claim to an ancient unity that has been lost, just as much as 'Ireland' for nationalists means a claim to a future in which Northern Ireland would become a part of the Republic.

In customary usage, both parties use the seemingly neutral terms of 'the North' and 'the South' to refer to Northern Ireland and the Republic respectively. While most of the Republic does lie to the south of Northern Ireland, this classification does not fit the situation in County Donegal, where the border divides Donegal in the west from Londonderry and Tyrone in the east. This point is crucial for understanding the situation in eastern Donegal, since many important social, economic, and religious ties joined this part of Donegal to its eastern neighbours and it was these ties that were originally cut or impeded by the partition. Historically, this part of Donegal was settled by immigrants from the south-west of Scotland and from England from the early seventeenth century onwards in the 'Plantation of Ireland' ordered by King James VI and I of Scotland and England. Battles between the monarch's forces and those of the Irish earls dating from Elizabethan times resulted in the famous 'flight of the Earls' from Donegal and the subsequent occupation of their lands by a variety of Scottish and English landowners and tenants, along with a smaller proportion of indigenous Irish who were granted tenancy and settlement rights while the bulk of the Irish speakers moved to the west of Donegal in the face of this new colonial encroachment (Hunter 1995; Robinson 2000). Donegal was de facto subsequently split between the settlers who occupied the fertile plains of the Laggan Valley, and the Irish Gaelic population of its mountainous and rocky west, where the land is less fertile but coastal areas provide opportunities for fishing. There has therefore been an internal split within Donegal that mirrors the wider partition of the island to some extent.

To these complexities, those of religious affiliation, so marked in the overall struggles within Ireland, have to be added. Our own fieldwork has been concentrated in the Laggan area, with some coverage also of Inishowen to its north and the Finn Valley to its south. The area between Londonderry/Derry and Lifford to its south, comprising rich farmlands and small towns such as Manorcunningham, Newtowncunningham, St Johnstown, Carrigans, Raphoe, and Convoy on the Republic side is the heartland of a phase of the Plantation settlement in which those granted the land and the followers who came with them were from Scotland's south-west, and brought to Donegal religious traditions closely associated with the Scottish Calvinist Reformation deriving from the times of John Knox and Andrew Melville (Lecky 1905).

In Scotland itself the seventeenth century was marked by religious upheavals that culminated in the eventual establishment of a Presbyterian Church of Scotland, with presbyteries, synods, and assemblies acting in a representative capacity without bishops and archbishops appointed by the throne. When an army was sent over to crush the Irish rebellion of 1641, Presbyterian ministers came along with Scottish contingents of troops, and from that time they began to organize church-centred groups in eastern Donegal. Military chaplains took on civil roles as ministers and stayed on after the rebellion was over (Davies 1999: 584; Lecky 1905).

Eastern Donegal thus acquired a Presbyterian character, and its inhabitants shared in the vicissitudes of Presbyterianism in general, continuing through to the contemporary period of the Troubles and their aftermath beginning with outbreaks in (London)Derry in the late 1960s. For example, in spite of the triumph of William of Orange against the Catholic King James VII and II (his own father-in-law, father of his wife Mary) in 1690 in Ireland, and the subsequent reconsolidation of Protestantism as the religion of the dominant political class, 'Protestantism' actually meant adherents of the established Anglican Church of Ireland (Tanner 2001: 165). Presbyterians and other Nonconformist Dissenters were by the Test Acts of 1702 onwards excluded from public office unless they were prepared to declare allegiance to Anglicanism (Strathern and Stewart 2001: 171). The same prohibition was applied to Roman Catholics, and these restrictions were not lifted until much later, in the case of Catholics stretching into the nineteenth century (Davies 1999: 725, on the Catholic Emancipation Act of 1829). Some dissenting Presbyterians of Scottish descent were motivated to join the 1798 rebellion against English-based rule in Ireland, a fact that contemporary historians have noted in the context of the later awkward rapprochement between Presbyterians and Anglicans under the banner of 'Protestantism' (Seery, Holmes, and Stewart 2000). Presbyterianism is associated with Scotland and its own uneasy incorporation into what became at the beginning of the nineteenth century the United Kingdom and the intensification of a sense of 'British' identity: a combination of acceptance and rebelliousness, a sense of isolation and ambiguity of identification (Strathern and Stewart 2001: 99–130).

All of these complex streams of historical influences flow into contemporary manifestations of conflicts and their memories. The hinterland of (London)Derry is affected every summer by the 'marching season', for example, extending through July until mid-August, and centring on formal occasions of celebrating the victory of William III at the battle of the Boyne, associated with the date of 12 July 1690,[1] and with the lifting of the siege of Derry instigated by James II and his troops, which took place on 28 July 1689 (Kelly 2001: 10; Davies 1999: 616). The celebrations are conducted by members of the Apprentice Boys' Clubs, first begun in 1813, and of the Loyal

Orange Order founded in 1795 after the Battle of the Diamond to defend 'Protestant' interests against those of the Catholics (McBride 1997; Walker 2001: 123–44).

Local Apprentice Boys groups and chapters of the Order take part in marches in the streets of Derry, marked by an escalation of tensions between 'the communities' (Catholics and Protestants) in the city, and associated with contests over the routes taken by marchers and the character of songs and emblems of a sectarian kind displayed at them (Jarman 1997; Bryan 2000). In more recent years, as part of the instituted Peace Process in Northern Ireland dating from the Good Friday or Belfast Agreement of 1998, explicit efforts have been made to lessen the tensions surrounding these marches (particularly in Derry and Belfast in 2005) and to ensure that they are by and large peaceful. They still remain the focus of markedly different evaluation by Catholics as against Protestants. The Orange Order comprises both Anglicans and Presbyterians, but the symbolic division between these is marked by the different decorations participants wear: bowler hats and dark suits primarily signifying Anglican traditions, and Highlands Scottish regalia of kilts, tartan sashes, and bagpipes primarily celebrating the Presbyterian heritage. Raphoe, St Johnstown, and Convoy all have Orange Order Lodges, and their bands customarily participate in the parades, as well as in festival competitions for bands elsewhere, for example in Antrim and in Glasgow, Scotland. The Order therefore represents an alliance between Presbyterians and Anglicans in ritual terms.

While these marches formally commemorate events of long ago, in practice they are deeply implicated with current struggles for overall power within local areas. Catholics/Nationalists view the marches as assertions of Protestant hegemony and dominance. In doing so, Catholic spokespersons, primarily Sinn Fein politicians or elected local officials, adopt the historical role of the victims, especially since the inception of the Troubles. Their statements are reported in newspapers such as the *Irish Independent* or the *Irish News*. But some Protestants also may see themselves as victims. During the marching season, rival newspapers with a sectarian inclination carry stories of families whose members call for justice in relation to deaths regarded as sectarian killings from the late 1960s or the 1970s. The same holds for stories of contemporary attacks. Each side asserts that the other's members are driving them out from their legitimate historical areas, in a kind of discursive tit-for-tat through which they construct themselves as unjustly subjected to the 'terror' exercised by the other side. Cases from the 1970s are juxtaposed with accounts of contemporary stonings or petrol bombings from contested city areas. These areas almost invariably relate to the bigger towns and cities, principally Belfast and Londonderry, where a good deal of the overt displays of violent behaviour generally take place; although perhaps the best-known venue of all the disputes specifically centred on parade routes belongs to Drumcree, or Portadown, in Armagh.

While the media blitz of stories rises and falls with the surge and ebb of the marching season itself, people keep these narratives year-round and retell them among themselves and to visitors whenever the topic of sectarian conflict comes up. On both sides, also, cynicism is often displayed about the roles played by the police. Some nationalists, mostly political spokespersons, say the police, specifically the Royal Ulster Constabulary, have in the recent past simply been the agents of terror imposed on them by the British state: this narrative is little altered by the changing of the name from the Royal Ulster Constabulary (RUC) to the Police Service of Northern Ireland (PSNI). They add that the RUC's officers have predominantly been Protestants. Many Protestants, however, have their own complaints, especially relating to the times since the Belfast Agreement. They may say that the police do not follow up cases against Catholics on their behalf, specifically so as not to interfere with the peace process itself. The impasse asserted here is of the Catch-22 type, since the pursuit of a complaint can also be relabelled as itself a sectarian act.

NARRATIVES OF BOMBINGS

Acts of bombing form a core of the historical experiences of terror and violence that feed into those contested domains of history-making. Bombings are obviously significant in this context. They are highly destructive and concentrated, they invariably produce shock and panic, and they have lasting results on people's consciousness. They destroy property as well as people, and can be seen as attacks that are a sign of dominance or simply as a mark of an historically established presence. They are memorable and not easy to forget. They can therefore form an experiential focus around which ideological attitudes can be reconfirmed and strengthened over time.

One such case, which came to our attention in 2002, was the bombing at the small town of Claudy, south-east of Londonderry. We received an account of this from someone with personal knowledge, belonging to the border area near to the city of Londonderry itself, on the Donegal side. This area is itself one that feels the regular backlash of events in the city, so that reports of attacks on property and harassment of people are often given a sectarian slant. The bombing in Claudy took place on 31 July 1972, during the marching season.[2] A car bomb exploded in the middle of the village, killing nine people including one nine-year-old girl. No warning had been given in advance, as was often the practice in incidents of this sort. The bombing was attributed to the Irish Republican Army (the IRA).

People working in nearby offices, including a local bank, were at risk from debris and were unable immediately to leave the area as the police took control and closed it off, so that distraught relatives were unable at first to locate their kinsfolk. The feelings of being trapped, of not knowing exactly what had happened, of being forced to witness the destruction, terror, and confusion, and panic: all these emerge from the accounts of the event itself.

Shortly after any such event there begins a long and indefinite aftermath. The event no longer pertains only to those immediately involved. The authorities, the churches, the media, political opponents, all take up positions in relation to what 'actually happened'. We have analysed processes of this kind elsewhere, focusing on contexts of ambiguity and uncertainty, and comparing acts of violence where the agents are hidden to contexts of witchcraft and sorcery (Stewart and Strathern 2004a). We are not so much concerned here with sectarian details as with the fundamental processes at work. We do not suggest that all Catholics or Protestants think in stereotypical ways about religion and politics, only that narratives inevitably are concerned with these forms of stereotyping.

While victims and the public generally saw the hand of the IRA in the Claudy attack, the IRA itself never admitted this, leaving room for speculation and a search for what had actually transpired. The year 1972 was stressful, with 470 people killed in sectarian contexts and almost 100 of these meeting their end during the month of July (BBC News, 23 December 2002, 10:35 GMT, Archives).[3] The motivation for the attack was unclear. Claudy, like many villages and towns near the border, has a mixed Catholic and Protestant population. The British army in the city of Derry were putting pressure on IRA units at the time and the attack may have been intended to divert their attention (BBC News, ibid.). The violence, as violence tends to do, seemed excessive. Three car bombs exploded, and the young girl who was killed was cleaning the windows of her parents' shop some distance away when she died in the blast.

The year 2002 saw further events that prompted people's memories and concerns over the Claudy bombing. These events lay at the back of the minds of the Donegal people who first, spontaneously and on their own initiative, had brought the matter up in conversation with us about border life in general. First the police revealed that the then Northern Ireland Secretary had discussed the responsibility for the bombing with the head of the Catholic Church in Ireland, a Cardinal. By implication, the Northern Ireland Secretary expressed concern about suspicions that a Catholic priest, stationed locally at the time of the bombing, had been in the IRA unit that carried out the act. Based on whatever 'local knowledge' existed, this priest's involvement had long been rumoured. Those with whom we discussed the matter took it as given that the priest had been guilty. The Cardinal, however, did nothing more than move him to one of the most remote parts of western Co. Donegal in the Republic, Malin Head, a long narrow promontory occupied predominantly by Catholics. There he died of cancer in March 1980 (TCM Archives, TCM Breaking News, 20/12/2002). Catholic church leaders said he had denied rumours of being a member of the IRA's South Derry Brigade. He had apparently not been questioned by police at the time of the attack, and neither he nor anyone else had ever been charged with the offence.

Here we see the beginning of a narrative of political cover-up that reveals people's disaffection not only from 'the other side' in the context of terror, but also from their own authorities. A story circulated – and we heard a version of it – that the priest under suspicion (TCM Breaking News, 20/12/2002) had written a letter to another priest whom he had met in Malin Head confessing his guilt before his death, including his involvement with the Provisional IRA in South Derry. There was some question about how genuine this story was, but the police agreed to reopen their inquiry in October 2002. Politicians moved in.

The then Ulster Unionist leader, David Trimble, called for an official judicial inquiry into allegations that the British government and the Catholic Church had colluded in a cover-up over the priest's involvement, presumably for fear of causing further sectarian trouble. He was followed shortly thereafter in a similar call by the Democratic Unionist party leader, Rev. Ian Paisley, who made it a part of his Christmas message. Both politicians added a further element. The British government had agreed to an inquiry (which became known as the Bloody Sunday inquiry) into the shooting of crowd members by British army security forces in Derry on 30 January 1972.[4] During the time of our fieldwork since the year 2000 this inquiry was proceeding, at considerable financial cost, and the conflicting evidence presented to it was reported regularly in the media. The Bloody Sunday inquiry had become a part of nationalists' representations of their victimhood and their cause for freedom.

The two Unionist politicians were demanding that the Claudy bombing be given parity to the Bloody Sunday inquiry. (The two events had taken place in the same year.) The people who told us about this in 2002 thought the same but they were not hopeful that anything would come of it. A year later, in July 2003, when we talked with them again, they reported that nothing at all had been done. While the accusations of a cover-up in the Bloody Sunday case had led to maximum judicial and media attention on behalf of nationalist/Catholic concerns, the concerns of Protestants over an imputed cover-up regarding Claudy were simply ignored, they said. What price, then, Unionist loyalty to the British government?

They were left with their own memories of terror and their image of themselves as minority victims, lacking the support of the very authority to which they traditionally would give their allegiance: a situation compounded by the fact that they lived in Donegal and belonged to the Republic in any case. Powerlessness, distrust, and insecurity are all expressed in this narrative of secret aggression and government inaction: products of the long aftermath of the shock of terror, to which people went back in their minds as the touchstone of 'what it all meant'.

The Claudy bombing belonged to the height of the Troubles and to one of the major hot-spots of conflict, (London)Derry, where even the name of the city encapsulates conflict and contradiction.[5] Our understanding of the meanings of these events to the local people stems from the narratives we received in 2002 and 2003, thirty years after the event. As is often the case, these narratives still captured the immediacy of the experience of terror, to which frameworks of assumption, rumour, and interpretation had accreted over the years. The theme of distrust of authority and the paradoxes of the peace process emerge even more clearly from the case of the Omagh car-bombing.[6]

The Omagh bombing took place in mid-August 1998,[7] and could be regarded as a last-ditch attempt by the breakaway Real IRA to derail the peace process set in hand that same year by the Good Friday Agreement and latterly invoked as a part of the rhetoric of power-sharing by both unionist and nationalist politicians keen to exercise political competition within a new framework of devolved politics centred on the Northern Irish parliament in Stormont.[8] A car packed with explosives was left in the middle of the town and an ambiguous message as to its location was supposedly phoned in by one of those who planned the attack. The bomb went off at a point other than was expected, killing 29 people and injuring 200 others.[9] This was one of the most devastatingly lethal attacks of the whole period of the Troubles and moreover happened after much of the violence had subsided.

In early July 2003 we were observing one of the Orange Order demonstrations, held in Rossnowlagh, in the far south-western coastal part of County Donegal. This parade is the only one that is regularly scheduled to take place in Donegal. Almost all parades take place within 'the North', even if contingents from east Donegal, notably Raphoe, attend them. It is recognized to be peaceful, because it takes place far away from immediately contested spaces. Rossnowlagh is a holiday village crammed with caravans. People from the North come there in large numbers on holiday and to watch the Rossnowlagh parade on the first Saturday in July each year. One leading Orangeman told us that he thought the event had been held there for at least 50 years. On this occasion, the atmosphere was quite relaxed. Families were gathered together, buying ice cream and trinkets from booths, and the weather was sunny. We started to make conversation with a middle-aged woman from the Sperrin hills in County Tyrone, an historic area of Presbyterian settlement.

We began by asking her if she knew about the Ulster-Scots movement in the Ulster region. This is a cross-border movement that aims to give a peaceful expression to aspects of culture derived from the Scottish settlers' traditions in Ulster as a whole. Yes, she said, they had had meetings and enjoyed performances of music, dance, and recited poetry, and had learned the term Ulster-Scots, referring, she said, primarily to 'the way we speak' – the Ulster-Scots language that dates from its importation by the early Scottish settlers. Then one of her daughters passed by, a slim young woman, and she told her to go off and get some iced lollies. She turned to us again and explained that the daughter had been 'blown up' in the Omagh attack. Her body had been torn open and a stranger had helped her to wrap it with a towel and taken her to a nearby hospital, saving her life, she said. All this she told us very matter-of-factly while waiting for the daughter to bring the lollies.

Then she went on to explain that the British government had instituted inquiries into claims that people had for compensation resulting from injuries or deaths. Because her daughter had recovered physically from her wounds, the authorities had been reluctant to give her any compensation. She had been interrogated by an all-male panel, who demanded to see her wound scars as proof of what she had undergone. Processes of decision-making were lengthy and reasons for decisions were not always given. The mother had directed her anguish and resentment on her daughter's behalf against the British authorities themselves. They were supposed to look after us, but did not, she explained. As for the perpetrators, it was all so pointless, she felt. What had anyone gained from it?

The 'peace process' was ineluctably pursued in preference to either the issue of victims' compensation or the job of bringing the perpetrators to trial. Although this latter point was not foregrounded, it perhaps was in her mind, contributing to her disillusionment. In mid-2004 the process of trying to obtain closure by seeing those responsible punished was still not completed. An activist group of family members petitioned the police and later the police ombudsman, arguing that the perpetrators were known and that the police, acting on government advice, had declined to pull them in because to do so might compromise the position of an informer who had infiltrated into the IRA camp: a familiar story replicated in other case histories.

The hidden enemy, the 'sorcerer', was escaping detection again, because of an odd collusion between enemies. Although Omagh is not immediately on the border, it is affected by north–south border issues of politics, in which the concerns of individuals and families are often overridden by political imperatives. The peace process here acquires a negative characteristic in the eyes of people caught up in atrocities, since it appears to require the negation of justice and a covering-up of what did happen, in the name of cross-border cooperation. It is the existence of the border itself that leads to this curious anomaly, since it is because of the border that people are asked to forgo the search for personal justice in order to facilitate political 'progress'.

NARRATIVES OF BURNING

The parades and celebrations relating to the marching season often prominently include the lighting of huge bonfires, constructed from wood and old car tyres. Around the time of the Apprentice Boys' march in Derry city in mid-August 2004 we were told that a particularly huge bonfire had been prepared there. The fires celebrate William of Orange's victory at the Boyne along with the relief of Derry itself. In addition to being celebratory, they are also clearly minatory, implying the burning of all that is opposed to the celebrants' cause. Similar bonfires are built by Protestant communities in Belfast and elsewhere. In July 2003 we heard about some of these from someone who had, for business reasons, to drive far into the North from Moville in the Inishowen area. Although Protestant (Methodist), she felt intimidated by these manifestations of political sentiment, especially since the licence plate on her car was from the Republic and might have become a target for stoning.

That same month, just after the parades had taken place peacefully enough throughout the North, the area near to Moville witnessed a retaliatory burning of a kind. A Presbyterian church hall a few miles south of Moville on the road into Derry was burned down. The minister who served this church is well-known for his broad-minded and ecumenical approach to inter-church relations. Who, then, could have decided to use this particular church hall as a target? The hall, although attached to the Presbyterian church, apparently had had no sectarian uses. It was not used for Orange Order purposes. However, the border itself attracts activities of this kind. Potentially lethal acts of aggression such as car-bombs are usually attributed by local people, openly or semi-openly, to the Real IRA (not the Provisionals, who had observed a cease-fire since 1998). The Real IRA are consigned by local people to the category of degenerates, drug-dealers, and criminals.

But Protestant people were doubtful whether burning down this church hall carried the mark of the IRA with it.

Our information in 2003 was gathered largely in Inishowen, where the emphasis was on peaceable interactions. Any intrusion into this emphasis was an uncomfortable reminder of the Troubles. People made efforts to put these reminders aside, and this influenced how they saw the burning of the Greenbank hall. While further down, in the Laggan area, Presbyterian people in St Johnstown openly said the burning was by sectarian louts, similar to those who, they said, were their own harassers there, people in Inishowen were concerned to play down any sectarian imputations: just a bunch of boys could have done it for mischief, many of them said.

This anodyne explanation was designed to deny any political power to the act. But the selection of a Presbyterian hall, and that in an area served by a minister with ecumenical principles, suggested that the act was at the very least designed, like the Omagh bombing, to hurt the process of peace and reconciliation between people. Also significant was that the burning occurred just after the 12 July marches/parades.

Closer to the city of Derry itself, a Masonic hall was also set alight that same evening, although it was not fully destroyed. Masonic halls belong to Protestants, and there is a similarity between Orange Order ritual and Masonic ritual. Action against two such targets on the same evening does not seem likely to have been random in intent. However, what interests us here is the narratives of explanation. Denying a sectarian link seems closely related to the precariousness of peace in the border areas. But, by the same token, the resulting ambiguity gives play for unarticulated suspicion, and this in turn can lead to retaliatory violence.

In August 2004 we heard a partial sequel, which fits into the narrative scenario of 'the police know who did it but would not do anything about it'. We were told that a youth had been struck and killed by a vehicle near to the church hall. His brother had seen who had done this and reported it to the police, but the police felt they lacked enough evidence to prosecute. People believed the killing was intentional, because the driver of the car was said to be a wastrel who had been denied a place to put a caravan by the family of the youth who had died. The same person was accused of responsibility for the arson that later destroyed the hall. As for the hall itself, many Catholics had rallied along with Presbyterians to donate money for its reconstruction, the mode of which was still under discussion. The narrative, again, replaces sectarianism with ecumenism, in an effort to make the border area where the hall is situated peaceful, purging it of its oppositional violence. The image of the Real IRA, as a transgressive incarnation of agency devoted to violent means at all costs to bring about the unification of the whole of Ireland, as opposed to devolution in the North and coexistence with the South, remains, however, like a ghost on the boundary.

BORDER NARRATIVES

The narratives we have given so far all relate to the border. The border itself is partly constituted, in a sense, in and through a violent history. Narratives given to us by some individuals either highlight this idea starkly, or they attempt to mediate and transcend this history of violence by substituting for it a cross-border narrative of shared coexistence. In this section we consider these two contrasting narrative forms. In this instance they belong to different sectors of the border itself. It should be stressed that we are not making generalizations here, but only discussing the symbolic construction of narratives in relation to the idea of the border in history.

1. Newtownbutler, Lisnaskea, and Enniskillen. Here in these southern parts of the North, marked by remote backroads and stretches of lake water, particular stories provide a sense of a constant backwoods struggle for control over the borderlands themselves, a microcosm of the larger struggle over the concept of 'Ireland' as a whole. The stories may relate to the time of the Troubles or to later periods. Three themes intersect. One is the theme of the enemy who attacks from across a border and then returns to safety, beyond jurisdiction. A second is the theme of struggles over land ownership, the putative reluctance of people to sell land to people of a different sectarian persuasion. The third is the theme of 'sectarian cleansing', and the methods used to pursue it, in which people's loyalties to family are pitted against their loyalties to the state system to which they belong. We encountered these themes in 2003, in narratives drawn from the experience of some farming people in Lisnaskea. Little surprise can attach, then, to the observation that when groups from these areas appeared marching in Scots regalia at Rossnowlagh in that same year, their banners proclaimed them as 'Border Defenders'.

The first theme is symbolically akin to that of the marauding alien sorcerer. We have seen how the Real IRA fits into this theme in the imagination of some people in Inishowen. Here the sorcerer appears in a more directly experienced form. He is portrayed as attacking farmers on their tractors working in their own fields. For that reason, they are said to often carry weapons as they work. (Many Nationalists, however, may see these farmers as agents of the colonial state, covertly co-opted into the RUC as 'B specials'. The 'B Specials' and the 'Real IRA' can be seen as constituting opposed categories of covert assassins/sorcerers in some people's imaginations.) The police, it is declared are never able to catch the IRA attackers, because they slip away beyond their jurisdiction, in spite of putative cross-border coordination of police activities. The same message percolates through general descriptions of IRA activities.

The second theme underpins this shadowy delineation of cross-border struggle. Farming land in Ireland is in many places fertile and valuable. Governmental and European Union subsidies underpin farming. The Republic government is sometimes said to have supported its farmers better than the UK government has done. Farms are sold only when a family dies out or moves. If a family decides to leave as a result of sectarian conflicts, including perhaps killings, others will try to buy their land. Sectarian conflict enters here because a Protestant farmer is said to be reluctant to sell to a Catholic, and vice versa. In the Fermanagh border context it is the Protestant farmers who are said to feel under pressure and are likely to leave, but narratives suggest that they must try to see to it that their land does not pass into Catholic hands. We were told that sets of Protestants may band together to buy land that comes on to the market in this way, in order to prevent Catholic encroachment. This is not simply a depiction of economic action. It acquires its significance from the symbolism of the border and the ideas of pollution and transgression associated with it, going back to the time of the original creation of the Irish Free State (see Harbinson 1960: 17 for one reflection of this theme). When Protestant farmers leave and say they have been driven out, they may speak of this process, borrowing terms from Balkans history, as 'ethnic cleansing' or, otherwise put, 'sectarian cleansing' (compare Tanner 2001: 6 on parallel processes in Derry City).

This is the third theme, then, the imaginative attribution of a total intention by one category of people to another in the border context. When we first heard of this issue in 2003, interestingly enough over in Scotland from someone whose family had recently left Fermanagh and sought a different life in Scotland, we thought that perhaps the idea was simply reflecting a unique situation. This, however, is not the case. Rather, the theme has a folkloric character. We found similar stories from an entirely different source in 2004, in Belfast, relating to experiences not in Lisnaskea but in Castlederg, a town that is close to the border with Donegal in County Tyrone. Central to the theme is the pitting of loyalties against each other in an impossible combination. In the imaginative construction of this theme, which has been narrated to us in several different contexts, a farmer is ambushed in his field, and a bomb is strapped to his tractor. The ambushers are then said to tell him he must drive it to the local police station and in effect act as a suicide bomber, crashing into the station and blowing it and himself up. If he does not do so, the narrative runs, the attackers say that they have captured his wife and children and that they will kill these family members, putting the person in a double-bind situation. Whether there are documented cases of this happening or not is not known to us, but the impact of the narrative theme in imparting a sense of terror is abundantly clear.

In Belfast we obtained some personal anecdotes that carried a certain sense of tense humour. For example, there was the story that some people found a car parked awkwardly in the driveway near to their pub one night, so they, without suspecting it had a bomb in it, decided just to push it across the street to a point in front of another pub, which just happened to be of the opposite sectarian persuasion to theirs. The car exploded, ironically causing damage to the property of the attacker's own side. These stories carry charges of morality, senses of revenge, and senses of unpredictability curiously combined with a feeling of fatality, giving a kind of contingent resonance to the notion of 'Border Defenders'.

2. The second kind of narrative form is one that we have spent most time following and pertains specifically to the part of Donegal where we work. This is a narrative of Ulster that seeks to give shape to a vision of peace-making by the recognition of cultural differences and similarities. Most specifically, it is a narrative that we have seen being developed between East Donegal and the counties of Londonderry and Tyrone that lie across its borders. One leading motif that the narrative is constructed around is that of the Ulster-Scots, based on the history of 'plantation' of the Scots in Ulster that we outlined earlier in this chapter. In a number of our writings, we have discussed the Ulster-Scots Movement and we have proposed the fundamental notion that the Ulster-Scot identity is one that is interstitial in character (see Stewart and Strathern 2003, 2004b, 2004c, 2004d, and Strathern and Stewart 2003, 2004, 2005). We call it a cross-border and trans-national concept. Employees of the Ulster-Scots Agency, a body set up under the Belfast Agreement on a North–South basis, promulgate the idea that the celebration of a Scots-based identity can be conducted for peaceful rather than belligerent purposes, and that recognition of this identity on the part of others can lead to mutual esteem and respect rather than denigration and conflict. But as we have pointed out, new conflicts and tensions have also arisen out of this process of 'identity promotion' (see Stewart and Strathern 2004c, and Strathern and Stewart 2005).

The approach itself has a number of aspects. One has to do with language and is fundamental to the idea of 'parity of esteem' between categories of people. As a part of cross-border initiatives stemming from the 1998 Belfast Agreement, Irish Gaelic is promoted as a language in the North as well as in the South, where it has been entrenched as a compulsory subject in schools; but Ulster-Scots as a form of language is also to be promoted in parts of the South as well as in the North. English does not enter into this arrangement, because English is recognized as the *lingua franca*. Irish Gaelic and Ulster-Scots are labelled as 'minority' or 'lesser used' languages and are recognized as such by the European Union, as are some other languages within the European Union countries. One of the difficulties here is that many opponents of this arrangement refused to recognize Ulster-Scots as a language on a par with Irish Gaelic, on the grounds that while Irish Gaelic is obviously radically different from English, Ulster-Scots is similar to English in many ways although its grammar is quite distinct (on this, see Robinson 1997). Some writers would classify Ulster-Scots as a dialect of 'English' rather than as a separate language. (This is not unlike the situation between Lowlands Scots, which is also recognized as a 'lesser used' language by the European Union, and English (see Strathern and Stewart 2001: 175–207).)

The problem appears semantic, but it is also highly political, and is exactly paralleled by the problematic status of Scots as a form of language in Scotland itself, where Scottish Gaelic also receives more government recognition and support than does Lowlands Scots. Some scholars of Lowlands Scots within Scotland, with whom we have discussed this issue, look askance at the relative success of Ulster-Scots activities in obtaining funding to promote their cause, claiming that they are drawing attention away from the cause of the language in its original homeland of Scotland. The Ulster-Scots Language Society, however, with funding assistance from the Ulster-Scots Agency, has sought to reverse a long trend of denigration of the language by assisting with the creation of a grammar, which was published some years ago under the authorship of Dr Philip Robinson, and a new dictionary, which is being prepared over a period of years through the Ulster Folk and Transport Museum near to Belfast (Robinson 1997). These are in the first place scholarly projects. However, linguistic and other identities are usually closely linked; and just as Irish Gaelic is unequivocally associated with the Republic and thus in secondary terms with a predominantly Catholic nationalism, so Ulster-Scots in the context of Northern politics has acquired an association with Protestant and Unionist tendencies. In a further set of overlaps, it is seen by many people as closely related to Presbyterian senses of identity, since these derive historically from Scottish contexts. And finally, there is, via Unionism, an overlap to some extent with Orange Order membership and in certain regards with the Democratic Unionist Party (DUP) rather than the Ulster Unionist Party of David Trimble (replaced in 2005 by Sir Reg Empey). As the DUP has recently grown in power, perforce the Language Society has come to look to the DUP for help for its cause, simply because DUP politicians have been more prepared to stake out a line in opposition to Sinn Fein and its Catholic Irish Republican agendas than David Trimble's Ulster Unionists, as news articles in Irish newspapers from August 2004 attest.

These considerations help one to realize why it is that the language aspect of the Ulster-Scots movement, designed to integrate in a linguistic community many people from the three Republic of Ireland Ulster counties with their fellow speakers of Ulster-Scots in the North, finds itself in difficulty. Nevertheless, the idea of shared language forms, and pride in these, is potentially a potent part of the overall narrative of mediating cross-border relations.

Other markers of identity are easier in some ways to promulgate, although controversy around these markers also exists. The main elements here include forms of dress (e.g. tartans) and musical instruments (e.g. bagpipes, drums, and fifes). The items chosen tend to derive from the Highlands of Scotland – this a little paradoxically because most of the original immigrants of the Plantation came from the Lowlands of Scotland. (Around the world, including in England, Scotland is often romanticized through the use of Highlands imagery, including by people of Lowlands Scots descent.) But we are dealing here with the appropriation and recreation of identities, so these forms of bricolage should not be surprising. The Ulster-Scots Agency successfully sponsors bands, and an orchestra that encompasses various instruments. One musical instrument, the Lambeg drum, which makes a very loud sound, is said to have associations with Lisburn, a town south-west of Belfast close to Armagh, but is cognate with large drums found also in Scotland and Holland. (William of Orange stopped at Lisburn on his way south to the Battle of the Boyne in 1690, and the Lambeg drum has strong links with Co. Armagh.) Such instruments and the bands that play them are often linked to Orange Order associations, but not exclusively; and as was pointed out to us by an official of the Ulster-Scots Agency employed in Donegal, the bands may play in an Orange demonstration on one day but on the next day be involved in playing for a charity or to raise money for a hospital.

In addition, the Ulster-Scots Agency has aimed to sponsor the spread of Robert Burns Supper clubs, on the model of those that operate in Scotland and worldwide in Scottish emigrant communities. These dinners celebrate the birth date of the eighteenth-century Scottish poet from Ayrshire, Robert Burns. Here there is a return to language issues, since Burns wrote many of his poems in the popular Lowlands Scots tongue of his region. These poems were also interspersed with 'elevated' eighteenth-century or 'Augustan' forms of English. Moreover, these clubs need not be based in any link with the Orange Order.

Figure 5.1 Orange Order march, 12 July 2003, Limavady, near the border with County Donegal. Limavady is in Northern Ireland, in the County of Londonderry. Donegal is in the Republic. Each group of marchers carries the flag of its Lodge. One in this picture carries the label 'City of Londonderry'. Some spectators hold the Union Jack, the British flag. The Orange Order is a Loyalist Protestant organization. Nowadays its marches are presented as peaceful, cultural occasions, although violence can in some locations easily be sparked in response to them. (Stewart/Strathern Archive)

Figure 5.2 Orange Order march, 12 July 2003, Limavady. Sashes represent Lodge memberships. Uniforms reflect either civic identities (suits and ties) or military associations (berets and drums). The Union Jack can be seen flying on a lamp-post. Spectators include young and old. (Stewart/Strathern Archive)

Figure 5.3 Flute-players' march, Orange Order, 12 July 2003. This group carries a large banner with 'Ballyquin Sons of Ulster L.O.L. (Loyal Order Lodge) 645' and at the bottom 'Limavady Dist(rict) No. 6'. In the centre of the banner is a picture of a triumphant William of Orange on a white horse. The 'marching season' commemorates, among other historical events, William's victory over the forces of King James II at the Battle of the Boyne in 1690. (Stewart/Strathern Archive)

Figure 5.4 Limavady Orange Order March, 12 July 2003. Visitors from Lodges in County Donegal came over the border for the occasion. The streets were heavily lined with spectators. This group's banner reads 'City of Londonderry Grand Orange Lodge'. Participants wear long white gloves. Traffic police were nearby on motorcycles, watchfully surveying the scene. (Stewart/Strathern Archive)

Further, the Ulster-Scots Agency has sponsored schemes to use Orange Halls as community halls open to Catholics as well as Protestants. In border contexts such a process can be quite successful. We heard of at least one case where this was happening, in Bready, in the North, and there were apparently similar initiatives afoot in

Figure 5.5   University of Ulster at Magee, in the City of Derry on the border between the Republic and Northern Ireland. Soldiers dressed in seventeenth-century uniform demonstrate the use of a gun from that period. The occasion was a seminar sponsored by the Institute of Ulster-Scots Studies at Magee on 'the Laggan Wars' of the 1640s, a part of struggles between settlers from the mainland and an Irish uprising of 1641. 'Laggan' here refers to East Donegal, whose farming population is connected historically to Scots settlement in the area from 1610 onward. (Stewart/Strathern Archive)

Donegal in the South. But shaking off the more oppositional aspects of the Orange Order, compounded with the radical history of the seventeenth-century Covenanters in the south-west of Scotland who opposed Episcopalianism on the grounds that it was too close to Catholicism, may be a difficult task (Strathern and Stewart 2001: 237–64). Nevertheless, this is among the tasks the Ulster-Scots Agency has clearly set itself to try to do.

In the broadest of terms, then, the Ulster-Scots Agency, and the movement it has generated, has set out to counter narratives founded

Figure 5.6 Scots influence and traditions show clearly in these kilted and bagpipe playing marchers at the Orange Order parade, Rossnowlagh, south-west County Donegal, 5 July 2003. The Rossnowlagh marches are known for being peaceful. At the rear of this group one man holds up a huge Lambeg drum, which he is playing. (Stewart/Strathern Archive)

on terror and violence from the past with cross-border narratives based on an imaginary scenario of peace linked to 'cultural heritage'. Interestingly, one of the most effective ways in which this new imaginary is being enacted is through artistic contexts. In Donegal we found a remarkable byway of this process in the shape of recitations of a folk ballad, the ballad of Stumpie's Brae, to which we now turn (see also Stewart and Strathern 2004b, 2004c, 2004d).

THE BALLAD OF STUMPIE'S BRAE

'Stumpie's Brae' is the local name given to a hill in between the towns of Lifford and St Johnstown, not far from the border of Donegal with the North. Its exact location is disputed by local residents between two hill crests on the same road, where from the southerly direction the road reaches a high point, then dips down to a bridge over a stream and from there climbs to the north up to a second high point. It is this northerly high point that we were told is the correct site. We were taken to the place and shown all of the various features of the landscape in relation to the details of the ballad. The hollow in the road is agreed to be the site where there was a small farmhouse in which the murder described in the ballad is said to have taken place. Nowadays this hollow is filled with nettles and other wild plants, but it is confidently pointed to and the house where the murder took place is still remembered. The ballad therefore has a clear local setting in the landscape, not far from the Foyle estuary, which marks the North–South border in this part of Donegal.

The ballad is said to have been composed or written down from folk recitation by a well-known nineteenth-century hymn-writer, Cecil Frances Alexander, who was married to Rev. William Alexander in Strabane near to Lifford. She spent some time living at Fahan near Lough Swilly in Donegal and also at Strabane. Her husband was appointed Anglican Bishop of Derry and Raphoe in 1867. Mrs Alexander lived from 1818 to 1915, thus covering most of the nineteenth century. She does not appear to have been of Scottish descent, and no record of her attribution as composer of this ballad seems to exist in most of the biographical materials that we have examined,[10] although her balladic work on the Siege of Derry is documented in her biographies. Given the folk character of the ballad and the fact that those who have the skill to recite it do not attribute it to her authorship, it seems possible that it in essence belongs to the traditions of the area we now label as Ulster-Scots in East Donegal. The version republished in *A Blad o Ulstèr-Scotch frae Ullans* (2003, originally in the magazine *Ullans*, no. 6, Spring 1998) is there attributed to Mrs Alexander, but also notes that 'this copy was sent in "Frae a guid freen" [from a good friend] "Sandy Jack of

Strabane"': in other words, from the area near to the *mise-en-scène* of the narrative and also where the hymn-writer herself had lived for some time. We suggest that she may have picked up the legend there in balladic form and worked it into a further literary form, but that versions of it have independently been transmitted in other ways, including orally. (We have ourselves heard different versions of the ballad of Stumpie's Brae recited over the years.) There is no way of knowing how old the ballad is. Its theme may predate the lifetime of Mrs Alexander. What is of interest is that it is seemingly unique, not part of a wide repertoire, and that it is clearly tied to the border area, where its message today carries a resonance that echoes loudly in the border relations of the Partition of Ulster.

The story of Stumpie's Brae is one that tells of how wrong actions can never be escaped. The story-line is of a farming couple who are visited by a pedlar or travelling salesman who wants to rest in their home overnight. The couple allow the man to stay but become envious of the wares that he has in his bag and they kill him while he sleeps and steal his goods. Thus, they were very bad hosts. They stuffed his body into the bag that the man had carried his goods in, but since he was too long for the bag they had to defile his body by cutting the legs off at the knees. After this act they buried the body on a nearby brae (Scottish for hillside) and returned to their home. But the unquiet spirit of the murdered man returned every night to haunt the couple. The ghost could be heard clomping across the wooden floors of the house as it moved on the bloody stumps of its legs. The ghost was referred to as Stumpie because of this. The story ends with the couple attempting to escape the ghost by emigrating to America but the ghost follows them across the sea and drives them insane and into an early grave.

The dramatic structure of the ballad is worth explaining here. It is a story of terror set into a framework of ineluctable retribution. The narrator speaks with the voice of a senior and wise person who is admonishing a younger person, telling them to sit down and listen, and then delivers the moral punch line before the story even begins:

> Young man, it's hard to strive wi' sin
> An the hardest strife of a'
> Is where the greed o' gain creeps in,
> An' drives God's grace awa'.
> Oh, it's quick tae do, but it's lang tae rue,
> When the punishment comes at last,
> And we would give the world tae undo
> The deed that's done an' past.

Then the scene and the events are depicted deftly and vividly. The pedlar comes in and the couple see how full his pack is of gear. The pedlar goes to rest, and:

> The man sat on by the dull fire flame
> When the pedlar went to rest
> Close till his ear the Devil came
> An' slipped intil his breast.

Prompted by the Devil, the couple readily agree to murder the pedlar and steal his wares, emptying them from his bag and cutting off his legs at the knees so as to stuff his body into it. They bury him up on the brae and leave, but when they are gone he sits up in the bag and declares:

> Ye think ye've laid me snugly here
> An' nane shall know my station.
> But I'll haunt ye far an' I'll haunt ye near,
> Father an' son, wi' terror and fear
> Til the nineteenth generation.

'Wi' terror and fear': the couple executed an act of terror, but the terror comes back to haunt not only them, but a long bloodline of theirs after they are dead. Moreover, the Devil both tempts them to kill their victim and gives his ghost the power to haunt them, it seems, since the ghost's return is a sign

> 'That the Evil one Had power'.

The man's gait became stooped and the woman's hair turned white overnight at the first haunting, and the ghost returned each night (this pattern is a feature in other ghost stories that we have collected from the Donegal area). The couple try to flee overseas,

> 'but who can flee
> His appointed punishment?'

It was to America, the land of new frontiers, they went, but the ghost came on the same ship with them, and:

> In the woods of wild America
> Their weary feet they set,
> But the Stumpie was there the first, they say
> And he haunted them on to their dying day
> And he follows their children yet.

Then the punch line is repeated at the end:

> I haud ye, never the voice of blood
> Call'd from the earth in vain;
> And never has crime won worldly good,
> But it brought its after-pain.

Similar narratives of 'wrong' actions haunting people to their graves are very much a part of contemporary narratives of sectarian violence. Often the stories tell of how a young man has killed a person or people on the 'opposite' side of a conflict and then left for America to take employment there for some time until the 'trouble' over the killing had gone away or at least cooled down somewhat. But it is frequently said that when these young men arrive in America they are haunted and return to Ireland in a coffin themselves. All of these stories are set into particularities of place that fix them in the landscape. Thus, we were taken on a tour to Stumpie's Brae and shown the former site of the house where the salesman was robbed and murdered. Complex issues of contemporary morality in the context of political conflict and the memories of killings become in this way attached to definite places, reminding people of their continuing significance.

These messages are messages of terror, but the terror is encompassed by a kind of theodicy based on a confluence of guilt, revenge, and justice. The border area where the story has flourished in popular consciousness is one that is populated by memories of killings during the Troubles and fears of cross-border incursions by the terrorizing activities of sectarian violence. Ghost stories take an expected place in popular consciousness in such areas, and we have found that there is a strong repertoire of such stories that underpins the visions of the ballad. One accomplished reciter of this ballad, now well into his eighties and a long-standing Presbyterian, nevertheless insisted to us that the story of the ballad is a true one (not 'a legend' in the sense of something fictional), and he also had a whole series of stories about ghosts from his own local knowledge. The incorporation of Stumpie's story into recitations on social nights sponsored by the Ulster-Scots Agency not only keeps alive the story and the language in which it is told, but also subtly underscores the idea that people need to exercise hospitality and respect to others across boundaries. If they do not do so, and turn to terror and violence instead, they will suffer terror themselves. Essentially, 'Stumpie's Brae' is a powerful exercise in the moral imagination, and its appropriation into the Ulster-Scots recitative repertoire forms a part of the general reimagining of political and historical space that the Ulster-Scots Agency has undertaken.

CONCLUSION: BORDERS AND IDENTITIES

At the outset of this chapter we suggested that borders generate ambiguities and conflict. They also reflect efforts to create clear-cut differences and to end conflicts (compare Donnan and Wilson 1999). The tension between these two processes often leads to a high degree of ritualized activity at border places. The traditions of marching by the Apprentice Boys in Derry city illustrate this process, for example. Derry, or Londonderry, at one time had a majority Protestant population, but this situation has long been reversed. The Derry marches, accused of perpetuating a Protestant, Orange Order-based, ascendancy, are, from another viewpoint, themselves enacted by a minority under siege in their own historic environment.[11] Celebrating the relief of the siege of Derry in 1689, they are struggling against a contemporary situation of siege in the position of Protestants in the border context: a siege marked by provocation and violent forays on both sides along with constant efforts to mediate these conflicts and move forward in peace. It is Derry/Londonderry's awkward position on the North/South border that leads to this regularly repeated process, one that we take to be paradigmatic of the border zones generally.

Figure 5.7   Another side of the Loyalist tradition. This plaque is set into the walls of the City of Derry, marked with the date 12 July 1937, commemorating the deaths of soldiers in the Great War 1914–18. Older people in County Donegal still mention the sacrifices made by 'Ulster men' at the Battle of the Somme. At the bottom of the plaque is the Latin motto 'Vita–Veritas–Victoria' (Life, Truth, Victory). The plaque was set up 'on behalf of the City of Derry Grand Lodge'. (Stewart/Strathern Archive)

Identities come into play here, not as assertions of absolute totalizing characteristics, but as partial and rhetorical attempts to deal with circumstances of conflict. The North/South divide becomes replicated in oversimplified divisions between Protestants and Catholics, Nationalists, and Unionists, British and Irish. The contingencies and exigencies of life break down and transcend these clear oppositions, but the oppositions also remain and energize much impassioned political activity as well as actual episodes of physical violence. It is in this context of what Michael Taussig might call 'epistemic murk'[12] that the imaginaries and the realities of terror are generated; and the heightened aura of consciousness that results makes the achievements of peaceful relations the more hazardous and uncertain.

The North–South body of the Ulster-Scots Agency represents an ingenious effort to straddle the North/South divide by foregrounding an identity that has a long historical background but has equally for long been submerged, if not dismissed as an entity. Populations under stress worldwide often reinvent traditions that give them a focus and a hope for a more definite stake in political processes, as well as a reason for being given monetary support for projects. Movements for 'indigeneity' all fall under this rubric, and the category of the Ulster-Scots is a highly complex case of such a reimagined form of indigeneity, standing in between British and Irish modes of consciousness, appealing to Scotland rather than England, and making links with the diaspora of the Scotch-Irish in the history of the United States of America and Canada.[13]

Ulster-Scots can claim that their religious and linguistic affiliations have been discriminated against in the past and deserve rehabilitation, just as do the proponents of the Irish Gaelic language and 'culture' movement, although their task of creating 'difference' for themselves is harder because of the obvious overlaps with the categories of English and 'British' identity. Moreover, by no means would all people of Ulster-Scots and Presbyterian backgrounds in Donegal identify with the Belfast-based church hierarchy or the connections with the Orange Order that intersect with a broader and deeper Ulster-Scots history in their area. Taken as a whole, however, the Ulster-Scots Agency's programmatic vision, as an act of creating a new social imaginary, is intriguing, and can be seen as an attempt to counter the narratives of terror with narratives of celebration: an effort to transform both politics and culture by stressing aspects of culture as the basis for a social identity at large.

Whether this broader vision can prevail in future remains to be seen. It can, at any rate, tap into some long-standing senses of consciousness. One senior man we met in Inishowen who was an enthusiast for Scottish-style music and dancing did not recognize the characterization of being an Ulster-Scot. What he did say was, 'Yes, they call us Planters, but we have been planted here for more than three hundred years.' 'Planted' but long-standing, immigrant but rooted in the Irish landscape and countryside, Irish but also Ulster-Scots: these symbolic notions can potentially act as bridges to mediate contradictions by embodying them. At the same time, the contradictions remain in latency and can be expressed again if circumstances favour this.

POSTSCRIPT

During our fieldwork in Ireland in July–August 2005 the IRA announced that it was forgoing its 'armed struggle', and the British government at once began to dismantle some of its own military posts in Northern Ireland. Unionists were frustrated by this turn of events. In September 2005 rioting broke out in Belfast over this and other issues that troubled Protestant areas. The 'peace process' continues to produce episodes of violence.

NOTES

1. Under the Julian calendar, the original date was 1 July, but when the Gregorian calendar was introduced in 1752, the battle was redated to 11 July and celebrations take place on the 12th.
2. This information regarding the Claudy bombing is taken from news archive sources on the Internet for 24/12/2002 (http://breaking.examiner. ie/2002/12/24/story81914.html); 20/12/2002 (http://archives.tcm.ie/ breakingnews/2002/12/20/story81528.asp; *ditto*/story81533.asp, *ditto*/ story81503.asp); 23/12/2002 (http://news.bbc.co.uk/1/hi/northern_ ireland/259213.stm). See also McKittrick and McVea 2001: 87, 254.
3. This news source is also referred to above in note 2. It is notable that the name Bloody Sunday, 30 January 1972 (referred to below in this section of our chapter), appears to encapsulate an echo of Bloody Sunday, 22 January 1905, when Russian police fired on and killed workers demonstrating in St Petersburg, giving rise to a violent period in the Russian Revolution (Encyclopedia Britannica 1990 edn, s.v.).
4. This was one of the dates that marked the early and most violent years of the Troubles in Northern Ireland. See McKittrick and McVea 2001: 76–8, 79.
5. *Doire*, the Irish Gaelic name, means 'Oak', referring to the ancient significance of this tree in Celtic ritual. 'Derry' is an Anglicization of this term. 'London-' was added to Derry at the time of the Plantation, signifying the interests of London-based trading companies in the city and the new county of Londonderry constructed around it. 'The city of Londonderry was to have 4,000 acres reserved on the Donegal side of the Foyle' (Robinson 2000: 81) for the new London-based Ulster Plantation Society to control. Subsequently this side of the city has become predominantly Catholic, belonging to what is called the Bogside area.
6. During May 2004 this bombing was made the subject of a special BBC 2 Television documentary-drama, revisiting the circumstances of the bombing and people's dissatisfactions with the work of the police who investigated it without being able to bring charges against its perpetrators.

7. See McKittrick and McVea 2001: 223–5. The bombing coincided in time with the annual Apprentice Boys' march celebrating the relief of Derry, which in 2004 was staged on 14 August.
8. McKittrick and McVea 2001.
9. The bomb was a 500 lb car bomb, and it exploded 'in a crowded street on a busy Saturday shopping afternoon' (McKittrick and McVea 2001: 223).
10. The hymn-writer's biographical materials mention the writing of numerous hymns and books, including her ballad on the Siege of Derry (see below), which contains the famous watch-word of 'No surrender!', emblematic of Protestant Unionist political concerns in the North. Lovell (1970: 13) does attribute 'Stumpie's Brae' to her, saying it was written 'in the local dialect of the time'.
11. This is also a familiar trope used in the rhetoric of Unionist politicians in Northern Ireland. It is actually a 'folk model'.
12. Taussig 1987: 121, 130–1. Taussig is referring to fears of real or imagined uprisings in colonial circumstances in Colombia, South America. There is a clear parallel in the incident of the 'Comber letter' recounted by A.T.Q. Stewart 1999: 64–5. This anonymous letter was discovered on the streets of Comber in County Down on Monday, 3 December 1688, addressed to a Protestant aristocrat and warning him of an uprising that was planned by Irish insurgents. The letter reached Derry by 7 December, causing panic and the shutting of the city's gates against an expected assault and so initiating the conditions of siege. On the power of rumour, see in general Stewart and Strathern 2004, with many examples parallel to this one.
13. The Ulster-Scots Agency in Belfast has produced numerous pamphlets for distribution stressing links with North America.

REFERENCES

Bryan, Dominic (2000) *Orange Parades. The Politics of Ritual, Tradition and Control*. London and Virginia: Pluto Press.

Davies, Norman (1999) *The Isles. A History*. Oxford: Oxford University Press.

Donnan, Hastings and Thomas M. Wilson (1999) *Borders. Frontiers of Identity, Nation, and State*. Oxford and New York: Berg.

Harbinson, Robert (1960) *Song of Erne*. London: Faber & Faber.

Hunter, Robert J. (1995) 'Plantation in Donegal'. In *Donegal: History and Society*, ed. W. Nortan, L Ronayne, and M. Dunlevy. Dublin: Geography Publications, pp. 283–324.

Jarman, Neil (1997) *Material Conflicts: Parades and Visual Displays in Northern Ireland*. Oxford and New York: Berg.

Kelly, William (ed.) (2001) *The Sieges of Derry*. Dublin: Four Courts Press.

Lecky, Rev. Alexander G. (1905) (repr. 1978). *Roots of Presbyterianism in Donegal*. Omagh: Graham and Sons.

Lovell, E.W. (1970) *A Green Hill Far Away. A Life of Mrs. C.F. Alexander*. Dublin: APCK.

McBride, Ian (1997) *The Siege of Derry in Ulster Protestant Mythology*. Dublin: Four Courts Press.

McKittrick, David and David McVea (2001) *Making Sense of the Troubles*. London: Penguin Books.

Robinson, Philip (1997) *Ulster-Scots. A Grammar of the Traditional Written and Spoken Language.* Belfast: The Ullans Press.

—— (2000) *The Plantation of Ulster. British Settlement in an Irish Landscape 1600–1670.* Belfast: Ulster Historical Foundation.

Seery, James, Finlay Holmes and A.T.Q. Stewart (2000) *Presbyterians, the United Irishmen and 1798.* Belfast: Presbyterian Historical Society of Ireland.

Stewart, A.T.Q. (1977) (repr. 1999). *The Narrow Ground. Aspects of Ulster 1609–1969.* Belfast: The Blackstaff Press.

Stewart, Pamela J. and Andrew Strathern (2003) 'Crossing Borders, Dividing States: Donegal, Ireland', article in *The European Union Center and Center for West European Studies Newsletter*, University Center for International Studies, University of Pittsburgh, April, pp. 1,7.

—— (2004a) *Witchcraft, Sorcery, Rumors, and Gossip.* Cambridge: Cambridge University Press.

—— (2004b) 'Ulster-Scots: Memory, History, and Imagination in the Construction of Irish Identity in the Border areas of Ireland'. Paper presented at the Institute of Ethnology, Academia Sinica, Taipei, Taiwan for the 'History, Memory, and Cultural Construction' Research Group, 5 January.

—— (2004c) 'The Ulster-Scotch Movement in Ireland: The Reassertion of a Minority Identity in the Context of the European Union'. Paper presented at the 14th Biennial Conference of Europeanists, Council for European Studies, 'Europe and the World: Integration, Interdependence, Exceptionalism?' in the panel 'History, Memory, and the Path to European Integration', at the Palmer House Hilton, Chicago, 11–13 March.

—— (2004d) 'Narratives of Violence and Perils of Peace-making in Irish Border Contexts: European Union Recognition of Diverse Identities'. Paper presented at the Colloquium on Europe, Dept. of Anthropology, University of Pittsburgh, 2 April.

Strathern, Andrew and Pamela J. Stewart (2001) *Minorities and Memories. Survivals and Extinctions in Scotland and Western Europe.* Durham, NC: Carolina Academic Press.

—— (2003) 'Epilogue'. In *Landscape, Memory, and History: Anthropological Perspectives*, ed. Pamela J. Stewart and Andrew Strathern. Sterling, Virginia and London: Pluto Press.

—— (2004) 'Scotland and Ireland: Identity, Diaspora, and Dislocation'. Paper presented to the Center for West European Studies / European Union Center, University of Pittsburgh, 30 March.

—— (2005) '"The Ulster-Scots": A Cross-Border and Trans-national Concept', *Journal of Ritual Studies* 19(2): 1–16.

Tanner, Marcus (2001) *Ireland's Holy Wars. The Struggle for a Nation's Soul 1500–2000.* New Haven and London: Yale University Press.

Taussig, Michael (1987) *Shamanism, Colonialism, and the Wild Man. A Study in Terror and Healing.* Chicago and London: University of Chicago Press.

Walker, Brian (2001) 'Remembering the siege of Derry: The rise of a popular religious and political tradition, 1689–1989'. In *The Sieges of Derry*, ed. W. Kelly. Dublin: Four Courts Press, pp. 123–44.

6 THE SIGN OF *KANAIMÀ*, THE SPACE OF GUAYANA, AND THE DEMONOLOGY OF DEVELOPMENT

Neil L. Whitehead

This chapter explores the way in which the shamanic complex of *kanaimà* becomes an articulation of the savagery and terror in both colonial and national cultures of north-eastern South America. The shamanic complex of *kanaimà* has become a central representation of the savage in both colonial and national cultures of north-eastern South America. Together with the cannibal sign, *kanaimà* is used to construct a vision of Satanic Majesty in Amazonia. This vision of a Satanic Majesty holding sway over indigenous cultures is used in turn to produce a demonology of development. This demonology pictures tradition and ritual as nothing but superstition and primitiveness, serving the ghoulish and violent desires emanating from this Satanic Majesty, who terrorizes the native population and is therefore the hidden enemy of development and progress. This idea of development, in Western discourse, alludes to forms of both material and spiritual redemption and advancement, and is understood here as part of the colonial and national conquest and incorporation of indigenous communities under the power of the state and government.

Kanaimà, a term that refers both to a practice and to its practitioners, is a form of mystical assault that ritually requires the extensive physical maiming of its victims in order that they may be produced as a divine food. This carnal violence, primarily a mutilation of mouth and anus, renders the victim near dead but the process of slow death that occurs allows the formation of the magic substance *maba* within the body of the victim. The putrefaction of the cadaver in its grave then completes the cooking of the *maba*, which the *kanaimà* shamans suck from the belly of the victim. This substance cools the heat of the killers, augments the senses and physical abilities of the *kanaimàs*, and facilitates the location, tracking, and eventual assault of future victims (Whitehead 2002a).

Kanaimà is currently deployed in the cultural practice of the Patamuna, Akawaio, and Makushi of the Pakaraima mountains, in various ways, but it is important to notice that it is not just a form of internal dialogue among 'natives' but also enters into the self-fashioning of the Guyanese, Venezuelans, and Brazilians. As a profoundly 'authentic' icon of Amerindian survival, it has been appropriated by the national societies of the region as a sign of their emplacement in the wild and alien landscapes of the 'interior'. This idea of the 'interior' posits Guyana as the end point of exploration, the counterpoint of modernity and the obstacle to development. Accordingly the language of conquest and occupation still suffuses the national imagining of this region, and *kanaimà* comes to stand for that alterity. In turn the terrifying encounter with *kanaimà* becomes a token of the traveller's, or anthropologist's, or missionary's, or miner's penetration to that inner mystery. In this way *kanaimà* becomes the metaphoric equivalent of the Conradian 'heart of darkness' where there is nothing but 'the horror, the horror', veritably a land of mystical terror and savage violence.

THE DEMON LANDSCAPE

This articulation of savagery through reference to *kanaimà* is culturally grounded, quite literally, in ideas and metaphors of physical space. Some recent work on the cartography of this cultural space in the eyes of colonial travellers such as Henry Bates (Raffles 2002), Robert Schomburgk (Burnett 2000), and Walter Ralegh (Whitehead 1997) allows more detailed connections to be made between this peculiarly Guyanese notion of the savage with the broader aims of colonial and national control of this permanently wild interior. This more detailed conjoining of the idea of Guayana with that of native savagery is not just the passing allusion of a few authors or travellers, but is a fundamental trope in the imagination of 'Guayana' from the inception of European exploration through to the present day (Lézy 2000; Whitehead 2002b, 2004a, 2004b). Nor is this imaginary confined to colonial mentalities alone, since *kanaimà* has also fed the national imagineries of Brazil, Venezuela, and Guyana.

The zone of *kanaimà* is thus both an intellectual construct and a physical space that comprises the geographical landscape of the region between the Orinoco and the Amazon rivers, defined to the west by the fluvial connection of those rivers via the Rio Negro and to the east by the Atlantic Ocean. In other works (Whitehead 1993a, 1994) I have referred to this physical space as 'Guayana', using the old Spanish spelling to indicate its epistemological priority over the colonial and national political territories of the Guianas (Guyana, Surinam, Guyane), and follow that usage here. In the earliest accounts of South America the land mass south of the Amazon was referred to as the 'Island of Brazil', and by extension the territories to the north were thought of also as an island. The fluvial orientation of human connections in this region also underwrites this perception phenomenologically since the rainy season inundates the rivers, creating for the traveller flooded vistas from which the land only intermittently rises such that 'islands' appear everywhere. In turn a political phenomenology of landscape was present in the forms of native topography such that key settlements were often designated using the suffix '-cai', a native word for island.

This meta-geography is also apparent in the continuing experience of place since the approach to the Orinoco from the north is quite dramatic for the way in which it is signalled by pronounced differences in landscape forms (Gibbs and Barron 1993). The flat, hard llanos, composed of greyish shale oil soils, are suddenly replaced by the red-earth that is indelibly Guayana. Such red laterite soils also feed ideas about the poverty of Amazon soils and are certainly of a morphological kind that challenges Western notions of agricultural productivity, but they are rich in minerals and the magic of gold. To the south such contrasts are repeated in the hydrological character of the south-flowing rivers that drain the hard old granitic heart of the Guiana Shield, which are filled with deep passages and narrow rapids, unlike the meandering and broad water courses that flow northwards into the Amazon channel. The deep green forest of the northern flanks of the Pakaraima mountains, which form the summit or the Guyanese Shield, along with the Parima chain, also contrasts strongly with the savannas that cover the southern flanks.

Rooted in these features of the physical landscape the idea of Guayana as insular is then understood, in both colonial and native thought, as distinct from its southern counterpart 'Brazil'. The Amazon river channel is thus a *frontier* not a centre in such continental systems. The 'civilized' chiefdoms to the south and west along the river, such as Tapojoso or Oniguayal, are then in opposition to those of the north bank, such as Arripuna, Conori, or Manoa, which become the wild and exotic lands of cannibals, amazons, and gold in the early colonial accounts (Whitehead 1994).

However, it is the emergence of Guayana as a demonic landscape, incompletely imagined through the cannibal, that is the subject of this chapter. Thus, the zone of the cannibal lies to the north and south of Guayana but is never clearly located within it, and then only as an invasive phenomenon. Cannibals in the Caribbean, the original site of this peculiarly American signifier, border Guayana to the north. Ancient cannibals were hypothesized to have brought their ritual proclivities to the shore of the Barima river as part of a wider invasive moment. The excavation of shell-middens in this region by the missionary William Brett (1851, 1881), during which human bones were recovered, apparently anchored this hypothesis with the evidence of archaeology.

Nineteenth-century colonial commentators thus constructed Guayana as resistant to this cultural proclivity until the demon Caribs, plundering and killing their way through the Caribbean islands and delta of the Orinoco, inflicted their warrior disciplines on the indolent indigenes, transforming the local Karinya from farmers of manioc into the 'red faces' of Warao legend who ate up the peoples of the Orinoco and interior. This was in itself but a mimesis of a European occupation that had already destroyed the majority of native cultures and had consumed their remnants in the pursuit of colonial development, firstly, through the system of plantation slavery that induced a dependency on the colonial regime through its payment for mercenary services in policing the interior for runaway slaves, and secondly, through the punitive slaving of certain Guayanese groups themselves, particularly the Makushi and other groups of the deep interior. Slaving then itself became a way of knowing and discovering, and slipped easily into evangelization as the economic stabilization of the colonial regimes in the region through the plantation economy supplanted the haphazard prior dependence on individual trade partnerships with native groups.

Likewise to the south, those gourmet cannibals the Tupi, who so fascinated the French commentators, were singular to their Brazilian location. Although early French ethnology tended to use categories derived from this Tupi encounter to describe the cultures of others in the Caribbean and even the land of the Iroquois, the attempt to implant such notions in Guayana, or to filter their experience there through this Tupian lens, resulted only in various infelicities in ethnological description. It proved all too facile to descry the ethnic dyads of Caribbean experience (Arawak vs Carib), in the dyadic logic of cannibalism and war among their allies in the region of Rio de Janeiro. In this way Guayana eluded the wider continental categories of conquest and knowledge such that native cultures in Guayana become the marginalia of evolving ethnological schemas in the nineteenth-century travelogues and the twentieth-century *Handbook of South American Indians* (Steward 1948).

A DEMONOLOGY OF DEVELOPMENT

The landscape is not a passive component of human socio-cultural processes, and so the way in which the colonial regimes of the region occupied and sought to reinscribe their own particular cultural meanings in the context of existing native practices has to be considered alongside the imaginary cartographies of the demonic that orientate colonial and national governments in their actions towards, and creation of, the indigenous (Whitehead 2003).

These constructions of the 'native' or 'indigenous', whether in public political discourse, the representations of the media, or in anthropological and ethnographic writing, have all served to enable and encourage violence against indigenous communities. From the initial charges of cannibalism made against Amazonian peoples in the sixteenth century to the supposed fierceness of the Yanomami, there has been a continuous external discourse on Native Amazonians' savagery and wildness, most usually demonstrated through their satanic proclivities (shamanism) and demonic customs (cannibalism). No less relevant to the fate of native peoples today than it was 500 years ago, this discursive production of 'natives' continues to create a broad cultural framework in which violence against indigenous persons can be more easily obscured or justified.

In Guayana successive waves of spiritual and material development have pounded native communities leading to the continuous ideological construction of indigenous peoples as obstacles to 'progress'. This is signalled by key cultural practices that have allowed the governmental regimes to separate out the 'good' and the 'bad' Amerindian. In Guayana this has proceeded along a number of axes that all reference spiritual and ritual forms of action as ciphers for the political opposition that given native groups showed towards these plans for their redemption and development. Most notorious was the dualistic ethnic typology, originated by Columbus, of Arawaks and Caribs. I have shown elsewhere (Whitehead 1995, 2002c) that this apparently objective ethno-linguistic distinction is in fact highly suspect and refers more to the exigencies of conquest than to native realities. However, this distinction became widespread across the region and in time a component of Amerindian identity itself. Colonial policy enshrined this scheme in legal statute – allowing plunder and slaving of those populations considered Carib. Arawak populations, both through selective alliance and the involvement of key Lokono clan leaders, were then understood as basically tractable and, given a system of raiding and warfare between key Carib and Arawak populations, such as the Karinya and the Lokono, such Arawaks were also considered to be self-interested, and so dependable, in their European alliances.

As missionaries began systematic evangelization in the seventeenth century along the Orinoco, this ready-made distinction became self-fulfilling since opposition to the missionaries was defined as Carib. In this way the Arawak, who accepted evangelization, were again seen as favourable to colonial development. But this distinction was, and still is, based on more than these competing representations of Amerindian tractability and intractability. The notions of Carib and Arawak refer also to spatial location and ritual proclivity. Consistent with the demonic nature of the colonial imagination of the space of Guayana, the Carib are pictured as interior bush-dwellers exemplifying the secretive, dangerous, and violent nature of the dark heart of the region. The Arawaks, coastal dwellers and even urbanites, in turn signal the possibility of indigenous redemption, reform, and development. These competing tropes of the indigenous can then be made to fit varying political and ethnic circumstance using linguistics to bolster the idea of a fundamental difference in the cultural ontologies of Arawaks and Caribs. Despite the fact that linguistic practices do not actually conform to this scheme it has remained a passionate debate in contemporary anthropology and archaeology (Whitehead 2002c).

Linguistics thus anchors a demonology of development in the ethnology of the region, but this demonology is not just a linguistic distinction correlated with a political opposition but also invokes apocalyptic visions of a threat to all social order, native, colonial or national, through the linguistically inscribed association of Caribs and cannibalism, the very terms being directly related etymologically through European usages. The production of cannibals was thus an economic and political interest, given the legal provisions that allowed special violence against them. It is also a central issue for anthropological interpretation, since, as Arens (1979) rightly indicates, this is the original anthropological question. As a result the literary and ethnological production of the cannibal has gone hand in hand with the military and political domination of the native population in this region of South America. The violence of conquest in the region mimetically referenced cannibalism as its justification, and representations of the native population suppressed description of Arawak torture and cannibalism, emphasizing rather the barbarity of the Carib.

It is therefore important to realize that in other contexts cannibalism *per se* simply did not function in this way as a justification for colonial or national violence against indigenous communities. The French commentaries on the Tupi of coastal Brazil from the sixteenth century thus also make a distinction between the good and bad Indian but do so with reference to the ritualization of the cannibal rite (Whitehead 2000). This resulted from the way in which the encounter with the Tupi provoked theological debate over the nature of the Catholic Eucharist and its doctrine of transubstantiation. In this scheme the elaboration of cannibal ritual, alleged among the allies of the French, and denied among the allies of the Portuguese, served to produce political and military distinctions among the native population. French collusion in the cannibalism of Portuguese prisoners of war should thus be understood as a way of sustaining a distinct kind of ethno-demonology, even if it was also was founded on the cannibal sign. In this way the very ritual practice that, to the north, was considered a defining characteristic, in any form, of a recalcitrance and hostility to colonial and national development, becomes an analogy of the Christian Eucharist in Brazil. The violence of the cannibal ritual was not problematic, but rather the nature of collective participation in that ritual violence. The participation of women and children implicitly undermined the colonial state's political justifications for its violent modes of control, the redemption of the heathen and rescue of the cannibal victim.

In the French sources (see also Lestringant 1997) the meaning and form of the Christian Eucharist is of greatest significance and is the starting point for Montaigne's consideration, 'De Les Cannibales' (in *Essais*, 1580). For Montaigne, both Tupi and Christian rules of cannibalism are communal, related to the worship of the dead and done in the hope of benefit to the group. But the key question for the differentiation of Catholic and Protestant liturgy then becomes – is this a literal homology present in the moment of transubstantiation or an analogy of spiritual nourishment that replenishes and feeds faith indefinitely? For Montaigne, as a Catholic, the assimilation of the Tupi practice to the Christian belief is an obstacle to the humanistic embrace of the Tupi. However, Montaigne fails finally to condemn the Tupi precisely because of the parallels in symbolic practice that other contemporary sources explicitly elaborate.

Without the possible religious significance of the parallels between Tupian and Christian Eucharist the subsequent fate of the cannibal is to be superfluous and so anachronistic, fit only for eradication, as with that 'exterminating angel' Robinson Crusoe (Lestringant 1997: 11). And so the cannibals come to be seen as responding to their bio-ecological conditions not their culture, or, in the act of erasure that Lestringant (1997: 12) rightly resists, the materiality of their acts is supplanted by the evanescence of a cultural discourse that 'shifts the noise of teeth and lips towards the domain of language'.

In his earliest work on Brazil, *Les Singularitez de la france Antarctique* (1558), André Thevet delineated a geography of man-eating that located the uncultured 'cannibals' to the north towards the Amazon river, and the ritualized 'anthropophages' in the orbit of French experience. Thus the former are characterized as cruel eaters of human flesh as a matter of diet, the latter as exponents of certain rituals of revenge. Not surprisingly this cannibal cosmography also conforms to the patterns of French trading and military alliances in the region (Whitehead 1993a). Thevet notes the progress of the cannibal rite in great detail and seems unable to resist an analogy with the preparation of roasting pig in French peasant culinary traditions. However, elaborate though this ritual becomes in Thevet's subsequent account in the *Cosmographie* (1575) and a manuscript work *Histoire de ... deux voyages*, it is clear that vengeance is the hermeneutic key to understanding the meaning of the cannibal act, such that description of the careful distribution of the victim's body parts and the embedding of the ritual in myth, becomes central to these later works.

Jean de Léry's account of this youthful adventure, *Histoire d'un voyage* (1578), was written some twenty years later, after he had become a pastor in the church in Geneva, and he was stimulated to do so not by the original encounter but by the events of later life. In Léry's writing the cannibal becomes a universal symbolic and tropic key; the central motivation of vengeance is made systematic through an examination of various aspects of Tupi culture, and he clearly allegorizes the act of eating. In this new framework of semiophagy the carnal and spiritual are expressed through the opposition of the raw and cooked. The northerly (or merely distant) bad cannibals, given specificity through the ethnological example of the Ouetacas, practise a cannibalism that shows no exercise of culinary, and so spiritual, art. However, a devolved cannibalism is also threateningly present inside, as well as outside, Tupi social space through the presence and enthusiastic participation of women in cannibal ritual. As a pastor Léry was also a witch-hunter of some enthusiasm in Europe, so that the imagery of life-sucking hecubas and witch cannibalism of the innocent, play easily into his representation of Tupian ritual, as they do strikingly in de Bry's illustrations of the same. This misogyny is given further inflection in Léry's own biography since he encountered survival cannibalism during the 1573 siege of Sancerre by Catholic forces, just before turning to write the *Histoire d'un voyage*.[1]

For Léry cannibalism can also symbolize cruelty, usury, and a lack of charity and, as the meaning of the cannibal sign universalizes, so debate over the Eucharist bloats Léry's account of the Tupi materials to the point that even Villegagnon, leader of the French colony of Rio de Janeiro during Léry's time there, is identified on account of his Catholic views as a *soi-disant* Ouetaca. So if the Tupian cannibal rite recapitulates at all points the Christian Eucharist, to prevent his readers turning away in ethnocentric disgust, Léry goes on to detail the unspeakable cruelties of European tyrants – including Dracula, by way of Vlad the Impaler. In this way Jean de Léry deterritorializes the cannibal who thus freed from the Brazil shore haunts the European and American imaginary (Lestringant 1997: 71). In the same way as cannibalism, *kanaimà* is disembodied in nineteenth-century ethnological writing through a refusal to accept the materiality of assault sorcery, the violence being seen as vengeful not mystical. This allowed a safe occupation of the demonic landscape from which such ghoulish remnants of native savagery have finally been exorcized.

By the end of the eighteenth century, however, as is evident from the French sources themselves, the 'cannibal' had begun to fade away into that mist of nostalgia and remorse for the pre-modern. The conquest and control of native societies had led to the virtual extermination of most autonomous native polities, leaving only relatively isolated remnants in the deep interior, or the emergent neoteric groups grounded in the social and cultural relations of the colonial world. In either case the spiritual practice of cannibalism, directly connected to the creation of political power, was therefore itself in decline. The previous ritual sponsors of such events were now engaged in the politics of incorporation within the burgeoning national societies of the region.

As a result the violence and barbarity of the intractable Indian became occluded and hidden, a matter of inner orientation and belief, no longer an aspect of public culture. Thus, with the suppression of native warfare, and the loss of autonomy that this implied, the uncontrolled and unknowable realm of spiritual and mystical assault emerges as the site of demonization. Whereas before the warrior or cannibal-killer was the object of colonial nightmare, in the new world of nineteenth-century progress the infrastructure of native autonomy was absent and so the mimesis of conquest becomes the skulking assassin, the vengeful and lone killer. In the demon landscape of Guayana the prominence given to the shamanic practices in the colonial literature, particularly *kanaimà*, also begins at this precise moment.

Kanaimà, depicted as vengeful assassination in the colonial literature, has subsequently become widespread in the cultural imagination of both national and indigenous populations of north-eastern Amazonia as a violent marker of both 'tradition' and 'indigeneity'. This process begins in the mid-nineteenth century as scientific explorers and missionaries wrote reports and travelogues of the relatively unknown interior peoples.

But, in the imagination of the Patamuna and other peoples of the highlands today, *kanaimà* is seen as emanating from the first time – a primordial force that has structured the universe and formed the world as we know it. *Kanaimà* is more ancient than warfare and more ancient than society itself. As a result *kanaimà* itself almost becomes outside history, or at least it is a universal and constant human possibility that is only contingently realized in the course of human history. In this way one may say that, while there is a history to the ritual practice of *kanaimà*, *kanaimà* as a way of being in the world is beyond time.

The temporal and spatial dislocation of *kanaimà* is therefore an integral part of its ritual and symbolic force, for practitioners are both able to travel vast distances in a short space of time and are able to expand their life-time and life-space by the means of the ritual practices that are involved in being *kanaimà* – that is, they have access to the plane of shamanic encounter and exploration (*karawali*), as well as being directly nourished by the production and consumption of the 'honey' of necrosis (*maba*), derived from the bodies of their victims.

In the early nineteenth century colonial sources assimilated *kanaimà* to notions of revenge more generally. As a result any instance of revenge became one of *kanaimà*. But this assimilation of *kanaimà* to all revenge killings meant that a vast array of different kinds of death were attributed to *kanaimà* when they may not have been ritual killings at all. Thus, as more systematic ethnographic observation began, and as the native discourse of *kanaimà* certainly would have raised the possibility of action by *kanaimàs* in all manner of deaths and injuries, it could appear that a *kanaimà* killing was no more than a vague attribution of sickness and injury to an all-encompassing evil force. Divested of its corporeal reality in native cultural practice, the symbolic force of *kanaimà* was then mimetically assimilated to the power of the colonial state itself.

In the external meanings and representations of *kanaimà* it will be apparent that this latter idea, of *kanaimà* as a native 'Satan' or evil spirit, was central to the ethnological and literary production of *kanaimà*. At the same time there was a symbolic convergence and mimetic elaboration of the category '*kanaimà*' in both native and colonial discourses (Whitehead 1997). This entailed that the wider cultural perception of *kanaimà* was as an example of the savagery of the native population. Nonetheless, *kanaimà* eventually transmutes in the ethnological literature into a functionalist mechanism for sustaining social order. The maiming and the killing become a kind of 'jungle justice', which, in the absence of the Hobbesian state and its police, regulates and punishes the 'criminal'. As a result the indigenous symbolic and ritual meanings of *kanaimà* were effectively overwritten or ignored, being understood as no more than an unfortunate welling up of latent Amerindian superstition and savagery.

The colonial gaze that produced this ethnological and literary view of *kanaimà* was certainly entranced by its violence, but *kanaimà* practice and its meaning was not properly understood. This was as much a limitation of the kinds of interaction that missionaries and others might have had with the interior peoples, as it was a conscious attempt to misrepresent what otherwise was evident. Even if the cultural importance of *kanaimà* violence was vividly represented as the 'oppressive nightmare' of the highland peoples, the cosmological significance of *kanaimà* as a shamanic practice was persistently overlooked.

Ethnological representation always emphasized apparent juridical features in *kanaimà*, picturing it as a codified system of revenge – a *lex talionsis*. This resulted principally from a failure to discriminate the various forms of shamanism and magical action. Although the *piya* (curing shaman) was seen as the key figure standing in the way of rapid and complete missionary conversion, in fact only a limited understanding of such 'weedy entanglements of evil' was required for its suppression. The highly physical nature of *kanaimà* killing and its connection to notions of revenge, or more exactly the rebounding violence of a challenge to social norms, therefore obscured its occult meanings for the colonial commentator. In this way *kanaimà* served as an answer to the puzzle of how native society might regulate itself, in the absence of formal institutions of law or criminal justice. As Thomas (1994: 127) has pointed out with regard to British missionary efforts elsewhere, each mission 'field' was apt to dramatize certain key cultural practices – such as head-hunting, cannibalism, or widow-burning – in order to provide an index of growing evangelical success. As a result these kinds of representation tend also to present the cultural practice in question as on the verge of extinction. This was very much how shamanism generally, including both *piya* and *kanaimà*, were presented.

Nonetheless *kanaimà* proved sufficiently elusive that it could not become a basis for the campaigns of cultural extirpation that are associated with other dramatized cultural practices, such as cannibalism. This elusiveness, coupled with pervasive native reference to *kanaimà*, meant that *kanaimà* still required some codification and so the legalistic interpretation was pursued by the major missionary and ethnological writers – William Brett (1868, 1851), Everard Im Thurn (1883), Walter Roth (1915), and John Gillin (1936).

The ferocity and horrific mutilations of a *kanaimà* attack nonetheless were impossible to ignore but they were seen as an almost laudable aspect of the rigour of native 'justice', provoking some authors to favourable comparison with 'tribal' Saxon and Judaic ideas of retaliation and recompense. The profound spirituality of *kanaimà* violence was in turn erased through its presentation as a folkloric belief, of uncertain corporeal reality, akin to the vampire or werewolf.

The beneficial effects of *kanaimà* in producing social order were identified in both its proto-legal functions and its supposed consequences for sustaining social distance and the particularity of 'tribal' identity. This analysis is given persistent emphasis, to the point that *kanaimà* becomes a particular instance of legal systems founded on retribution and punishment; the only distinction with Western society is that it is the retributive force of government and society, rather than that of the clan or family, that is being expressed. In the twentieth-century imagining of *kanaimà* this notion has been taken to its conclusion and, as the State supplants Religion, so *kanaimà* becomes a particular instance of the way in which the 'capriciousness' of the cosmos may be represented (Simpson 1964: 4–7).

Unlike sixteenth-century Spanish attempts to delineate American 'cannibalism' or nineteenth- and twentieth-century British attempts to determine the 'reality' of African witchcraft, *kanaimà* was not the subject of 'official investigation'. However, as in Evans-Pritchard's (1937) classic work on Azande sorcery, the ethnology of *kanaimà* shamanism 'reveals' itself as a system of justice and legality. In this way the cultural force of *kanaimà*, which so manifestly entrances and troubles the colonial imagination, is shown to be a matter of the ineffable and irrational nature of colonial subjects. That primitive mystery is then made less threatening through the 'science' of ethnological description, which sanitizes sorcery through its selective re-presentation in familiar, intelligible and comforting terms – as a form of law and order.

This literary and observational process is underwritten also by a high degree of inter-textuality among the colonial authors. Certain key accounts, especially those of the Schomburgks (Whitehead 2002a: 56), are constantly recycled thereby progressively constricting the interpretive space for subsequent new descriptions or information. As a result, by the end of the nineteenth century, the colonial imagining of *kanaimà* becomes embalmed in the textual record and later accounts have largely failed to escape this rendition.

In sum, *kanaimà* was clearly misrepresented in the colonial sources, and that was done in ways that enabled the progress of colonial administration, especially through missionary evangelism but also through the imposition of colonial legal codes. It is notable that a number of the authors depict *kanaimà* as an institution of primitive law, thereby also laying the groundwork for a later appeal to colonial justice as an advance on this primitive, if somewhat admirable, law of blood-revenge.

In indigenous counter-representation, tales of whites killed by *kanaimà* and the possibility that whites might be susceptible to the physical mutilations, though not the occult meanings, of *kanaimà* attack are to the fore. But such threatening meanings are averted in colonial mentality by the reassuring suggestion that the 'white man' might act as a final court of appeal in the jungle justice of the blood feud. This ethnological representation also allows the 'naturalization' of retributive law and capital punishment, so that *kanaimà* aids the cultural project of government in the metropolitan as much as the colonial setting. At the same time, this very focus on *piya* and *kanaimà* shamanism signalled the significance of spiritual practice for the colonial regime and so encouraged the expression of resistance or opposition in these modes. This attitude in itself gave an external importance to *kanaimà* that has fed into its current resurgence in native communities.

Kanaimà practice itself has become closely attuned to the violence of the development frontier and thus symbolically, as well as materially, directly engages with this external discourse of savagery. Modernity, development and *kanaimà* violence are all related in current Patamuna thinking. On the one hand they are keenly aware of the way in which development, both now and in the past, seems to have passed them by, eluded them and made necessary efforts to go and 'fetch it up' from Georgetown. On the other hand, and conscious of the power of anthropology as the arbiter of 'culture', the Patamuna are also keenly aware of the potential for a loss of tradition, a distinct way of 'being Amerindian', which, paradoxically perhaps, the ritual skills of the *kanaimà* or *piya* – death or resurrection – best express. In the face of modernity *kanaimà* becomes a potent symbol of continuity with the past.

For us too, 'modernity' is a much-debated concept and, by way of definitions it needs to be said that the idea of 'modernity' employed here is one that emerges only in opposition to the notion of 'tradition'. In other words, I do not think that 'modernity' can be understood apart from those social and cultural processes that, in any particular situation, also give meaning and content to the idea of 'tradition'. In this sense 'modernity' is both ancient and plural, an aspect of the continuous construction of tradition. The meaning of these categories is therefore closely interrelated and historically contingent, the mutual condition of their possibility.

As a result local ideas of the modern and traditional may not be heavily inflected by the original Western content of such globalized notions, and there has not been that 'convergence' of modernities in the manner suggested by both Marx and Durkheim, to produce a global social and cultural uniformity, but rather an explosion of alternative modernities.

Consistent with this view experience of modernity in Guyana has largely been in terms of the spread of 'governmentality' – the apparatus of state by which we are all rendered 'citizens' (Foucault 1994). However, despite being repeatedly surveyed, classified and converted, the systems of law, education, sanitation, and economy, which were supposed to bring the Patamuna the fruits of development and progress, have failed to materialize. As in other colonial and post-colonial contexts, industrial capital and Western democracy have appeared wearing the differing costumes and masks of evangelical redemption, medical services, schooling, economic development, democratic rights – the full regalia of modernity, as it were. In the case of the Patamuna, and other peoples of the highlands, the experiences of such successive modernities has been highly episodic and fleeting, a series of one-night shows, short runs, and rapidly folding productions. Nonetheless, the fact that the theatre of modernity has been trying to establish itself in the highlands over the last two centuries means that Patamuna conceptions of the traditional and the modern are more complex and sophisticated than a simple opposition of, say, feathers and loincloths to trousers and shirts.

In response to this repeated failure of modernity to establish itself a 'hyper-traditionality' has emerged that is inimical to both external *and indigenous* notions of modernity. This persistence of a notion of modernity is manifested in a cultural consensus, shared by most Amerindians and other Guyanese alike, as to the relevance of these convergent, globalized ideas of tradition and modernity, those 'costumes and masks' referred to above.

This by no means entails that there is any consensus over how those shared conceptions might be realized or enacted, but it does underline their co-evalness. The cultural and political trajectory of *kanaimà* in the face of these multiple modernities in all their scene and costume changes has been violent resistance.

This needs to be understood as a persistent enactment of a notion of 'tradition' rather than some active counter-programme of 'modernity'. This resistance has become more potent as the idea of 'tradition', especially 'authentic', 'pre-modern' tradition as often derived from Amazonia itself, has become widespread in modernist society. Given the anti-modernist rhetoric of much of the 'new age' interest in shamanic tradition, perhaps we should after all consider *kanaimà* a truly post-modern development; an alternative traditionality in response to an indigenous modernity. Either way designer tribalism and ethnic chic are well established cultural tropes for us, and the production of tradition among people like the Patamuna is likewise an issue of cultural persistence and affirmation.

The external projection of *kanaimà* as a cultural tradition and its meaning for practitioners and their victims have therefore become increasingly entwined. As a result there has been a notable literary use of the idea of *kanaimà*, from the missionary William Brett's (1880: 152–4) poetical work, *Kànaima* (see Appendix 1), to Romulo Gallegos's (1935) novel *Canaima*, as well as Wilson Harris's (1995) short story, but the symbolic force of *kanaimà*, potent enough within an indigenous poetic of violent death and already reflected in these mimetic cultural productions of outsiders, continues to haunt the modernist cultural imagination.

In this sense the *kanaimà* takes his place alongside the 'thuggee', 'bogeyman', 'cannibal', 'head-hunter', 'zombie' , 'vampire', and now 'terrorist' as another ghoul in the colonial and modern nightmare of irrational, cultic violence that springs from enigmatic and atavistic cultural proclivities. This usage occurs in more sensationalist presentations, such as the pulp-novel *Skull of Kanaima*, by Victor Norwood and other recent materials, such as Brazilian role-playing games, which feature '*Kanaimà*' as a game-player identity, or the Ukrainian Death Metal band, *Tessaract*, which presents a song *Black Kanaimà* (see Appendix 2). However, reactions are not restricted to the cultural lexicon of colonialism or modernism, and the anti-modernist search for other kinds of meaning can represent the *kanaimà* as a figure that is inspiring in virtue of its very cultural opacity, as in the case of the poetry of Pascale Petit (1998).

In these ways scientific tropes of evolution, literary metaphors of wildness and the anthropological categories of culture and society have eased the assaults of development by providing an intellectual

Figure 6.1 Kanaimà in the Brazilian cultural imaginary: Illustration from an RPG (role-playing game). [http://www. geocities.com/SoHo/4113/kanaima2.html]

framework for the comprehension and control of the native. This programme is then made manifest in the policies of development, which become a material realization of this imagery of indigeneity. However, the practice of *kanaimà* constricts and chokes off the space for material and spiritual redemption through progress, for it is a counter-discourse on modernity in which the promise of development is violently rejected in favour of a new kind of tradition. The value of this tradition is precisely the way in which it eludes external attempts to classify and analyse native society – for it is beyond the visible and material, as well as of them.

Such material relations of representation in turn recreate native and colonial or national realities, such that these representational practices achieve an ontological status as ethnological 'fact', evidenced in the cultural practice of development and the counter-performance of a *kanaimà* killing. To be brutally short, representation is not just 'about' violence but is also part of violence, allowing terror to be projected beyond the materiality of physical violence into the very foundations of emotive and imaginative life.

APPENDIX 1

William Brett, *Legends and Myths of the Aboriginal Indians of British Guiana* (1880: 152–4). This work versifies various indigenous 'myths', and in the section devoted to the 'Legends of the Acawoios' appears the following:

KANÁIMA

From the base of high Roráima
To the widespread Eastern sea,
Votaries of dread Kanáima
Track their victims secretly.
Deadly vow must each fulfill,
Real or fancied foe to kill.

He who that dread vow is taking,
Family and friends must leave;
Wife and children all forsaking,
No discharge can he receive.
Still around his victim's way,
Hovering night and day to slay.

If the victim warned of danger,
To some other place should fly,
Soon th'assassin, though a stranger,
Will to that retreat draw nigh,
Patiently he bides his time,
Waiting to commit the crime.

Stealthily each step he traces,
Hiding till he strikes the blow.
Poison in the mouth he places

Of his victim, lying low.
Then if found with swollen tongue,
None will know who did him wrong.

When the grave has closed upon him,
The destroyer hovers round:
Dread Kanáima's spell is on him;
By it he must still be bound,
Till he pierce, with pointed wood,
Through the grave, and *taste the blood.*

Stern *Kanáima* thus appeasing,
Who withdraws his direful aid,
All his horrid influence ceasing
When that off'ring has been made.
Uncontrolled, the votary then,
Goes, and lives with other men.

One who passed us on the water,[2]
Had his victim lately slain;
There triumphant, fresh from slaughter,
He was hast'ning home again.
Feathered crown adorned his head–
Bright red spots his skin o'erspread–

Spots, to show that, nightly ranging
(So do their sorcerers declare),
He, into a jaguar changing,
Could his victims seize and tear.[3]
As the 'were-wolf' of the East
Prowls, on human flesh to feast.

*   *   *   *   *

Should the victim 'scape him living,
Or, if dead, be borne away;
He, no horrid off'ring giving,
Finds Kanáima on him stay.
Still the spell upon him lies;
Mad, he wanders till he dies.

One, who sank with forests round him,
To our Mission hill was borne;
First, an ocelot, which found him,
Horribly his head had torn.
Head and hands he raised in pain,
Scared the beast, then sank again.

Sank – for life no longer striving,
Christian Indians found him then.
Arawâks, his strength reviving,
Bore him to his countrymen.
Healed and fed, *Kanáima* still,
Christians all he vowed to kill!

APPENDIX 2

Lyrics from Tessaract, 'Groundless Translethargical Groaning' demo, 1992 (MC 2000 – Bloodhead Productions)

BLACK KANAIMA

Ritual dance accursed voice
Millions moans of Indians
Iron rumble with hawking of dog's
Feeling the death. Ceaseless

Jaguar's skull on long pole
Symbol of death and psychotic ghoul
Black Kanaima murder in him
Send to Indians emaciating dread

Wild jungle unnerving Indians
Owing to Kanaima incursion
Black vice born the fear
That live in the brain dungeons

Spacious virgin nature in night
Glimmer by death in ritual fight
Tribe wizard gabbing in dance
Blows of drum, calling to death!

Jaguar's skull on long pole
Symbol of death and psychotic ghoul
Black Kanaima murder in him
Send to Indians emaciating dread

Jaguar's skull on long pole
Throwing the power from eyehole
Dark energy from infernal skull
Burn flowing blood at human fall

Fume of burning blood
Above Amazonian forest
Throbbing according drum
Ritual drum of possessed wizard!

Earthquake
Rage of Kanaima
Flame from ground
Nowhere asylum

Sacrifice
Kanaima vengeance
Blood of child
Sacrilege vice

Obliteration of the Indians!
Tropical death irruption!

Jaguar's skull on long pole
Glimmer by empty of eyeholes
Show the fangs in frightful smile
Gnash under wind and wait for you die!

NOTES

1. A family was caught preparing to eat their dead child, a scene to which Léry (1574) was eyewitness. In his account the ethical scene is broken down into the criminal and diabolical, with the old woman of the house bearing the full weight of Léry's witch-centred view of female corruption. Indeed the trauma of this event, for so Léry represents it, is plausibly directly connected to his literary return to the Brazil shore of his youth (Lestringant 1977: 74–80). Here Tupi cannibalism, as a rite of men and controlled and shaped by their desires, becomes acceptable in a way that the female seduction of masculinity and youth was not in Sancerre.
2. 'Archdeacon Jones and myself, on the Upper Demerara, in 1865. That *'Kanáima'* murderer, we found, had followed his victim and friends from the vicinity of Roráima to Georgetown and back, killing him on his return' (Brett 1880).
3. 'A set of jaguar's claws, hung up in the sorcerers hut, have the same threatening signification' (Brett 1880).

REFERENCES

Arens, William (1979) *The Man Eating Myth: Anthropology & Anthropophagy*. New York: Oxford University Press.
Brett, William H. (1851) *Indian Missions in Guiana*. London: George Bell.
—— (1868) *The Indian Tribes of Guiana*. London: Bell & Daldy.
—— (1880) *Legends and Myths of the Aboriginal Indians of British Guiana*. London: William Wells Gardner.
—— (1881) *Mission Work in the Forests of Guiana*. London / New York: Society for Promoting Christian Knowledge / E. & J.B. Young & Co.
Burnett, David. G (2000) *Masters of All they Surveyed. Exploration, Geography, and a British El Dorado*. Chicago: Chicago University Press.
Dance, Charles Daniel (1881) *Chapters from a Guianese Log-Book*. Georgetown: Royal Gazette.
Evans-Pritchard, Edward E. (1937) *Witchcraft, Oracles and Magic among the Azande*. Oxford: Clarendon Press.
Foucault, Michel (1994) *The Order of Things*. New York: Vintage Books.
Gallegos, Romulo (1935) *Canaima*. Barcelona: Araluce.
Gibbs, Allan K. and Christopher N. Barron (1993) *The Geology of the Guiana Shield*. New York: Oxford University Press.
Gillin, John (1936) *The Barama River Caribs of British Guiana*. Papers of the Peabody Museum, XIV(2). Cambridge, MA: Peabody Museum.
Harris, Wilson (1995) *Kanaima*. In *Concert of Voices*, ed. V.J. Ramraj. Peterborough: Broadview, pp. 145–51.
Im Thurn, E. (1883) *Among the Indians of Guiana*. London: Kegan, Paul, Trench, & Co.
Léry, Jean de (1574) *Histoire memorable de la ville de Sancerre*. Geneva.
—— (1578) *Histoire d'un voyage faict en al terre du Brésil*. Geneva: Antoine Chuppin.
Lestringant, Frank (1997) *Cannibals*. Berkeley: University of California Press.
Lézy, Emmanuel (2000) *Guyane, Guyanes: Une géographie sauvage de l'Orénoque à l'Amazone*. Paris: Belin.
Montaigne, Michel de (1580) *Essais*. Paris.

Petit, Pascale (1998) *Heart of a Deer*. London: Enitharmon Press.

Raffles, Hugh (2002) *In Amazonia. A Natural History*. Princeton: Princeton University Press.

Roth, Walter E. (1915) *An Inquiry into the Animism and Folk-Lore of the Guiana Indians*. 30th Annual report of the Bureau of American Ethnology, 1908–9. Washington, DC: Smithsonian Institution.

Simpson, George Gaylord (1964) *This View of Life; The world of an evolutionist*. New York: Harcourt, Brace & World.

Steward, Julian (ed.), (1948) *Handbook of South American Indians (4), The Tropical Forest Tribes*. Washington, DC: Smithsonian Institution.

Thevet, André (1558) *Les Singularitez de la france Antarctique, autrement nommée Amerique: & de plusieurs Terres & Isles decouvertes de nostre temps*. Paris: Chez les Heritiers de maurice de la Porte.

Thomas, Nicholas (1994) *Colonialism's Culture. Anthropology, Travel and Government*. Princeton: Princeton University Press.

Whitehead, Neil L. (1993a) 'Historical Discontinuity and Ethnic Transformation in Native Amazonia and Guyana, 1500–1900'. *L'Homme*, 28: 289–309.

—— (1993b) 'Native American Cultures along the Atlantic Littoral of South America, 1499–1650', *Proceedings of the British Academy*, 81: 197–231.

—— (1994) 'The Ancient Amerindian Polities of the lower Orinoco, Amazon and Guayana coast. A preliminary analysis of their passage from antiquity to extinction'. In *Amazonian Indians. From Prehistory to the Present*, ed. A.C. Roosevelt. Tucson, AZ: University of Arizona Press.

—— (1995) 'The Island Carib as Anthropological Icon'. In *Wolves from the Sea. Readings in the Archaeology and Anthropology of the Island Carib*, ed. N.L. Whitehead. Leiden: KITLV Press.

—— (1996) 'The Mazaruni Dragon. Golden Metals and Elite Exchanges in the Caribbean, Orinoco, and the Amazon'. In *Chieftains, Power & Trade: Regional Interaction in the Intermediate Area of the Americas*, ed. C.H. Langebaek and F.C-Arroyo. Bogota, Colombia: Departamento de Antropologia, Universidad de los Andes, pp. 107–32.

—— (1997) 'Monstrosity & Marvel: Symbolic Convergence and Mimetic Elaboration in Trans-Cultural Representation'. *Studies in Travel Writing*, 1: 72–96.

—— (1998a) 'Indigenous Cartography in Lowland South America and the Caribbean'. In *The History of Cartography*, vol. II(3), ed. D. Woodward and G.M. Lewis. Chicago: University of Chicago Press, pp. 301–26.

—— (1998b) 'The Crises and Transformations of Invaded Societies (1492–1580) – The Caribbean'. In *The Cambridge History of Native American Peoples*, vol.III, ed. F. Salomon and S. Schwartz. Cambridge: Cambridge University Press, ch. 10.

—— (1998c) 'Lowland Peoples Confront Colonial Regimes in Northern South America, 1550–1900'. In *The Cambridge History of Native American Peoples*, vol.III, ed. F. Salomon and S. Schwartz. Cambridge: Cambridge University Press, ch. 14.

—— (1998d) 'Colonial Chieftains of the Lower Orinoco and Guayana Coast'. In *Chiefdoms and Chieftaincy in the Americas*, ed. E. Redmond. Gainesville, FL: University Press of Florida, pp. 150–63.

—— (1999) 'Native Society and the European Occupation of the Caribbean Islands and Coastal Tierra Firme, 1492–1650'. In *A General History of the Caribbean*, vol. III, ed. C. Damas and P. Emmer. London: UNESCO Publications, pp. 180–200.

—— (2000) 'Hans Staden and the Cultural Politics of Cannibalism'. *Hispanic American Historical Review*, 70(4): 41–71.

—— (2001) *Beyond the Visible and the Material* (ed. with Laura Rival). Oxford: Oxford University Press.

—— (2002a) *Dark Shamans. Kanaimà and the Poetics of Violent Death*. Durham, NC: Duke University Press.

—— (2002b) 'South America/The Amazon: The Forest of Marvels'. In *The Cambridge Companion to Travel Writing*, ed. Peter Hulme and Tim Youngs. Cambridge: Cambridge University Press.

—— (2002c) 'Arawak Linguistic and Cultural Identity through Time – Contact, Colonialism, and Creolization'. In *Comparative Arawakan Histories*, ed. F. Santos-Granero and J. Hill. Champaign, IL: University of Illinois Press.

—— (2003) *Histories and Historicities in Amazonia*. Lincoln, NB: University of Nebraska Press.

—— (2004a) *In Darkness and Secrecy. The Anthropology of Assault Sorcery and Witchcraft in Amazonia* (ed. with Robin Wright). Durham, NC: Duke University Press.

—— (2004b) *Nineteenth-Century Travels, Explorations and Empires: Writings from the Era of Imperial Consolidation, 1835–1910, Part II, Volume 8: South America*. London: Pickering & Chatto.

7 IMAGINARY VIOLENCE AND THE TERRIBLE MOTHER: THE IMAGERY OF BALINESE WITCHCRAFT[1]

Michele Stephen

At the beginning of the twentieth century Freud introduced a new view of the human psyche as torn by unconscious conflicts and driven by sexuality and aggression. Even civilization itself could achieve no more than a sublimation of these instinctual desires and energies, which remain barely restrained beneath the surface of consciousness, ever ready to burst through the ego's shallow defences (Freud 1928). This pessimistic view of human nature challenged any utopian hopes for the perfectibility of human kind. At the beginning of the twenty-first century, after decades of escalating global conflicts, our world is experiencing a new wave of warfare, violence and terrorism, and any hopes that 'civilization' might bring about world peace and a new era of enlightened unity seem at best, dim. Freud's view that the human psyche stumbles blindly in a pursuit of pleasure yet is wracked by the painful consequences of its own destructive urges, is perhaps more compelling than ever before. Drawing upon Freud's insights, but developing them in an original way, the founder of the objects relations school of psychoanalysis, Melanie Klein, also saw the human psyche as torn between life and death instincts (Hinshelwood 1991: 367–8; 266–70). For Klein, however, the psyche developed in relationship, and ultimately is impelled to seek relationships with its internal and external 'objects'. This requires engaging in a continuous process of repairing and rebuilding emotional ties with important others, a process Klein (1937) referred to as 'reparation'. For Klein, the dynamic behind cultural construction is not sublimation of instinctual energies, but rather the need to make reparation for damage done to loved others. Thus to give back, to rebuild, to repair and to create are deeply rooted in the most basic levels of the psyche. Split between destructive and reparative urges, the human psyche struggles with its own rage, and fears of retaliatory rage, and its need to repair the damage it has done, so that it can maintain its good 'objects', both inner and outer – in other words, its own internal feelings of worth and strength and its positive relationships with close others. Klein's view is thus a more complex and a more hopeful one than Freud's, since she envisages the psyche's selfish drives as balanced by the equally pressing primal need to make reparation.

The anthropological and historical records clearly show that, strange as it might seem, human cultures are not content merely with engaging in physical violence in the form of assault, murder, mutilation, torture, warfare, cannibalism, head-hunting, human sacrifice and the like, they also construct elaborate belief systems concerning mystical violence committed by human beings upon their fellows. What, we might well wonder, is the relation between the very widespread beliefs about mystical attack and violence perpetrated by witches and sorcerers, and the prevalence of physical violence? Or to put it another way, why are human cultures so concerned with imaginary violence? Simple substitution is not a satisfactory answer since anthropological evidence reveals that such beliefs as often lead to violence as substitute for it (Stephen 1987a: 8–9; 1999: 722–3).

Beliefs concerning witches and sorcerers are so widely found across human culture that some scholars, including myself, have suggested that they appear to be basic patterns of the human imagination (Needham 1978; Stephen 1987b, 1999). I have previously argued on the basis of Melanesian data (Stephen 1987b) that sorcery and witchcraft beliefs involve two significantly different configurations of mystical violence, although one can blur into the other in actual situations. One is associated with malevolent power out of control, and is usually linked to women, deviants or socially marginal males; the other is associated with male power and authority, and the status quo. I refer to the former as 'witchcraft' and the latter as 'sorcery'. The utility of such a basic distinction will emerge more clearly, I hope, in the discussion to follow.[2]

As a way of reflecting upon what these imaginary forms of violence might have to reveal about the nature of human violence in general and the terror it inspires, I am going to attempt a Kleinian interpretation of Balinese sorcery and witchcraft. My aim is to show how Klein's psychoanalytic theories alert us not only to the nature of the destructive imagery involved, but also help us to understand the ritual means employed to deal with the suspected perpetrators, serving to contain the physical violence that open accusations would provoke. Before turning to my ethnographic example, I will very briefly outline Kleinian theory as it pertains to imaginary violence.

KLEIN AND THE TERRIBLE MOTHER

Klein (1946: 8ff.) presents us with a picture of the early emotional life of the human infant that is filled with images of murderous rage, of cannibalistic desires, of phantasies[3] of invading the mother's body to suck, scoop, devour, and rob it of its contents and all the riches it is believed to contain. These horrific desires in turn give rise to paranoid fears of retaliatory attacks by the mother – and later both parental figures – in which the infant expects to be ripped, torn, sucked, devoured, attacked with explosive faeces, drowned in urine, and poisoned with dangerous body substances (Klein 1989: 128–9, 132–3).

Such images, according to Klein, pervade the first six months of life. Since the infant has yet to acquire language, its thought processes during this early period take the form of imagery attached to feeling states (Klein 1937: 308). It is at first unable to perceive whole objects, or to distinguish between inner and outer images. Its own bodily feelings of pleasure, satisfaction, and comfort give rise to positive emotions and associated imagery; when it is hungry, cold, or in pain these bodily sensations provoke rage and aggression, accompanied by imagery of destroying by whatever means possible the source of its frustrations. Klein (1952: 63ff.) argues that the infant forms in its mind images of what she refers to as the 'good breast', the source of all pleasure and satisfaction, and an image of the 'bad breast', the source of all painful and frustrating sensations. As intensely as it desires to receive the love and comfort of the 'good breast', so it fiercely desires to destroy the 'bad breast'. In turn, the child expects retaliatory revenge from the object of its hatred and is overcome by persecutory fears.

If we consider the picture which exists in the infant's mind – as we see it retrospectively in the analyses of children and adults – we find that the hated breast has acquired the oral-destructive qualities of the infant's own impulses when he is in states of frustration and hatred. In his destructive phantasies he bites and tears up the breast, devours it, annihilates it; and he feels that the breast will attack him in the same way. As urethral- and anal-sadistic impulses gain in strength, the infant in his mind attacks the breast with poisonous urine and explosive faeces, and therefore expects it to be poisonous and explosive towards him. The details of his sadistic phantasies determine the content of his fear of internal and external persecutors ... Since the phantasied attacks on the object are influenced by greed, the fear of the object's greed, owing to projection, is an essential element in persecutory anxiety: the bad breast will devour him in the same greedy way as he desires to devour it. (Klein 1952: 63–4)

This early phase, dominated by sadistic phantasies and persecutory fears, Klein (1946) termed the paranoid-schizoid position. Klein's findings were even more horrific than Freud's, since not only a sensual and sexual being, as Freud would have it, the angelic infant was now attributed with the most horrific aggressive desires – and aimed at nothing less than the mother! All the gruesome violence of adult criminals was to be found in the phantasies of infants and toddlers according to Klein (1927).

As the infant's mind develops, it begins to perceive whole objects, and at about six months of age it enters a new phase of development. Klein (1940: 345) termed this the depressive position. Now the child, having realized that the good breast and the bad breast are but aspects of the one person, the mother, fears that in destructive rage against the bad breast, it had damaged or destroyed the good along with it. The child now experiences feelings of loss and pining and guilt for its own destructive rage. To deal with its intense feelings of guilt and loss, the child attempts in phantasy to repair the damage it has done to its inner objects – the good mother. This repairing or putting back together in phantasy the damaged body of the mother constitutes what Klein (1937, 1940) refers to as the process of reparation. The capacity to make reparation is essential to the child's working through the depressive position, and continues in adult life to be of central importance in dealing with grief and loss. Indeed, Klein argued that need for reparation underlies creative processes in general, including artistic endeavour, and the very production of culture itself (Hinshelwood 1991: 412–16).

If Klein is correct, then the powerful imagery of violence – cannibalism, burning poisons (urine), exploding projectiles (faeces), ripping teeth, tearing nails, body invasion – is already laid down in the infantile imagination in the first few months of life. Of course, it must be kept in mind that such images are just that – imaginary. The terrible mother is an image – an unconscious imago[4] – not the actual mother.

Hinshelwood (1991: 423) observes, 'extreme cruelty is attributed, in Kleinian thought, to the basic instinctual endowment of human beings ... The prevalence, therefore, of all these impulses of cruel aggression is extremely wide ...' One of the main themes underlying my discussion in this chapter is our need to recognize how deeply and pervasively sadistic violence is rooted in the human psyche, and thus how easily cultural forms might serve to tap into it.

BALINESE IMAGES OF THE DEVOURING MOTHER

Bali, a tiny island of Indonesia, presents us with some extraordinary imaginary figures of terror that display all the classical features of both the witch of ethnography and of the terrible mother of Kleinian theory.[5]

One of the most striking performances given in Balinese temples involves a confrontation between Rangda, a hideous hag usually described as the 'queen of the witches', and a strutting hairy monster decked with gold and mica decorations, called Barong. Usually, but too simplistically, the dance is interpreted as a battle between good and evil in which neither side wins (for a summary of previous scholarly interpretations, see Stephen 2001: 137–40). The association with witchcraft is common knowledge, but precisely what is the connection and how the ritual dance serves to combat witchcraft is all too vague in most accounts. Depictions of Rangda and her followers, the *leyak*, are to be found profusely in temple reliefs and statuary, and in traditional paintings and carvings – and today commonly adorn even articles produced for the tourist trade. Although Rangda and her followers are usually identified in the literature as 'witches', it is important for my argument that I carefully describe what constitutes a 'leyak' before assuming any simple equivalence with English terms and concepts.

Rangda, the 'queen' of the *leyak*, is depicted as a female of monstrously ugly form, with a huge bulging body, pendulous breasts, a shaggy mane of hair, and long, sharp teeth and claws. During the performance she leaps about menacingly, snorts, grunts, and emits high-pitched unnerving shrieks, a nightmare figure indeed. Deciphering her meaning is no easy task (Stephen 2001), but since she provides the model for the human *leyak*, it is worthwhile paying careful attention to her symbolism and iconography. Although only a few Western scholars seem to have recognized her identity, Rangda represents the goddess Durga in her most dangerous and uncontrolled form (Stephen 2001: 148–54).

In Balinese Hinduism,[6] the goddess Durga is the terrible form taken by the creator goddess Uma, consort of the high god, Siwa (Shiva). Creation myths tell of how the cosmos emerged from the yoga of Siwa and his Sakti, or female energy, Uma (Hooykaas 1974). After the heavens and the earth had emerged, Uma turned to look back at her creations and a sudden change came over her. She became enraged and, taking the terrible form of Durga, she began to wreak havoc on the world she had just created. In philosophical terms, Durga is the divine creative power of Siwa's consort turned destructive. She is the reverse side of the beautiful mother goddess Uma. The Balinese Durga has several forms, including Berawi Durga,[7] who is found in the cemetery with her followers the *leyak*, devouring human corpses. Berawi Durga thus represents that aspect of cosmic power that smelts down (*lebur*) dead matter and returns it to its original condition.[8] The Rangda of temple performance represents Durga in this dangerous manifestation when she is loose in the cemetery with her followers.

Figure 7.1 shows Durga as represented in a Balinese temple carving. Some European interpreters, perhaps influenced by Western notions of witches, have asserted that Rangda represents a post-menopausal hag, who devours infants out of jealousy since she is no longer able to bear them. On the contrary, Durga/Rangda is the fertile mother, with her heavy breasts and belly, and her great lolling tongue symbolizing desire, greed, blood, and fire. Fire is her element, the fire of passion, of anger, and of the red female reproductive substance (*kama bang*). Flames can be seen in the palms of her hands, on her tongue and rising from her head. Her huge teeth and tusks emphasize animal greed and aggression, and her bestiality is highlighted in the hair that sprouts from her face, and the sharp claws on her hands and feet. Her bulging eyes and snout-like nose further underline her animal nature. Long matted locks of hair envelop her and sway about her

Figure 7.1 The Goddess Durga (Balinese temple carving).

ankles. Durga/Rangda is bursting with fierce energy. She is drenched
in blood, garlanded with entrails, and dances in the graveyard (the
stance assumed by the figure is a dancing position). In short, Durga
personifies cosmic creative energy wildly out of control.[9]

The minions of Durga include the *leyak*, human beings who by the
grace of Durga become her followers and share in her terrible powers.
The *lontar* text,[10] *Siwagama*, recounts the story of how they originated
in the world.[11] After a quarrel with her husband, Siwa, the goddess
Uma descended to earth in anger taking the form of the terrible
Durga. Arriving at the cemetery, she encountered her daughter, Kalika,
also in demonic form, who with the demonic forces, the *bhuta kala*,
were ravaging the earth with disease and feasting themselves on the
dead. Kalika begged her mother to teach her powers to the human
women who had become her (Kalika's) followers. Durga consented
and in return for her lessons, she ordered the women to pay with
the flesh of their own relatives, including their husbands, children
and grandchildren, so that her minions, the *bhuta kala*, might eat the
corpses. The women agreed to the pact, whereupon Durga granted
them all kinds of powers to inflict disease and death. Such is the
mythic origin of human powers to kill by magical means. The first
leyak were women who used their powers to kill their own children
and relatives to feed Durga's minions.

Leyak are attributed with the power to transform themselves into
frightful shapes resembling that of their leader, Durga.[12] Paintings
and carvings depict them as monstrous female forms, with heavy
breasts, sharp talons, and great protruding teeth and tusks, between
which hang grotesquely long lapping tongues. Fire, which is their
element, bursts from their heads, tongues and other parts of their
bodies. Their tastes are as bestial as their appearance. They too feast
on human flesh, especially that of babies. (See Figure 7.2, where a
leyak is wrapping her long tongue around the corpse of an infant she
holds in one arm, and Figure 7.3 of another smaller figure clutching
a child's severed head.) They are attracted to dead matter and rotting
smells. Their favourite haunt is the cemetery, where they gather in
search of new corpses to devour. They go about at night, invisible,
and are believed to fly through the air as moving lights (the fire
issuing from their bodily orifices). As well as transformations into
the shape of Durga, which is achieved by only the most practised
adepts, witches can take the form of animals, in particular monkeys
and night birds. *Leyak* act out of sheer cannibalistic greed – and those
they attack, as we have seen in the mythic account of origins, are
their own close family members, children, and grandchildren. The
form of attack consists of an invisible devouring of the inside of the
body of the victim that later manifests itself as a physical disease.

Figure 7.2 A *leyak* holding the corpse of an infant.

Evidently, *leyak* are in essence female. According to the myth, human *women* were granted powers directly by the goddess Durga to inflict disease and death. Becoming a *leyak* means to take on the form of the goddess Durga. Women are said to have a special proclivity to become *leyak* as they are more greedy, more ambitious and more concerned with material things than men. It must be stressed at this point that Balinese philosophy does not emphasize only the negative aspects of female reproductive power: the female energy of the god, his *sakti*, is seen as the origin of all existence. Without the Sakti, no world would have been created and the original unity of the divine would never have been divided. The Sakti is the origin of all material things. Many of my Balinese informants spoke of the 'power of the

Figure 7.3   A *leyak* clutching a child's severed head.

mother', the source of all material existence, but this, they emphasized, becomes a terrible power when uncontrolled, just as fire, the element of female cosmic power, destroys all in its path if unchecked (Stephen 2001: 150–3). Human women, since they participate in this power by giving birth, are part of the cosmic flow of forces that have both creative and destructive aspects. Human women begin as beautiful mothers, like the lovely Uma, but may degenerate into fiendesses like Durga.

All human beings, however, are embodied creatures and thus subject to base desires such as greed, sloth, jealousy, anger, and lust. Accordingly, the man who chooses to develop this potential within himself can also become a *leyak*; but since men are associated with the male cosmic principle of spirit, as opposed to matter, they are thought to be less inherently suited to the role. The Balinese cosmos consists of three levels or worlds – *bhur, bwah,* and *swah.* The lowest level of animal instinct and energy and the realm of the *bhuta kala,* the demonic forces, is *bhur;* the human level is *bwah,* and the divine is *swah.* Human beings possess a threefold nature, with an instinctual, a human, and a divine potential, and it is up to each person which potential they choose to develop. The person who seeks to become a *leyak* deliberately develops the lowest instinctual, brute level of the self.

The terms used to refer to destructive magic are many – such as *desti, bebai, teluh, tranjana*[13] – and it is difficult to determine their precise meanings, but what is clear is that the powers of the *leyak* are but one of many types of destructive magic, or perhaps it would be better to say that the term designates a particular technique of harmful magic. A basic distinction in Balinese terminology is between *pengiwa,* magical knowledge of the left hand, and *penengen,* knowledge of the right hand. The powers of the *leyak* belong to the left hand, *pengiwa,* while the knowledge and practice of healing belongs to the right, as does protective magic of various kinds.

There are many different kinds of Balinese healers, usually termed *balian,* and it is difficult to make a brief summary of them (Stephen and Suryani 2000: 7–8). Furthermore, as well as persons designated 'balian' there are others who can heal, including village priests (*pemangku*), Brahmana priests (*pedanda*), and puppeteer priests (*dalang*). However, healing is specifically the role of the *balian,* while those other persons who possess healing powers do so tangentially to more priestly functions. Although there are many types of *balian* specializing in different kinds of treatments, a basic division exists between those whose powers are based upon the study of the sacred *lontar* texts, and those who obtain the ability to heal through some kind of spiritual experience involving a direct communication of knowledge, as in a dream, trance or vision, from a supernatural source.

Medical texts, the *usada,* constitute an important part of the sacred *lontar* literature. There are also *lontar* compendiums of magical diagrams, potions, and spells (Hooykaas 1978, 1980). The healer is believed to require a knowledge of destructive magic in order to be able to counteract it. Thus although this is rarely mentioned openly, it is well known that the healer can harm as well as heal. Indeed, knowledgeable people told me, in confidence, that healers often work hand in hand with *leyak,* and while one makes people sick, the other is paid to heal them.

At this point the difference between the left- and right-hand paths seems to blur, but the distinguishing feature is that the healer can both harm and heal, whereas the *leyak* possess only destructive powers. Evidently the role of the healer is to control the *leyak.* In this context, the healer is associated with the male concept of spirit and the god, Siwa, while the *leyak* is associated with the female energy turned destructive, and thus the goddess Durga. It is the role of the former to bring under control the destructive power of the latter. The *lontar, Tutur Kandaning Catur Bhumi*,[14] explains that after Durga had inflicted disease on the world, Siwa descended to earth and brought to human beings the knowledge of healing so they could cure themselves of the afflictions caused by his terrible spouse. The same theme of male cosmic power bringing under control female creative energy is acted out in the meeting in temple performance of Rangda/Durga with the monster, Barong, as we shall see later.

All harmful magical powers emanate from Durga. They can be acquired by praying to Durga in the cemetery, meditating there and receiving a special gift (*anugrah*) or a magical amulet of some kind, such as a special stone (*pica*). The powers can be learned by studying the sacred *lontar* texts for oneself, or by studying with a teacher, by buying charms and amulets from a knowledgeable person, usually a *balian*. Only those who are able to read the sacred texts are capable of obtaining the highest knowledge, but since the texts are written in Kawi, a language inaccessible to most Balinese, this knowledge is limited to a small elite, usually of Brahmana priests and scholars. Nevertheless even illiterate persons can receive oral instruction from teachers in the spells and required rituals, and, at the lowest level, one can buy amulets and charms that serve to activate one's lowest animal nature and thus the potential to become a *leyak*.

Ultimately, no matter how the powers are acquired, becoming a *leyak* involves a special kind of identification with the goddess Durga. In a written *mantra* (prayer or spell) entitled *Durga Murti* (Durga takes physical form), to be used on the magically powerful date of Kajeng Kliwon when *leyak* are believed to be abroad, the magician declares:

Om, in my inner concentration I take the form of Durga-Murti [then names all the parts of the body to be invested with demonic entities].

I am Kalika, I am the goddess Kali, I am the goddess Sapuhjagat [a name often given to Rangda masks], I am the Goddess, Berawi Durga, I return home to the supernatural world and become the goddess of the Pura Dalem [Durga], I am the leader of the world, I am the leader Durga, all the Durgas pray to me – all success![15]

We see here that the would-be *leyak*, even if male, mystically takes on the very form of the terrible goddess.

It is by now evident that Balinese beliefs about witches and harmful magic are embedded in the complex mythic, philosophical, and mystical traditions that constitute Balinese Hinduism.[16] In Balinese philosophy, the Sakti – the creative energy of the high god, Siwa – is the source of all material existence, but she is also the principle that leads to the destruction of the physical world. Her human followers, the *leyak*, when confined to the graveyard, play a necessary part in the process of *lebur*, of returning matter to its original pure condition. But if humankind is not to be wiped out, the actions of Durga and the *leyak* must be kept in control. The meeting in dance of Barong and Rangda is intended to achieve precisely this end, as we shall see later.

THE SOCIAL REALITY OF BALINESE MYSTICAL VIOLENCE

How do these cultural beliefs – elaborated in myth, in philosophy, in ritual, in art, and in the sacred texts – manifest in popular belief and action? In Bali today beliefs in the ability of some human beings to kill others by magical means are by no means simply a matter of abstract belief, or of fairy tale and legend. There is, as Wikan (1990) has shown, an undercurrent of fear of violence – mystical violence, that is – that permeates all Balinese social interaction.

We need to keep in mind that the term 'leyak' does not include all forms of destructive magic. It represents a specific technique involving a transformation into a being that resembles the terrible goddess, Durga, and that becomes her follower. A person may possess the power to 'ngleyak', a verbal form that actually refers to changing shape,[17] but in addition possess other harmful powers, and furthermore have abilities to heal. Such a person is not likely to be identified as a 'leyak'. When a Balinese admits to fears that someone is employing harmful magic against him or her, this does not necessarily imply that the suspected perpetrator is a *leyak*. As I have already noted, the healers who base their practice on written texts must also possess a knowledge of destructive magic. People may hire *balian* to harm neighbours or enemies, or buy from them a charm or amulet to achieve the desired result. Likewise priests and other persons who study the sacred texts may have knowledge of harmful techniques and can use them on their own behalf, or on the behalf of others. But such persons balance these destructive powers with healing and protective magic.

The situation is complex, and further obscured by the fact that most Balinese are very reluctant to talk openly about such matters. However, if we attend to which persons are actually designated as 'leyak' or as possessing the power to 'ngleyak', a clearer picture emerges.

The community with which I am most familiar, which is close to the tourist centre of Ubud, has had extensive contact with westerners over the last 20 to 30 years, and would certainly be considered progressive, but fears of witchcraft are rife, although such matters are always covert. Foreigners asking about such matters are likely to be told, 'There are no *leyak* here – maybe in the past there were some, but not now.' Such answers seem only appropriate in a community where general levels of education are high, but in fact beliefs in *leyak* and *pengiwa* are pervasive, even among the most highly educated.

One thing that struck me was that those persons in the community most often referred to as being *leyak* were women. All the accounts I heard where a particular person was identified centred on women, usually old or middle-aged, who to all intent and purposes appeared to be simple, unlettered housewives, mothers, and grandmothers. The persons identifying these women were usually members of the same household,[18] and close relatives of the suspect, who might be their aunt, adoptive mother, mother-in-law, or grandmother. When I asked a young unmarried woman well known to me, who at the time suffered at the hands of tyrannical adoptive mother, whether there were many *leyak* in the community, she replied emphatically, 'A lot!' And when I asked whether they were men or women, she exclaimed as if it were obvious 'All of them are females!' I pressed her further, 'How do we know whether a person is a *leyak* or not?' The answer was quick in coming, 'X and Y (naming the two male healers in the community), *they* know who is.' Implied in her answer is that the two healers know as it is their job to try to cure the illness caused by the *leyak*.

To illustrate the beliefs in action I will describe three examples from the community with which I am most familiar.

Case A: A childless woman in her 70s married to a village priest (*pemangku*), the adoptive mother of the young woman just quoted. Now physically frail and ailing, this old lady is nevertheless feared by her family. She is attributed with the deaths of at least three wives within her husband's extended family. Her motive is said to be desire for power within the extended family. For many decades she has imposed her will on the house compound, which includes the wives, children, and grandchildren of her husband's two older brothers. Although the wife of the youngest brother, it is said that she controlled family finances and matters for many years, using her power to siphon off resources to her natal household, since she herself had no children. The women whose deaths are attributed to her were the wives of her husband's nephews. Younger members of the family were warned by their mothers not to anger or cross the older woman, thus reinforcing her control. In terms of her behaviour, she is at times very abusive verbally to family members, particularly the younger females, and her irritability and strangeness always increases around the time of Kajeng Kliwon, a magically significant date occurring once every 15 days. Her powers are said to derive from her father who was a man knowledgeable in the sacred texts and in matters pertaining to magic. The woman herself is unable to read the *lontar* texts, but is said to have been given by her father a special amulet, usually referred to as a *sabuk* (belt) containing the power to enable her to *ngleyak*. This is the basis of her power, which has increased over time, although some family members says that now she is getting older, the power of the *sabuk* is beginning to turn upon her, and will eventually eat her as she is no longer strong enough to control it. This is said to be the normal course of events and that eventually the power of the *sabuk* devours its owner as she gets older and weaker. Crazy, senile old women were sometimes pointed out to me as evidence of the fact that the woman who develops her capacity as a *leyak* is eventually eaten up and destroyed by these very powers.

Case B: A widow in her mid-50s. She is attributed with the deaths of many children in her husband's family, including her own grandchildren. Her son, with tears in his eyes, and desperation in his voice, described his mother's activities to me shortly after the death of his newborn son, his first child. He had no doubt his mother was responsible for the child's death, and he described to me how also his brother's wife had had numerous miscarriages over many years and still had not succeeded in giving birth to a live child. If the son had had any doubt at all about his mother's guilt, the death of his next child, a year later, dispelled them. I visited the hospital a few hours after the child's birth – a large and perfectly formed son. The baby died two days later, as had the first child. For the second time the bereaved father unburdened to me his sorrow not only at his child's death, but at his mother's complicity in it. The sincerity of his conviction that his mother had killed his own and his brother's children was undeniable. I tried to ask about the possible motive. The son answered that his mother and her sister, who had both married into the same family, wanted to destroy that family by making sure there were no heirs, or perhaps they were simply looking for victims as a means of repaying the goddess Durga for their powers (referring here to the idea that women must pay with human victims for the magical powers they obtain from Durga). The son also ventured to me the possibility that his mother was not consciously aware of her actions. He stressed how much he loved his mother and how close he had been to her before these awful events. His father had died when he was a child and now it began to emerge that he believed his father had also been a victim of the mother's attacks. In response to my puzzlement, my informant explained that sometimes women become *leyak* without being aware of it, so that at night they see their husbands, children, and grandchildren as meat to eat, and so devour them, with the result that the victim soon sickens and dies. Many other people confirmed these ideas about women who change into *leyak* at night, unaware, and devour their families. The young man also told me that during her pregnancy his wife had experienced many dreams in which her mother-in-law came to her wanting something. The couple had removed themselves from the family home when the second pregnancy was confirmed, but their attempts to thus avoid the cannibalistic attacks were to no avail.

The two cases just described involve persons well known to me personally over the last five years. As is usually the case, the horrendous fears that people harbour concerning the actions of their own relatives, even their own mother, are simply borne in silence. The most drastic action to be taken might be to move away from the house compound of the putative *leyak*, as in Case B, but this is not always an option, and basically people must learn to live with their fears as best they can without taking any overt action against the suspected culprit. Only very occasionally are suspects physically attacked by others. My final example is an account of such an occasion reported to me some years after the event by neighbours of the protagonists.

Case C: A man who had attacked and killed a woman many years before was released from jail during my fieldwork, which was how I came to learn of the incident. Several of the man's children had died in succession, and suspicion fell on one of his female neighbours, who was also a relative. One day he discovered a monkey (a form often assumed by *leyak*) in his house compound, and when the animal bounded off he followed it, only to find it entering his neighbour's house. As he watched, hidden, the monkey changed itself back into a woman. In uncontrollable fury at having discovered the *leyak* in the very act, he fell upon the woman and bludgeoned her to death. Later he was tried and convicted of murder. Although the community sympathized with the man's actions, as he was convinced he had destroyed the malevolent creature responsible for the deaths of his children, no one condoned the act, or felt that this was the appropriate means of dealing with the culprit.

These three examples serve to illustrate the kinds of circumstances in which fears and suspicions of *leyak* operate. The focus on women – close relatives and neighbours – is evident. In all the cases I know of where an actual death is attributed to a known person in the community, that person was a woman. Deaths of women and children, in particular, are attributed to female *leyak*. Those suspected are typically ordinary wives and mothers who possess no important ritual knowledge or learning. Since the source of all ritual knowledge, including *pengiwa*, is believed to be the *lontar* texts, this might appear to be an anomaly. Such women are said to acquire their powers in two ways: they can purchase the power in the form of an amulet, which usually includes spells written on paper or palm leaf, or inscribed in metal, and they can seek direct empowerment from the goddess Durga by praying in the cemetery or the Pura Dalem, the temple devoted to Durga. However, as we have seen in Case B, some women who become *leyak* are not in fact aware of their powers, and thus did not deliberately set out to acquire them. This situation can come about when a woman buys a charm intended for a different purpose, such as attracting customers to her shop or food stall, or to regain a husband's straying attention. Gradually over time the content of such a charm begins to influence the lower aspects of the owner's character, to the point that she finds herself transforming into a *leyak* unawares. What had started off as a means of attracting others, serves to increase the woman's own greed and desire until she becomes the epitome of greed, the *leyak* who perceives her own offspring as meat to eat.[19]

The women identified as *leyak* are evidently associated with unconscious, uncontrolled destructive powers of a non-human sort, they do not possess other ritual knowledge, or positive powers, they exercise little social power beyond the family or house compound,[20] and they are the ones who are likely to be physically attacked in the rare case where violence is used against the suspect.

Men also may be identified as possessing the power of *leyak*, but in their case a very different picture emerges. Such men are usually literate in the sacred texts, and possess other important ritual knowledge and powers by which they are publicly identified. Thus *pedanda* (Brahmana priests), *pemangku* (village priests), *balian* (healers), *dalang* (puppeteer priests), and others who study the sacred *lontar* texts, may be attributed with the power to *ngleyak*. Such respected ritual experts have knowledge of both *pengiwa* and *penengen*. Thus they are able to inflict sickness, illness, and injury, but they are also able to heal; this is in sharp contrast to the women attributed with *leyak* powers, who are seen as possessing negative powers only. These influential male ritual experts are not, to my knowledge, attributed with deaths of women and children in their own families.[21] Their victims are other magicians, rivals – and the effects of their magical attacks on each other are presented as battles between equals or contests between spiritual warriors. No one would dare attack such a ritually powerful person, except an equally powerful magician.

There is never any identifying of who is the victor in these mystical battles; thus many men might be thought to have *ngleyak* as part of their magical armoury, but they are never identified as individuals in the way the women suspects are. In fact such men are not identified as *leyak*, but rather as *anak sakti* – people possessing magical power in general (which may include the shape-changing power of *ngleyak*). There are many rumours of the *siat malam*, or night battles, in which powerful magicians engage in duels to the death by transforming themselves in various forms, including the goddess Durga. The battles can sometimes been seen, it is said, as fireballs crossing the sky at night. If one were to ask, 'Who participates in the *siat malam*?' one could expect at best evasive or only very general answers. Only in the context of actual events does specific information emerge. The following example illustrates this point.

Case D: K.S. was a man in his 50s known as a *balian usada* (healer who bases his practice on textual knowledge) in his community. His death occurred while I was in the process of writing this chapter. At the time a friend from Bali was staying with me in Australia. When he telephoned home he learned that K.S. had died the night before. About three weeks earlier K.S. had fallen ill. As a *balian* he had been called upon to treat a patient in Tabanan, a district at some distance from his home. The night before he set out for Tabanan he had a dream warning him not to go. In the morning on the way to his destination he was attacked by a crow at a crossroads, whereupon he fell ill, had to return home and was taken to hospital. After a few days he was discharged apparently cured. Three weeks later, he suddenly dropped dead. My friend explained that it was clear K.S. had been defeated in a night battle with another magician. When a magician loses the battle, his spirit has already departed, and within a month his physical body will die. K.S.'s death had occurred three weeks after he had received warning not to treat the patient in Tabanan, and the attack by the crow. He had made the mistake of trying to heal a patient whose illness had been caused by a more powerful magician, and in the attempt to battle for the patient's life had lost his own.

Here we see that treating a patient may involve engaging in a night battle with the magician responsible for inflicting the illness.[22] I referred earlier to the idea of a pact between the healer and the witch wherein the two connive to use their different powers to make money, one inflicting the illness, the other curing it – for a price. Often the course of treatment may require the patient returning again and again to the healer. Balinese make a rhyming pun on the term, referring to 'balian maalihan-alihan',[23] implying that the healer is a trader chasing a profit by keeping his clients dependent on him. We have also seen that the women suspected of being *leyak* are thought to have acquired their powers from *balian*, and thus are in their debt, if not under their control. *Balian* are also said to operate in pairs or networks so that while one is attempting to treat a patient, his friend or partner will provide protection against rivals who may wish to keep the patient sick. Thus the very process of healing begins to be revealed as a contest of mystical powers between groups of competing *balian* and their assistant *leyak*.

A knowledgeable friend explained to me that these contests were not simply between two rival *anak sakti*, but rather involved a whole host of dangerous forces. The leaders (*balian* or other powerful men) are accompanied by their assistants, as well as those persons who had been given amulets conferring *leyak* powers. These included the old women identified in the community as *leyak*, but they are in fact only followers. At this point I asked with surprise whether this meant that the leaders of the *leyak* were in fact powerful men, such as *balian* and priests.[24] 'Precisely', my friend answered. But this, he further explained, was only in accordance with the basic cosmic ordering whereby destructive female energy must be brought under control by the masculine principle of spirit. Thus although the male practitioners may use their powers to destructive ends, they also possess positive powers – they can kill and revive. This capacity is demonstrated in the famous tale of magic, Calon Arang, where the widow of Dirah, who has taken the form of Rangda, is challenged to a contest of powers by the wise man, Empu Bharada. He burns down a tree with his magic and challenges her to do the same. She quickly burns down a great tree with her fire, but when Empu Bharada revives his tree and challenges her to follow, she is unable to do so.[25]

The situation I have described, some might object, is confounded by the fact that not only men are healers, many women are also *balian*, particularly those who work primarily as spirit mediums communicating with the ancestors. Women rarely if ever base their practice on a knowledge of written texts, and their vocation depends on some kind of spontaneous inspiration or revelation from supernatural sources. Yet such women, although acknowledged to have positive abilities to heal, are not usually thought to have abilities to harm. Often they are seen, and perceive themselves, as vessels through which a higher power operates spontaneously and without their control.[26] The female *balian* is in a sense not responsible for her actions as a healer – she is often in trance and thus not even consciously aware of what she says and does in a healing session. Control once again seems to be the issue here – females possess great power but do not control it; this is the role of the masculine principle of spirit.

In philosophical terms, magically powerful men gain their power from the Sakti but at a higher level represented by the benign goddess, Saraswati. Balinese mystical knowledge has many levels, from harmful to protective magic, to rituals ultimately aimed at the achievement of yogic liberation. Such men, usually termed *anak sakti*, may obtain some powers from the terrible goddess Durga, but they have also achieved a high level of spiritual development, balancing their destructive capacities with positive ones, their final goal being spiritual enlightenment.[27]

In short, men suspected of having the power to *ngleyak* are respected and powerful ritual experts, possessing positive powers to balance their destructive ones; their knowledge is based, ideally, on study of the sacred texts, and their destructive powers are not used to attack innocent people or members of their families but rather are deployed in contests of powers between rivals and equals. For such men, to use powers of *ngleyak* is a way to demonstrate to others their level of mystical power. Persons who become too attached to this level of mystical power are said to preclude themselves from reaching the highest levels of spiritual attainment, but nevertheless they are perceived quite differently from the old women who are thought to attack and kill their own families.

Despite the terminological difficulties involved, it is clear that Balinese suspicions concerning holders of harmful magic are directed towards two quite different groups of people and have different social consequences. We are evidently not dealing with clearly ascribed social roles, but rather with fluid ideologies that when used in practice are coloured by rumour, personal fears, and rivalries, and the valences of family and local politics. What is said about a person in public is a very different matter from what is confessed in private. Particular individuals, depending on their personalities and abilities, may manipulate these ideologies to their own ends, or become the victims of them. My point is that there exists a basic split in beliefs

about the nature of harmful magic that enables them to be used in
two quite opposite ways: conferring power and social influence on
the person believed to possess them or resulting in social castigation
and blame. These distinctions might blur and overlap in practice but
the basic polarity is evident. In Bali, as in many cultures (Barfield
1997: 493) including early modern Europe (Hodgkin 2001: 219),
women are usually the focus of blame and scapegoating, while men
usually gain influence and respect as a result of such attributions. I
will return to this issue later.

HOW TO DEAL WITH *LEYAK*?

Now we are in a position to return to the question of why it is that
the meeting in dance of Barong and Rangda is the appropriate means
to deal with *leyak*.[28]

As we have seen, attacking or killing persons suspected of being
leyak is not deemed by Balinese to be the appropriate way to deal
with them. Often the actual circumstances of the situation make
this impossible, as we saw in the example of the young man who
believed that his widowed mother was responsible for the deaths of
his two infant children. Despite his grief and anger, he assured me
that he still loved his mother; killing her was not a possible solution
to the problem, even if he were to go on losing his newborn children.
Nor was it likely that a young woman would even contemplate the
thought of doing violence to her adoptive mother, as much as she
feared and hated her. The relationships between victim and suspected
attacker are so close that any violent action of revenge could only
bring further sorrow to all involved. Where violence does break out,
as in Case C, it is a spontaneous action of an individual on the spur
of the moment, not a calculated assault. The social reality of fears
of *leyak* thus underlines the cultural philosophy that the power of
the Mother/Sakti, who gives birth to us, and to all material things,
has a destructive aspect that must be controlled. As one of my most
knowledgeable informants expressed it, 'The power of the Mother is
very, very important, but it is also dangerous, it must be controlled.
But if we kill the Mother, we kill ourselves.' He was responding to
my questions about the ritual meeting between Barong and Rangda,
in which I was asking him why Rangda was not defeated or killed at
the end of the performance.

How then is this power to be controlled? The simple answer is
via ritual. In the Balinese worldview, the cosmos moves between
phases of creation and destruction, as the process of creating
material entities degenerates. Much of Balinese ritual life, in all its
amazing complexity, is to halt the process downwards and return
the dangerous and destructive forces generated by the Sakti back to

their divine source, so that a new pure phase of creation can begin again (Stephen 2002, 2005).

The myths concerning the origin of all the dangerous and destructive forces in the world, the *bhuta kala*, also explains the origin of *caru*, the rituals used to deal with them (Stephen 2002: 73–82). Uma, the beautiful creatrix, was cursed by her husband Siwa and she descended to the earth as Durga, where she multiplied into five, one for each of the cardinal directions and one in the centre. Missing his wife, Siwa cursed himself and descended to the earth in the terrible form of Kala Rudra. He met the five Durgas at the crossroads and from their meetings were spawned legions of demonic and dangerous forces, the *bhuta kala*. With their creators, they began to lay waste to the earth and devour humankind. Fearing the destruction of the world, the Tri Semaya (the gods Brahma, Wisnu and Iswara) descended to the earth in the form of Brahmana priests to teach human beings how to stop the devastation. The king of the land was shown by the three gods how men could become priests, how to make the *caru* offerings of meat and blood for the demonic hosts, and how to stage performances to bring Kala Rudra and Durga to awareness of their terrible actions. When the rituals were completed an astonishing transformation was achieved: Kala Rudra, Durga, and the *bhuta kala* all returned to their gentle forms of Siwa, Uma, and the angels of heaven (*bidedara-dedari*).[29] Although *caru* rituals have often been interpreted by foreign scholars as a means of placating and thus dispersing the demonic forces, the myth just quoted and other Balinese texts make it clear that the aim and purpose of the ritual is to transform dangerous entities back to their original pure and benign state (Stephen 2002). Dangerous and demonic entities are thus not destroyed or simply chased away; they are transformed back into that from which they originated. The frightful Durga becomes the beautiful mother Uma again, the hideous Kala Rudra becomes the divine Siwa, and their demonic minions become the heavenly hosts.

Caru rituals are performed regularly as the necessary preliminary part of most ritual occasions in Bali. It is usually said that their purpose is to 'clean' or 'purify' the area, which is correct, but westerners are likely to misinterpret this as removing evil and dangerous influences, when what is actually aimed at is a reabsorption of those influences back to their pure origins (see Stephen 2005, Chapter 5).

There are also rituals directed specifically to bringing *leyak* under control. These consist of performances, either masked dances or shadow puppet plays, in which Rangda/Durga is confronted by the monster Barong. According to my most knowledgeable Balinese informants, what is taking place in this meeting is a transformation and reabsorption of the destructive power of Durga/Rangda, and of her students, the human *leyak*. Barong represents Siwa in monstrous form come to meet his spouse and bring her under control (Stephen 2001: 154–8, 177–84). In fact the monster Barong is not fighting Rangda but courting her, and his intention is to unite with her so as to end her anger and thus return her to her benign form of Uma. In terms of Balinese philosophy, Rangda represents the element fire (the female cosmic principle), and the mystic sound, Ang. Barong represents the element water (the male principle) and the mystic sound Ah. Together they constitute Rwa-Bineda, the two different principles, which unite to form vapour, a more refined, that is, less material entity (Stephen 2001: 179–80). This symbolizes the reabsorption of the multiplicity of the coarse, material world back into an undifferentiated, spiritual unity.

As Rangda/Durga is transformed through this ritual meeting, at the same time the destructive powers that her human followers have obtained from her are reabsorbed into their source. In other words, the terrible mother is returned to her positive form, along with her minions, the *leyak* – just as the *bhuta kala* are returned to being the angels of heaven by means of the *caru* rituals. Towards the end of the performance, Rangda calls to all the *leyak*, summoning them to her. Her action has been variously interpreted as a call for help or as a challenge (H. Geertz 1994: 81) to the *leyak* to fight her. In my view, she is summoning the *leyak* so as to absorb back their destructive powers into herself, so that they are returned to the human beings from which they degenerated, just as she is returned to the gentle Uma.

One cannot kill Rangda any more than one can kill one's own mother; to do so would be to try to kill one's self, since the Mother/ Sakti is the origin of all embodied existence. This is symbolized during the performance in the attacks upon Rangda by the *kris* dancers, who attempt to stab Rangda with their long daggers. But Rangda turns upon them and they fall into trance, turning their blades upon themselves in paroxysms of self-stabbing. Likewise people cannot kill those mothers and grandmothers who invisibly feast upon the flesh of their own families, but, through the appropriate ritual, they strive to return them to their human form. In the natural course of things, just as Uma keeps returning to the earth as Durga, just as the process of material creation inevitably becomes destructive after it reaches a certain point, so the rituals to deal with *leyak* must be periodically repeated. The ritual transformation to benign form is temporary. For a time the *leyak* will cease to be troublesome but as the ritual cycle of 210 days progresses dangerous influences will build up again.[30]

THE DEVOURING MOTHER, SPLITTING, AND REPARATION

At this point I want to return to Klein's theories to show how they might relate to the Balinese ethnographic data.

1. *The striking resemblance between the Balinese* leyak *and the Kleinian devouring mother of unconscious phantasy.*

The iconography of the Balinese Durga/Rangda and her students, the human *leyak*, provide startlingly vivid images of ogresses with huge fangs, tearing claws and great lolling tongues, caught in the act of devouring infants. The phantasies Klein describes could hardly have a more direct representation and realization in concrete form. The infant, who desires in rage and hatred to destroy the bad mother, expects retaliatory attack in the same form – being sucked dry, bitten, torn by nails and teeth, and devoured. The emphasis on the teeth, tongue and claws of Rangda – and her great hanging breasts – seem hardly coincidental from a Kleinian viewpoint. As we have seen, Durga/Rangda represents a whole complex of ideas concerning the dangerous aspect of female cosmic power out of control. The symbolic form here has been developed into a complex philosophical concept, but its psychogenic (Obeyesekere 1990) roots remain obvious.

2. *The radical splitting of the mother figure in Bali into the hideous Durga and the beautiful Uma.*

Kleinian notions of the splitting of the mother figure are vividly portrayed in the Balinese cultural images of Durga and Uma.[31] Uma represents the 'good mother' who creates the world and everything in it. She has many refractions in Bali: Saraswati, goddess of knowledge; Dewi Sri, goddess of the rice fields; Dewi Danau, goddess of the Lake; and others. All material riches, wealth, and good things stem from her. She is represented as a young, slender, beautiful girl, dressed like a queen. Not only is the split clearly recognized in Balinese iconography, but so is the identity of the two equally apparent: when Uma becomes angry she transforms into Durga and descends to earth. Knowledgeable Balinese informed me that Uma is always in Heaven, and when she descends to the earth she becomes Durga. This reflects the philosophical view that all material creation begins with a pure spiritual source, Uma, but as it progresses it descends into increasingly coarse and ultimately dangerous entities.

3. *The ritual means of dealing with Durga and the* leyak *closely parallel Klein's theory of reparation, whereby the damaged mother must be made whole again in phantasy.*

Earlier in this chapter I referred to the importance in Kleinian theory of the process of reparation, whereby the infant tries to repair the damage done in phantasy to its inner and outer objects (Hinshelwood 1991: 412–16). The early paranoid schizoid phase, where the mother is split into two totally different entities, one all good, one all bad, is gradually replaced by what Klein terms the Depressive position (Hinshelwood 1991: 138ff.). By about six months of age, the child is becoming capable of perceiving whole rather than part objects, and it begins to fear that in its previous attempts to destroy the 'bad breast' it has damaged or destroyed the 'good breast'. This leads into the Depressive position, where the child pines for the lost good mother and in phantasy attempts to repair the damage done to her. In this way the child is able to restore, and thus regain its good inner objects, that is, its internal images of good and helpful figures (Klein 1940).

If we approach from this perspective the Balinese rituals used to deal with *leyak*, we can see that these rituals aim precisely at making Durga happy, that is, reverse Uma's anger, and thus return her to the beautiful, smiling young mother who returns to Heaven. The ritual is intended to bring about a transformation from monstrous to beautiful form. The terrible devouring mother is not killed in the ritual performance – the *kris* dancers try to stab Rangda but cannot.[32] Nor does Barong harm or defeat her, rather he flirts with her for he is Siwa come to woo his angry spouse. According to the myths, it is Siwa himself who caused Uma's anger by cursing her, and so it is up to him to make good the damage he has done. Human ritual strives to create a context in which Siwa curses himself to take monstrous shape as Barong, and as such can make love with his wife Durga again, remove the curse on her and return her to her original beautiful form of Uma. The damaged and injured mother is thus, via cultural phantasy, made whole and good again.[33]

With respect to all three of the above characteristics, we can see that Balinese beliefs concerning *leyak* closely parallel unconscious phantasy processes identified by Klein. Not only does the 'primordial character' (Needham 1978) of the witch match the phantasy figure described by Klein, but the cultural means of dealing with it makes good psychological sense in terms of Kleinian theory.

At this point, I think it is also possible to offer some suggestions as to why the witch figure, despite the terror it invokes, may or may not provoke actual physical violence. In the Balinese case we see that despite the vivid images of the devouring mother that is the goddess Durga and her human minions, and despite ever-present fears of actual mothers and grandmothers as cannibalistic witches, Balinese rarely inflict violence on suspected *leyak*. Instead the appropriate way to deal with them is via rituals of reparation. By such means the paranoid fears provoked by the terrible mother can be mitigated.

Accordingly, we might expect that in cultures lacking ritual means of reparation open violence is more likely. I have argued the devouring mother is a central figure of unconscious phantasy that is reactivated in adult life by bereavement and loss (Stephen 1999). Where cultural beliefs in witches exist, individual unconscious phantasies of the terrible mother feed into them, giving them life. Once activated, guilt and fears of retaliatory attacks by the witch (mother) create an unbearable emotional situation that must seek some release. In such situations, if no means of reparation are available or can be found, violent revenge against the witch provides the only outlet for unbearable guilt and paranoid fears.

KLEIN AND GENDER DIFFERENCES IN ATTRIBUTIONS OF WITCHCRAFT AND SORCERY

Kleinian theory can also throw some light on the differences in Balinese attributions of destructive powers, as well as on previous distinctions I have attempted to make between witchcraft and sorcery (Stephen 1987b, 1999). Why should women consistently receive negative projections and be subjected to blame and scapegoating, while men attributed with the same destructive powers are usually respected, even admired? Of course, this may in part reflect social realities wherein males have social power and prestige that females lack, but I suspect that the matter goes rather deeper than this (the position of women generally in Balinese culture is known to be high).

I think that women are more likely to be perceived in negative terms because in unconscious phantasy the image of a terrible devouring mother is formed in earliest childhood experience and it continues to exist as an unconscious imago to be dealt with throughout life. The father figure is also important, but secondary; he is often seen as part of or contained within the mother, in what Klein terms the 'combined parental figure' (Hinshelwood 1991: 242–3). This figure, too, is the focus of intense rage and hatred, and thus of paranoid fears of retaliatory attacks. But here the father is rather a content of the mother's body that the infant desires to rob, possess or devour, than a separate entity. Thus the primary image of terror is the *mother*. The cultural image of a female witch figure activates unconscious paranoid fears of retaliatory attacks by the terrible mother. The male attributed with destructive magical powers is at a symbolic remove from this female figure of primary horror.

I see this division reflected in the emphasis on *control* of powers that is evident in the Balinese as well as in the Melanesian data. Evans-Pritchard's (1937) description of sorcery and witchcraft among the Azande, which provided a model for many subsequent anthropological studies and then came to be rejected as too culture-bound, was based upon just such a distinction. The witch's powers constitute inherent capacities and act even without the witch being aware, whereas the sorcerer's abilities are acquired as the result of studying the necessary spells, potions, and rituals; one is an inherent propensity to cause mystical harm, the other a learned capacity deliberately exercised. It might be thought that on this basis all

Balinese *leyak* are properly termed 'sorcerers', since the power of *ngleyak* must be obtained through some kind of deliberate effort or study, but this overlooks the important difference between those persons who have only destructive powers and those who balance destructive powers with positive ones. The female *leyak* represents desire, greed, and materiality spiralling out of control; she ultimately becomes the victim of her own base nature. She can only inflict disease and death, whereas the man attributed with such destructive powers can heal and protect as well as harm.[34] The important point here is not the difference between learnt or inherent abilities, but what this symbolism implies – *the perceived degree of conscious, intentional control over the capacity to cause harm.* The distinction pointed to by Evans-Pritchard was correct, the only problem being that many subsequent ethnographers have interpreted it too literally, rather than appreciating its metaphorical sense.

Another significant difference can be discerned in the cross-cultural data: the capacities of the witch are usually far more fantastical than those attributed to sorcerers. Witches fly through the air, change into animal and other shapes, engage in cannibalism and incest. Sorcerers are more prosaic creatures who achieve their ends via ritual actions that constitute a mystical attack on the victim but do not necessarily involve the transformation of the practitioner himself into something less than human. As I have argued elsewhere (Stephen 1999: 727–8) the sorcerer appropriates for himself the power of the devouring mother, although he remains at one step removed from the absolute terror she inspires. The sorcerer, whatever his evil actions, is believed to be a human being, whereas the witch is thought to be either inhabited by some demonic creature, or else capable of transforming into a non-human entity.

In the Balinese case we see that becoming a *leyak* involves the magician taking on the form of the dreadful Durga herself; this is clearly stated in the spell 'Durga-Murti' and in the depictions in art of *leyak* – they all have female form, with pronounced sexual characteristics. Thus there can be little doubt that the man who employs the power of *ngleyak* deliberately identifies himself with the terrible mother. There is a kind of logic here that the man who can achieve this pinnacle of destructive power – as long as he can continue to balance it with his more positive powers – becomes a kind of grand master of magic and the leader of the hosts of *leyak* that participate in the night battles. Whereas a sorcerer merely appropriates the mother's power – often using female reproductive substances and the corpses of babies for his lethal potions (Lovric 1987) – this grand master both appropriates, and identifies with, the power of the terrible mother.[35]

Without the benefit of Kleinian theory, I have argued that the unconscious roots of sorcery might lie in infantile dependency needs for a father figure, whereas witchcraft represented a projection of guilt that served to defend the self and the group (Stephen 1987b: 288–93). Now, on the basis of Kleinian ideas, I have reached the conclusion that beliefs in both sorcery and witchcraft draw upon the same unconscious imago – the mother – but represent different appropriations of it. Those who have social power, usually men, can seek to acquire the punitive powers of the terrible mother in order to increase their prestige; or, alternatively, the terrifying image can be projected by the group on to a scapegoat, usually a woman.

Where attributions of harmful magic bring blame and scapegoating, I argue that we are dealing with what is appropriately termed 'witchcraft'. The essential feature of witchcraft is the uncontrolled and inhuman nature of the powers involved; thus it may be symbolized as an innate capacity, as a supernatural entity that enters the human host's body, as an uncontrollable greed or maliciousness, or as an unconscious capacity to harm others that acts even without the perpetrator's conscious awareness. In my view, the witch is a cultural projection of unconscious fears concerning the terrible mother. Where, on the other hand, attributions of harmful magic bring social influence and respect, we are dealing with what is appropriately termed 'sorcery'. The essential feature of sorcery is the fact that it is controlled to human ends. This may be symbolized in the learned rather than innate nature of sorcery powers, the deliberate performance of complex ritual and spells, and/or the fact that it is used to punish wrongdoers rather than being a purely malicious act. Sorcery represents an appropriation of the power of the terrible mother usually by males, who control it to group ends.

However, in situations where witch fears greatly escalate, men also may be accused; and men occupying structurally inferior social positions or deviants may become the focus of suspicion.[36] This does not vitiate the general preponderance of women perceived as witches. Furthermore, where epidemics, famine, and other changes lead to dramatically escalating death rates, male sorcerers are in danger of losing their perceived legitimacy as it seems that they have lost control of their capacity for destruction.[37] It should be kept in mind, however, that these labels are analytic categories that we as ethnographers are applying to our cultural data. Emic categories may not precisely match with our distinctions, as the Balinese data shows. It is apparent that witches and sorcerers in terms of my definitions exist in Bali, although the one term 'leyak' may be used in various circumstances with reference to both.

I have argued that the witch figure is not simply a means of explaining misfortune, or merely a reflection of social conflicts, although it is linked to both. Rather it constitutes an imaginary potential arising out of unconscious phantasies generated in the primal experiences of the human infant's relationship to the mother. The terrible mother imago is so compelling that every culture needs to engage with it in some way. Witch beliefs are one of these ways. If we are inclined to assume that contemporary Western culture is an exception, we might pause to reflect upon our own fascination with witches and sorcerers in television, film, and popular literature.

WITCHCRAFT AND HISTORICAL CHANGE

My argument is not that cultural forms are predetermined by unconscious phantasy but that such phantasy provides an important part of the raw material culture draws upon (Obeyesekere 1990). Furthermore, I propose a feedback between the cultural forms and the individual's emotional development, so that the unconscious material incorporated into cultural forms subsequently serves to shape, influence, and direct the phantasies of individuals. Different cultures take up and embellish different aspects of unconscious phantasy, thus channelling in different directions the unconscious processes of their members. I am not suggesting that static forms and images are involved, but rather shifting symbolic expressions centring on certain basic themes linked to the mother imago. This is perhaps best illustrated in situations of social change over time.

As I do not have data from Bali on this point, I now turn to recent important work by Stewart and Strathern on changing images of witchcraft and sorcery in the New Guinea Highlands. Focusing on three regions, Pangia, Hagen, and Lake Kopiago, Stewart and Strathern (1999: 664) have identified changes in these regions that have brought about a post-colonial situation wherein sorcery and witchcraft have 'mutated and spread'. While their research demonstrates the changes in beliefs that have taken place over time, they also point to recurring themes that resonate strongly with the Kleinian theories I have been discussing.

They begin by identifying ideas about bodily invasion as providing a key metaphor for beliefs in assault sorcery and cannibalistic witchcraft in the three regions they examine. Despite differences in detail, the common theme linking these beliefs is 'that of bodily invasion, resulting in either destruction of or in consumption of bodily parts themselves' (Stewart and Strathern 1999: 646). They go on to point out the appropriateness of such imagery in relation to anthropological perceptions concerning social conflict and the permeability of the boundaries of the body, and relate this to anxieties created by changing political boundaries brought about by colonial efforts at 'pacification' beginning in the 1950s. They conclude that as local groups lost their capacity to define their own political boundaries through warfare, so these insecurities began to be reflected in growing fears of bodily invasion by mystical means. In the Pangia district, concerns over political and territorial boundaries were reflected in escalating fears about assault sorcery perpetrated by lone male sorcerers from enemy groups. The Pangia assault sorcerer was believed to suffocate his victims with his 'heat', then removed the internal organs of the body, replacing them with leaves, and finally stuffed the kidneys in the victim's mouth and ordered him or her to return home (Stewart and Strathern 2001: 68–9). On reaching home, the dazed victims began to cook and eat their own kidney, revealing a 'state of disorientation, being no longer aware of what is inside or outside or how to relate himself or herself temporally or spatially to the surroundings' (Stewart and Strathern 1999: 653).

Stewart and Strathern demonstrate convincingly the appropriateness of the metaphorical parallel between Pangia fears concerning actual territorial boundaries and fears concerning mystical invasion of the body and self. The question in my mind is: does the external threat to political boundaries actually create the image of body invasion, or rather does it merely activate or connect to a complex of unconscious imagery relating to fears about attacks on the body? Why, I wonder, do the imagined attacks on the body focus on the ripping out or cannibalizing of body contents, internal organs, rather than for instance attacks on the head, the limbs, or the skin (which, as Stewart and Strathern 2001: 72–3 also point out, often refers to boundaries of the body)? It is not that the internal organs seem inappropriate, but why are they privileged as a symbolic representation? Furthermore, why does the *cannibalizing* of them feature so prominently when surely there are many other possible modes of attack? The primitive oral aggression depicted here so vividly seems to point to unconscious sources.

Of course, from a Kleinian perspective, fears about the invasion of the body, especially attempts to scoop or suck out, or devour body contents, is the key phantasy of the infantile paranoid/schizoid phase. The infant's phantasized attacks upon the frustrating 'bad breast' where it desires to scoop, suck it dry, and devour it, later move on to an awareness of the mother's body as a whole and the desire to rob, rip, and tear out all the desirable things it is thought to contain, including food, faeces, babies, and the father's penis. To these oral aggressive urges are then added anal sadism, at which stage the child phantasizes attacking the mother's body (or the combined parental figure) with explosive faeces and poisonous urine. In return, the child fears retaliatory attacks from the mother via precisely the same means it had used to penetrate and rob her body. Klein, unlike Freud, rarely made reference to other cultures, but she herself noted that the basis of beliefs in black magic seemed clearly prefigured in anal phantasies of attacking the mother's body.[38]

Stewart and Strathern (1999) refer to the similarities and differences between cultural beliefs concerning assault sorcery, as among the Wiru of Pangia and cannibalistic witchcraft among the Melpa and Duna. In my view, beliefs in assault sorcery draw upon phantasies of anal attacks upon the mother's body, which give rise to fears of similar attacks upon the self; whereas fears of cannibalistic witches arise out of oral aggression directed at the mother's body and the expected retaliation by the mother. Both kinds of aggressive phantasies exist in the unconscious, and, as Stewart and Strathern show, in some cultures such as the Duna beliefs in both assault sorcery and cannibalistic witches can exist side by side. The unconscious potential is there to create both figures of imaginary violence. The linkage of assault sorcery with male perpetrators is also understandable in psychoanalytic terms since the anal stage is concerned with gaining control over self and the external world. The assault sorcerer is believed to deliberately implement his attacks, in an appropriation of the powers of the terrible mother. The Pangia assault sorcerer, it appears, represents a projection of power on to an external figure, which suggests to me that he retains a degree of legitimacy. Under the political changes brought by colonial control, his numbers are believed to have increased enormously, suggesting not just that fears concerning the breaching of political boundaries have increased but that confusion with regard to what is and is not legitimate action in relation to boundary maintenance is also at issue. In each case we must look to the particular external circumstances (as of course Stewart and Strathern do) that serve to activate specific unconscious imagery.

In the Melpa case, greed is the 'core idea in notions of witchcraft' (Stewart and Strathern 1999: 654), and changes in witch beliefs since the 1960s can be understood in terms of economic shifts that have created new anxieties concerning consumption and exchange patterns in the region. As is by now surely evident, greed – the greedy attacks upon the breast and the mother's body as a whole – is indeed at the very core of unconscious guilt and fears concerning attacks by the terrible mother. Oral greed – very explicitly taken up in the Hagen beliefs about cannibal witches – is a key element in unconscious phantasies concerning attacks upon the mother's body. Furthermore, the Melpa beliefs that originally dead bodies were considered fit to eat and then later were replaced by an exchange of valuables on a death also point to processes of reparation – the dead body, standing in the unconscious for the mother's body, being reconstituted as wealth/ valuables (for a discussion of Melpa exchange from this perspective, see Stephen 2000: 135–8).

Changes in the Melpa exchange system as a result of the introduction of a cash economy through the buying and selling of coffee (Stewart and

Strathern 1999: 656) provoked 'fears of greed and excessive consumption' that were reflected in an increase in fears of witches. Previously such fears had been confined to the idea that a few women in each clan were witches who devoured corpses; now it was believed that witchcraft was rapidly spreading, many people of both genders being affected as a result of contaminated drinking water, and that now the witches were actually killing people as there were not enough corpses to satisfy their hunger. This is similar to the Balinese belief, discussed earlier, that when witches satisfy their hunger by eating corpses they serve a useful function in the returning of dead matter to its source, but when they get out of control and start killing to satisfy their greed, then ritual action must be taken. For Melpa, the idea that some women were cannibal witches was tolerable but when deaths began to escalate as a result of disease epidemics, people became convinced that the witches themselves were multiplying and killing to satisfy the increased need for human 'meat' to satisfy their ever-growing hunger. From a Kleinian perspective, we can see that the increased death rate activated unconscious fears that already had cultural expression in the form of the female cannibal witch. I have elsewhere (Stephen 1999) discussed in detail how bereavement reactivates in the unconscious mind all the guilt, fear, and anxiety associated with the mother imago. The cultural figure of the witch not only reflects unconscious fears of the terrible mother but also, as scapegoat, provides a means of projecting the guilt experienced by the bereaved on to an external figure. When a death occurs in the community unconscious phantasies concerning the terrible mother activate the cultural image of the witch, giving it new force; when multiple deaths occur, paranoid fears are built up to the point that witches are now seen everywhere and anyone might become a witch.

Among the Duna people of Lake Kopiago beliefs in male assault sorcery and female witchcraft have escalated in the 1990s in ways that correlate with changes in gender politics and the weakening of male dominance over women. Stewart and Strathern (1999: 659) show that the new fears concerning the increase in attacks by outsider male sorcerers and insider female witches were manipulated to justify attempts by men to reinforce their authority over females. As in Melpa, the underlying issue with respect to female witchcraft was greed – specifically desire for pork, which in pre-colonial times was denied to women. Disease epidemics and famine were also afflicting the region, along with other changes in local politics and leadership that had eroded male dominance. Stewart and Strathern are able to identify specific historical circumstances that provoked male insecurities with regard to women. From a Kleinian viewpoint fear concerning greedy and terrifying women/mothers constitutes a basic substratum of the imaginal. It is little wonder that in such male-dominated societies as the Duna any threat to male control would activate this unconscious potential, giving rise to a conscious wave of fears of witches.

My point is not that Stewart and Strathern fail to offer satisfying explanations of the increase and mutations of witchcraft beliefs, since clearly they do. What I am arguing is that the external circumstances of change they describe touch upon precisely those themes that most closely cluster around the mother imago – greed, cannibalism, consumption, body invasion, death and bereavement, and the power of the mother.

Stewart and Strathern also provide evidence revealing that unconscious sources are being drawn upon in the cultural construction of these changing beliefs concerning imaginary violence in the New Guinea Highlands. They refer to the role of dreams, for example in the emergence of new ritual methods to deal with new threats of witchcraft, and they note the importance of dreams generally in Melpa culture (Stewart and Strathern 2001: 76–9), a circumstance noted for many other New Guinea cultures (Stephen 1979, 1995; Lohmann 2000). Here we see how unconscious phantasy products, dreams, are being directly incorporated into cultural belief and woven into existing cultural practices. Given the high evaluation of dreams in these cultures, especially in situations of change, it is not difficult to see how unconscious phantasies continuously feed into culture, providing the basis for new cultural symbols and beliefs, yet still centring on certain basic primal themes. Innovations emerge, involving novel combinations of new and old elements, such as the claim by a Duna aid post orderly that instead of the traditional sago-spine dart used to pierce the victim's body by assault sorcerers, he and his squads of trained followers employed hypodermic syringes to the same end (Stewart and Strathern 1999: 659). This kind of 'cultural bricolage', where the changing details of everyday life are mixed together and recombined with unconscious material, I have referred to as the product of 'autonomous imagination' (Stephen 1989a, 1989b, 1995). Via the processes of autonomous imagining – in dreams, trance, visions – new configurations of external reality shaped by inner desires are sought and found.

Images of witchcraft and sorcery change and mutate in changing circumstances – creating the bricolage effect – but the primal themes that the beliefs cluster around remain the same.

CONCLUSION: THE MOTHER IMAGO AND TERRORISM

Social anthropologists argue that society provides the model for symbolic forms. Since symbols reflect society, they arise from a view of reality predicated by the nature of that society. The body politic is invaded, giving rise to ideas about the invasion of the body of the individual. Thus it would appear that sorcery and witchcraft are reflections of social relationships and circumstances. Yet if this is so, why do so many vastly different social structures give rise to essentially the same beliefs concerning mystical power to harm? In my view, social structures and changes in them – through internal tensions or external forces for change – do not determine these beliefs but rather touch upon and evoke deep unconscious potentials to construct images of mystical violence.

I have argued that sorcery and witchcraft represent an imaginary potential of images of terror and violence that can be used by different cultures in different ways, but the core of these images relates to unconscious persecutory fears concerning the mother imago, and cluster around oral and anal sadistic attacks upon the mother's body projected upon the self and the group. This leads me to reflect on the link between the mother imago, primal images of terror, and modern terrorism.

Hanna Segal (1997), a prominent Kleinian analyst, has drawn attention to the ambivalence and guilt that warfare generates in a populace, creating a situation in which the paranoid-schizoid defence mechanisms of splitting and projection are brought to the fore. She argues that the threat of nuclear warfare which emerged in the last century presents even greater dangers since the possibility of total annihilation that it brings 'mobilizes those mechanisms to a far greater extent' (Segal 1997: 156). Segal believes that by facing nuclear threats with the primitive defence mechanism of splitting and projection, so that totally evil enemies are set up – the 'empires of evil' – that become carriers for all our own projected fear and guilt, we have brought about a situation in which a nuclear holocaust becomes almost inevitable.

At the beginning of the twenty-first century, terrorism is adding yet a new and possibly even more dangerous element to this already intolerable situation. The theme of bodily invasion (Stewart and Strathern 1999) provides a link between imaginary violence and modern terrorism. Threats from an external enemy that can be identified and acted against by conventional military means are one thing, but when attacked by unknown assassins who have invisibly penetrated the interior of the body politic, then the likelihood of provoking the most primitive levels of paranoid fears and defences seems obvious. The terrorist throwing bombs and poison gas becomes the infant attacking the parental imago with explosive faeces and poisonous urine – and expecting terrible vengeance in return. Both victims and aggressors are thrown back into the paranoid schizoid position of early childhood in their extreme emotional responses. The task of controlling or breaking the cycle of violence and the need for revenge is thus even more difficult to achieve than in conventional, even nuclear, warfare.

Yet if this is so, a Kleinian perspective on human aggression indicates that although such is inherent in the human psyche, so also is the urge to repair and make good the damage done. We need to find the cultural means to make reparation, and thereby confront and deal with our own persecutory fears and guilt.

When on 12 October 2002 terrorist bombs killed over 200 people in Kuta, a tourist district in Bali, the Balinese response was not to seek revenge or to give way to despair. Instead, after an appropriate interval, Balinese performed a series of *caru* rituals. Such rituals (of which there are many levels) are, as described earlier, directed to transforming the dangerous and disruptive forces in the world generated by the goddess Durga and her spouse, Kala Rudra, back to their pure and benign forms. Some might object that such actions can have no effect on terrorists, and I could not dispute this, but for the Balinese who had experienced the horror, the rituals served an important psychological need, preventing an escalating of paranoid fears and helping people to begin the difficult psychic process of restoring their good inner objects and rebuilding their inner world through making reparation.

NOTES

1. Acknowledgments: I wish to thank the Indonesian Istitute of the Sciences (LIPI) for their sponsorship of my fieldwork in Bali from 1996 to 1999, on which this chapter is based. Funding for the fieldwork was provided by a Large Grant from the Australian Research Council. For their valuable comments on an earlier version of this paper, I thank the editors of this volume, Pamela Stewart and Andrew Strathern.

2. For recent discussions of these definitional problems, see Ellen 1993: 6–11; Stewart and Strathern 1999: 645–9; Strathern and Stewart 2000: 101–2; Stewart and Strathern 2001.

3. 'Phantasy', as distinct from 'fantasy', refers to 'the imaginative activity which underlies all thought and feeling' (Rycroft 1972: 118) and is a technical term used by Kleinians. Hinshelwood (1991: 32) defines it thus: 'Unconscious phantasies underlie every mental process, and accompany all mental activity. They are mental representations of those somatic events in the body which comprise the instincts, and are physical sensations interpreted as relationships with objects that cause those sensations.' I have followed this usage throughout this chapter.

4. Rycroft (1972: 69) defines 'imago' as 'a term used by Freud to describe (unconscious) object-representations'. It is a term frequently used by Klein with reference to unconscious phantasy concerning parental figures.

5. I have elsewhere (Stephen 1999) described the close parallels between the imagery of unconscious phantasies described by Klein and beliefs concerning witches to be found cross-culturally. The discussion of

Balinese witchcraft was based upon the published literature, as it was written prior to my doing fieldwork in Bali. The present chapter is based upon my three and a half years' fieldwork in Bali, from January 1996 to July 1999.

6. Hinduism was introduced to Bali, first probably directly from India and later via Java, sometime prior to the ninth century A.D. (Ramseyer 2002: 35–6). Intermixing with Buddhism and with indigenous Indonesian elements, Hinduism took on unique local forms, and in Bali evolved over more than a millennium to create the distinctly Balinese forms of beliefs and rituals that are practised today. As Hildred Geertz (1994) explains: 'The people of Bali today call their religion "Balinese Hinduism" after a major strand in a complexly woven web of symbols, ideas, and ceremonies ... these Hindu traces today have very different meanings than in India.'

7. 'Berawi' is presumably derived from the Sanskrit 'Bhairavi', a terrible form taken by Shiva's consort (Kinsley 1986: 163); 'Bhairava' is a terrible form of Shiva himself. The Balinese Berawi Durga resembles the Indian goddess Kali, rather than the Indian Durga. In Bali, however, an important role is played by the god Kala, son of Siwa and Uma, who is the lord of all terrible and destructive forces in the world (Stephen 2002: 66–73).

8. In Bali Siwa (Shiva) is often referred to as 'pelebur', in his role of destroyer of the world.

9. The Balinese Durga is described thus in a creation myth:

> Her teeth were long and sharp, like tusks,
> Her mouth an abyss in between,
> Her eyes shone, they were like twin suns.
> Her nostrils, deep and cavernous.
>
> Her ears stood like two thighs, straight up,
> Matted and twisted was Her hair;
> Her body was misshapen, huge,
> There was nothing that broke its height. (Hooykaas 1974: 64–5)
>
> With blood, as ashes, She was smeared,
> And garlanded with human skulls.
> Intestines were draped over Her,
> She wore a scarf of red and black.
>
> Her minions were escorting Her,
> The creatures of the God Kala,
> With all their brood attending them,
> Then in the graveyard She did dwell. (Hooykaas 1974: 71)

10. The *lontar* are manuscripts made of palm leaf. See Hooykaas (1978: 2–3) for a description of the different kinds of texts that comprise the Balinese written tradition.

11. *Siwagama*, Pusat Dokumentasi Kebudayan Bali, Denpasar, Ida Pedanda Sideman, Geria Sanur, typed by Ni Made Sarini, 31 August 1988, no number. I obtained a copy of this document at the Gedong Kirtya Lontar Library, Singaraja, Bali. It consists of a collection of several myths concerning the high god, Siwa, and was compiled by a famous Brahmana high priest, Ida Pedanda Sideman. See Stephen (2002: 82–5) for a more detailed discussion of this and other texts describing the origins of destructive magic.

12. Many impressive images of *leyak* are to be found in H. Geertz 1994. See also Hooykaas 1980. For general descriptions of Balinese beliefs concerning *leyak*, see Covarrubias [1937] 1989; Hooykaas 1978; Howe 1984; Lovric 1987; Wikan 1990; H. Geertz 1994.

13. *Desti* is a term used to refer to destructive magic in general; *bebai* is a specific technique that involves obtaining the corpse of a baby, giving it magical life, and then causing it to possess a person; *teluh* and *tranjana* are terms that appear in texts, but it is uncertain whether they refer to specific techniques or harmful magic in general.

14. *Tutur Kandaning Catur Bhumi*, Geria Tandeg, Kaba-Kaba, Kediri, Tabanan, typed by Made Pardika, 21 June 2001. Indonesian translation by Nyoman Suarka (pp. 25–6). I obtained this document at the Gedong Kirtya Lontar Library, Singaraja, Bali.

15. *Durga-Murti*, Anak Agung Gede Oka, Sidan, Gianyar, typed 10 August 1976 by I.K. Windia. I obtained this document at Gedong Kirtya Lontar Library, Singaraja, Bali. It was translated into Indonesian by I. Nyoman Suarka. There are not one but five forms of Durga, one for each cardinal direction and the centre.

16. Ellen (1993: 11–13) notes the interweaving of sorcery and witchcraft beliefs with the great religious traditions, including Buddhism and Hinduism, in Southeast Asia. The Tantric cast of Balinese Hinduism (Lovric 1987; Stephen 2005) seems to fit especially well with ideas about magic, sorcery, and witchcraft.

17. 'Ngleyak' is a verbal form that refers to changing shape or form in general. It can be used, for example, to refer to transforming raw rice grain (*beras*) into cooked, edible rice (*nasi*). When applied to the mystical transformations undergone by certain human beings, it refers to assuming animal and even more monstrous forms, ultimately that of the terrible goddess Durga herself.

18. Balinese live in extended families occupying what are usually referred to as 'house compounds'. Several agnatically related nuclear families usually occupy the one house compound, each family possessing its own kitchen and sleeping areas, and sharing certain ceremonial structures.

19. Men are also said to buy charms (*sabuk*) for protection, usually against physical attack. Such devices can also react upon their owners, especially if not handled properly, but in the case of men the effect is not to turn them into *leyak*, but rather to send them crazy (*amok*), so that they become wild and aggressive in actual behaviour, attacking and possibly killing others.

20. Clifford Geertz (1975: 385) describes the marked separation 'both conceptually and institutionally' of public and private life in Balinese culture. The house compound is private, familial space and it is to this area that the female *leyak*'s influence is thought to be restricted. Lovric (1987) also refers to the domestic contexts in which fears and accusations concerning *leyak* usually operate.

21. There probably are, of course, some exceptions to this, but I have heard of no actual examples. In general, men are said to use the power of *ngleyak* against rivals and enemies.

22. Ginzburg's (1992) study of witchcraft in early modern Europe comes to mind here, with its descriptions of the 'night battles' waged by anti-witches to protect their communities against witches and wizards.

23. The root word is 'alih', which means to look for something, to try to get something, thus the *balian* is not simply trying to heal, but rather is looking out to make a profit.

24. Balinese concern with social hierarchies and their reflection in concepts of divine ordering, described for example by C. Geertz (1975: 387–8), seems to be emphasized in these ideas about mystical power possessed by human beings. Legions of powerful magicians are thought to be competing against each other, thus the unseen realm is filled with competitions of supernatural power.

25. H. Geertz (1994: 75–6) recounts this episode of the story of Calon Arang. There are many versions of the story (see Hooykaas 1978).

26. In terms of the cultural belief system, it is difficult to say more about why these women are not thought to have negative capacities, but certainly given the view that women have a special proclivity for harmful magic, female healers might see it in their best interests to deny all but positive capacities. For healers who base their ability on the written texts, who are considered to be by far the more powerful, knowledge of both negative and positive capacities is essential, but in the case of spontaneous inspiration, this is not so. We also glimpse here the control of mystical knowledge by a literate elite. In the past, even in the case of the Brahmana caste of priests and scholars, who possess the most extensive access to the textual sources of knowledge, women were largely excluded from studying the texts.

27. The importance of magic in Tantric mystical thought is demonstrated by Goudriaan (1978, 1979). For a discussion of Balinese magic in this context, see Stephen (2005).

28. One might ask: what level of *leyak* is being aimed at? I think that the ritual is intended to influence not so much individuals as the mystical creatures, *leyak*, that cause disease and death – these might be women or men. Yet I have sat through a shadow puppet theatre performance of Calon Arang into the early hours of the morning listening to my research assistant comment knowingly on the reactions of various old ladies sitting in the audience who were widely believed by the community to be *leyak*. On this occasion people commented that the *dalang* (puppeteer) had been especially daring in his challenges to the *leyak*, and that he might well suffer later as a consequence.

29. This version of the myth is summarized from the *lontar* text, *Siwagama* (Pusat Dokumentasi Kebudayan Bali, Denpasar, Ida Pedanda Sideman, Geria Sanur, typed by Ni Made Sarini, 31 August 1988, no number). Obtained from Gedong Kirtya Lontar Library.

30. The Balinese possess a very complex calendrical system that basically consists of two calendars, one the Saka lunar calendar and the 210-day Pawukon (Eiseman 1990: 172–92).

31. Belo (1966: 38–9) noted the splitting of the mother image in Balinese culture, as had Bateson and Mead (1942).

32. The importance of Oedipal issues is also evident in the actions of the *kris* dancers, who attempt to stab Rangda (see Stephen 2001: 189).

33. The meeting of Barong and Rangda might also be seen to be linked to the Kleinian theme of the combined parental figure (Hinshelwood 1991: 242–3). The parents who have been separated now are ritually brought together and united. If we return to the iconography of Durga/Rangda,

with her great snake-like tongue, we might also consider that the tongue has a phallic significance and that Durga's attributes thus reveal her as a cultural depiction of the Kleinian mother with a penis (Hinshelwood 1991: 388).

34. In this context it should be recalled that female healers (*balian*) are usually thought to have positive powers only, and are seen to operate as mediums or channels for higher powers, rather than as agents in full control of their capacities. This further suggests that whether constructive or destructive powers are involved, the important consideration is the control that the person can exert over them.

35. In unconscious phantasy, the father figure (Hinshelwood 1991: 308–9), when he becomes separated from the combined parental imago, represents a move away from the primal world of the mother. He comes to stand for the external, cultural world.

36. For example, among the Nage of eastern Indonesia (Strathern and Stewart 2000: 115), those accused of witchcraft may be males or females, but witchcraft is thought to be an inherited capacity of the descendants of slaves. Thus a marked structural inequality in Nage society is linked to witchcraft suspicions and accusations of males. I have previously described how in situations where disease and other factors result in a high mortality rate and drastic depopulation, accusations against witches increase, and may focus on men as well as women, as with the Etoro and Kaluli of Papua (Stephen 1987b: 282–3).

37. I have discussed at some length (Stephen 1987b: 277–88) the effects of historical changes, including disease epidemics and depopulation on increases in fears of witchcraft and sorcery, and the effects these changes have on the perceived legitimacy of the sorcerer. And *pace* Stewart and Strathern (1999: 649), I do not assume a static pre-colonial society, but rather suggest that there always was an inherent ambiguity in the sorcerer's claims; furthermore, many of the examples I discuss involve changes prior to European intervention. It remains true, however, as Stewart and Strathern note, that our evidence of change comes mainly from the colonial and post-colonial period.

38. Klein (1989: 145) observes, 'in its phantasies the child uses feces as persecuting agencies against its objects and secretly and surreptitiously inserts them by a kind of magic (which I consider to be the basis of black magic) into the anus and other bodily apertures of those objects …'

REFERENCES

Barfield, Thomas (ed.) (1997) *The Dictionary of Anthropology*. New York: Pergamon Press.

Bateson, Gregory and Margaret Mead (1942) *Balinese Character: A Photographic Analysis*. New York: New York Academy of Sciences.

Belo, Jane (1966) *Bali: Rangda and Barong*. Monographs of the American Ethnological Society. Seattle and London: University of Washington Press.

Covarrubias, Miguel [1937] (1989) *Island of Bali*. Singapore: Oxford University Press.

Eiseman, Fred B. (1990) *Bali: Sekala and Niskala. Volume I: Essays on Religion, Ritual, and Art*. Hong Kong: Periplus.

Ellen, Roy (1993) 'Introduction'. In *Understanding Witchcraft and Sorcery in Southeast Asia*, ed. C.W. Watson and Roy Ellen. Honolulu: University of Hawaii Press, pp. 1–25.

Evans-Pritchard, Sir Edward E. (1937) *Witchcraft, Oracles and Magic among the Azande*. Oxford: Clarendon Press.

Freud, Sigmund [1928] (1989) *Civilization and its Discontents*, ed. James Strachey. New York: Norton, Harmondsworth: Penguin Books.

Geertz, Clifford (1975) 'Person, Time and Conduct in Bali'. In *The Interpretation of Cultures*. London: Hutchinson & Co., pp. 360–411.

Geertz, Hildred (1994) *Images of Power: Balinese Paintings Made for Gregory Bateson and Margaret Mead*. Honolulu: University of Hawaii Press.

Ginzburg, Carlo (1992) *The Night Battles: Witchcraft and Agrarian Cults in the Sixteenth and Seventeenth Centuries*. Baltimore: Johns Hopkins University Press.

Goudriaan, Teun (1978) *Māyā Divine and Human*. Delhi: Motilal Banarsidass.

—— (1979) 'Introduction. Tantrism in History, The Place of Tantrism in Hindu Religious Speculation'. In *Hindu Tantrism*, by Sanjukta Gupta, Dirk Jan Hoens and Teun Goudriaan. Leiden: E.J. Brill, pp. 3–67.

Hinshelwood, Robert (1991) *A Dictionary of Kleinian Thought*. London: Aronson.

Hodgkin, Katharine (2001) 'Reasoning with Unreason: Vision, Witchcraft, and Madness in Early Modern England'. In *Languages of Witchcraft: Narrative, Ideology and Meaning in Early Modern Culture*, ed. Stuart Clark. London: Macmillan Press, pp. 217–36.

Hooykaas, Christiaan (1974) *Cosmogony and Creation in Balinese Tradition*. The Hague: Martinus Nijhoff.

—— (1978) *The Balinese Poem Basur: An Introduction to Magic*. The Hague: Martinus Nijhoff.

—— (1980) *Drawings of Balinese Sorcery*. Leiden: E.J. Brill.

Howe, L.E.A. (1984) 'Gods, People, Spirits and Witches: The Balinese System of Personal Definition'. *Bijdragen Tot de Taal-, Land- en Volkenkunde*, vol. 140. Gravenhage: Martinus Nijhoff, pp. 193–222.

Kinsley, David R. (1986) *Hindu Goddesses: Visions of the Divine Feminine in the Hindu Religious Tradition*. Berkeley and Los Angeles: University of California Press.

Klein, Melanie [1927] (1988) 'Criminal Tendencies in Normal Children'. In *Love, Guilt and Reparation: and Other Works 1921–1945*. London: Virago Press, pp. 170–85.

—— [1937] (1988) 'Love, Guilt and Reparation'. In *Love, Guilt and Reparation: and Other Works 1921–1945*. London: Virago Press, pp. 306–43.

—— [1940] (1988) 'Mourning and its Relation to Manic-Depressive States'. In *Love, Guilt and Reparation: and Other Works 1921–1945*. London: Virago Press, pp. 344–69.

—— [1946] (1988) 'Notes on Some Schizoid Mechanisms'. In *Envy and Gratitude: and Other Works 1946–1963*. London: Virago Press, pp. 1–24.

—— [1952] (1988) 'Some Theoretical Conclusions Regarding the Emotional Life of the Infant'. In *Envy and Gratitude: and Other Works 1946–1963*. London: Virago Press, pp. 61–93.

—— (1989) *The Psycho-Analysis of Children*. London: Virago Press.

Lohmann, Roger I. (2000) 'The Role of Dreams in Religious Enculturation among the Asabano of Papua New Guinea'. *Ethos*, 28(1): 75–102.

Lovric, Barbara (1987) 'Rhetoric and Reality'. Unpublished Ph.D. thesis, Sydney: University of Sydney.

Needham, Rodney (1978) *Primordial Characters*. Charlottesville, VA: University of Virginia Press.

Obeyesekere, Gananath (1990) *The Work of Culture: Symbolic Transformations in Psychoanalysis and Anthropology*. Chicago: University of Chicago Press.

Ramseyer, Urs (2002) *The Art and Culture of Bali*. Basel: Museum der Kulturen.

Rycroft, Charles (1972) *A Critical Dictionary of Psychoanalysis*. Harmondsworth: Penguin Books.

Segal, Hanna (1997) *Psychoanalysis, Literature and War: Papers 1972–1995*. ed. John Steiner. London: Routledge.

Stephen, Michele (1979) 'Dreams of Change: The Innovative Role of Altered States of Consciousness in Traditional Melanesian Religion'. *Oceania* 50: 3–22.

—— (1987a) 'Introduction'. In *Sorcerer and Witch in Melanesia*, ed. Michele Stephen. New Brunswick and London: Rutgers University Press, pp. 1–14.

—— (1987b) 'Contrasting Images of Power'. In *Sorcerer and Witch in Melanesia*, ed. Michele Stephen. New Brunswick and London: Rutgers University Press, pp. 249–304.

—— (1989a) 'Self, the Sacred Other, and Autonomous Imagination'. In *The Religious Imagination in New Guinea*, ed. Gilbert Herdt and Michele Stephen. New Brunswick: Rutgers University Press, pp. 41–64.

—— (1989b) 'Constructing Sacred Worlds and Autonomous Imagining in New Guinea'. In *The Religious Imagination in New Guinea*, ed. Gilbert Herdt and Michele Stephen. New Brunswick: Rutgers University Press, pp. 211–36.

—— (1995) *A'Aisa's Gifts: A Study of Magic and the Self*. Berkeley: University of California Press.

—— (1999) 'Witchcraft, Grief and the Ambivalence of Emotion'. *American Ethnologist*, 26(3): 711–37.

—— (2000) 'Reparation and the Gift'. *Ethos*, 28(2): 119–46.

—— (2001) 'Barong and Rangda in the Context of Balinese Religion'. *Rima*, 35(1) (Winter): 137–93 (Sydney: The University of Sydney).

—— (2002) 'Returning to Original Form'. *Bijdragen tot de Taal-, Land-en Volkenkunde*, 158(1): 61–94 (Leiden: KITLV Press).

—— (2005) *Desire, Divine and Demonic: Balinese Mysticism in the Paintings of I. Ketut Budiana and I. Gusti Nyoman Mirdiana*. Honolulu, HA: University of Hawai'i Press.

Stephen, Michele and Luh Ketut Suryani (2000) 'Shamanism, Psychosis and Autonomous Imagination'. *Culture Medicine and Psychiatry*, 24: 5–40 (Kluwer Academic Publishers).

Stewart, Pamela J. and Andrew Strathern (1999) 'Feasting on my Enemy: Images of Violence and Change in the New Guinea Highlands'. *Ethnohistory*, 46(4): 645–69 (American Society for Ethnohistory).

—— (eds) (2001) *Humors and Substances: Ideas of the Body in New Guinea*. Connecticut and London: Bergin & Garvey.

Strathern, Andrew and Pamela J. Stewart (2000) *The Python's Back: Pathways of Comparison Between Indonesia and Melanesia*. Connecticut and London: Bergin & Garvey.

Wikan, Unni (1990) *Managing Turbulent Hearts: A Balinese Formula for Living*. Chicago: University of Chicago Press.

AFTERWORD
THE TASTE OF DEATH

Neil L. Whitehead

> Cowards die many times before their deaths,
> The valiant never taste of death but once.
>
> William Shakespeare, Julius Caesar, II, ii, 32–7

Terror and violence occupy central places in our contemporary cultural imaginary and we all die many times before our deaths as we contemplate and, even more crucially, anticipate the possible consequences of terrorist attack. This constant imaginative rehearsal of certain forms of death and dying reflects not just some greater awareness of the use of shocking and outrageous forms of violence as a means of political and cultural assertion, but also the avowedly conscious construction of violent strategies of such assertion. This has occurred most notably in the context of post-colonial conflicts such as Bosnia, Sri Lanka, and Rwanda, as well as in contexts of 'terrorist' actions, particularly suicide bombings, in Chechnya, Iraq, and Palestine. Such violence is overtly designed to achieve an impact on the cultural imagination of the 'West'.

Recent revelations of prisoner abuse and humiliation by US forces at Abu-Ghraib in turn pointedly raise the issue of whether this torture was an outcome of individual psycho-pathology or part of a systematic military policy for interrogation. Such revelations also underline the importance of understanding how violence works both as part of the individual imagination and as part of the cultural order, since the form of abuse practised by individual US soldiers reflected particular kinds of cultural values emphasizing certain forms of sexualized humiliation rather than, say, gross physical injury. It is part of the teaching of interrogation techniques that torture and abuse in these senses simply do not work as effective means of intelligence-gathering. It thus follows that the purpose of such abuse must be analysed by reference to the way in which the cultural meaning of the 'War on Terror' in Iraq, and the cultural place of the military in US society, interrelate. In this light 'Homeland

Security', and preparedness for terrorist attack, are no less part of a cultural performance of our own violent socio-cultural order through the 'software' of our imaginations, than the constant display and homoerotic appreciation of the 'hardware' of Hummers, tanks, automatic weapons, precision rockets, and bombs.

However, the media dominance of Euro-American commentary on 'violence' and 'terrorism', as well as their supposed ideological and psychological bases, in 'radical Islam', or other unfamiliar political ideologies, can be considered part of that violence for the way in which it directly feeds the cultural imaginary of media consumers around the globe. From comic books to movies and music, no less than news and media analysis TV, the imagination of violence and terror is not just about violence but is actually integral to it. The physicality of violent assault cannot be limited to its destruction of human bodies but, necessarily, must also be related to the way violence persists as memory, trauma, and in the intimate understanding of one's self-identity.

Violent acts may embody complex aspects of symbolism that relate to both order and disorder in a given social context, and it is these symbolic aspects that give violence its many potential meanings in the formation of the cultural imaginary. This is a particularly important point when we consider the violent acts taken by peoples around the world in the name of a particular religion, or in a belief that these acts conform to a set of 'moral' or 'patriotic' teachings directly linked to specific ideologies. When atrocity or murder take place they feed into the world of the iconic imagination. Imagination transcends reality and its rational articulation, but in doing so it can bring further violent realities into being.

Ethnographically anthropology has proved hesitant to try and understand the ferocity and forms of such violence since witnessing such acts is problematic in itself, to say nothing of the direct challenges to the practice of ethnography that violent cultural practices inherently present. The ethnographer can just as easily be a victim of violence as an observer of it, and observation itself contributes to the cultural meaning of violent acts, no less than their perpetration. The chapters in this volume clearly show the importance of attempting to grapple with these issues since they all emphasize in varying degrees the relevance of changing global conditions to the violent contestation of nationalism, ethnicity, and state control. Crucially they also address the question as to why such violence might take particular cultural forms – such as specific kinds of mutilation, 'ethnic cleansing', or other modes of community terror. Such an approach has not been adequately integrated into wider anthropological theory despite the pioneering work of relatively few authors, but it is only in this way that the links between acts of violence and their imagination and anticipation can be drawn out. The significance of this linkage should not be underestimated and has been a key focus in this volume. As was the case under early modern European regimes of torture, simply to be shown the instruments of torment was often sufficient to produce the required confession of heresy or apostasy. So today, simply to be shown the aftermath of 'terrorism' invites each citizen to rehearse their complex political commitments to 'freedom' and 'democracy', which in turn sustain those regimes of political power that locate and identify the terrorist threat at the very gates of society, political stability, and economic prosperity.

This kind of approach requires a more explicit anthropology of experience and imagination in which individual meanings, emotive forces, and bodily practices become central to the interpretation of violent acts. This also implies a recognition of the need to interpret violence as a discursive practice, whose symbols and rituals are as relevant to its enactment as its instrumental aspects. How and when violence is culturally appropriate, why it is only appropriate for certain individuals and the significance of those enabling ideas of cultural appropriateness to a given cultural tradition as a whole, are therefore among the key questions that have been addressed in this volume. Until now there have been few attempts to map how cultural conceptions of violence are used discursively to amplify and extend the cultural force of violent acts or how those violent acts themselves can generate a shared idiom of meaning for violent death – and this discursive amplification is precisely what is meant by the poetics of violent practice. By bringing together questions as to how violence is legitimated, and by relating the contest for such legitimacy to a wider field of cultural meaning and imagination, the chapters here take an important step forward in developing such an anthropology of experience.

Anthropological research on violence also has the potential to make an important impact on anthropology's understanding of neo-liberal development and democratization more widely, since it is in those economic and political margins of the global order that violence becomes an inevitable, and legitimated, form of cultural affirmation and expression of identity to counter or compensate for a felt loss of 'tradition' or challenge to collective identity. Unless anthropology can develop ethnographic approaches and theoretical frameworks for engagement with such violent contexts then it risks being intellectually marginal to both the subjects and consumers of its texts.

In many popular and conventional presentations of indigenous or 'tribal' life ways the more or less overt message is normally to the effect that the lives being witnessed are subject to the kinds of arbitrary violence and terror that Western liberal democracy has otherwise banished from our everyday existence. Of course, other kinds of tropes are used in the various forms of programming on TV that suggest a more positive aspect to the lives of others – their harmony with nature, the beauty and satisfaction derived from tradition and custom – but even here the implicit meaning of the representation is that it is an anachronistic route to human happiness and contentment. Accordingly, the pervasive threat of the Hobbesian condition – a war of all men against all men – with the inevitable consequence – that the life of most men is nasty, brutish and short – repeatedly ensues. This mode of representation, and the imagination of other's subjectivities it entails, is particularly evident in the treatment of topics such as sorcery and witchcraft, and other televisual dioramas of 'traditional' violence, such as initiation ceremonies, mystical practices of self-mutilation or pain endurance, and so forth.[1] What such portrayals neglect in their urgent concern to convince us of the degree to which such lives are immured in superstition and fear is that we too live in a state of constant fear and terror, kept active in public consciousness by such devices as government-issued threat levels, civic exercises in preparedness for attack or disaster, and the nightly news bulletins and TV dramas. For even if we are somewhat defended against the terrorist of yesterday, the potential for similar violent disruptions of normalcy is nevertheless constantly rehearsed in crime dramas, documentaries, and reportage on the imminence of all kinds of natural and social disaster.[2]

However, as the chapters here suggest, not only (of course) is this to overlook the way in which states of terror and acts of violence are entangled with the social and political order, but also how those apparently negative and undesirable conditions are nonetheless valorized as the context for the expression of ultimate cultural value – be that heroism and self-sacrifice, or physical endurance and indifference to pain. Moreover, the meanings of the televisual contrasts between savage and violent others and our pacific and sophisticated selves are not just linked to an implicit endorsement of a 'Western way'. They are also linked to the effacement of our own social and cultural capacities for, and institutions of, violence with a resulting enfeeblement of the individual in the face of, or prospect of, the exercise of violence. We sit entranced by the sights and sounds of 'terrorist violence' – the twisted piles of metal and rubble, the wailing of women, the shouting of men, and the shots of tell-tale blood pools, which visually confirm the overriding importance of this kind of violence as a token of the perpetrators' barbarity, and the occasion for our condemnation. In this way we are implicitly invited to infer the relative insignificance of our own counter-violence, rarely itself so starkly presented, in defeating the monstrous perpetrators of such acts. We also learn that we are dependent on the professionals of violence to achieve that end.

This is partly why the visual materials emanating from the torture camp at Abu Ghraib prison were so shocking and incommensurable with our understanding of the meaning of violence when we deploy it. Although US cultural values were overtly shaping the forms of violence – all the torturers wore plastic gloves, focused on sexualized humiliation, and generally gave off the impression that this was merely a frat party or hazing event – it was the automatic response of commentators that either the perpetrators were individually psychopathic or that higher authority was aberrant, but understandably so, since the aim of defeating terror was a far more important political goal. Moreover, even recent liberal-inspired commentary focuses on a validation of US government and the nation's body politic by suggesting a balancing out of the 'mistakes' of Abu Ghraib by the process of free journalist inquiry and a Freedom of Information Act that uncovers the 'truth' of such abuse and torture – presumably then the detainees at Guantanamo Bay are doing just fine.[3]

Of course, the latest terrorist pandemonium is in many ways just a reinscription of pervasive and limitless threats that were earlier evident in the supposed imminence of total global holocaust that was constantly paraded during the era of nuclear confrontation between the United States and Soviet Union. Now 'Weapons of Mass Destruction' are back in vogue again to suggest the imminent possibility of terrorist catastrophe in the vein of the 9/11 attacks, if not the emergence of a Cold War style stand-off with North Korea or Iran. Clearly, though, certain forms of violent 'terrorist' action cannot serve this cultural purpose since such responses to Timothy McVeigh's bombing of a Federal building in Oklahoma have been noted but not introduced into the wider public discourse on the 'War on Terror', precisely highlighting the difference between personal safety and national security as relating to different realms of political thinking and priority. Security is the politico-military prerogative of government while safety remains a culturally diverse and individualized idea. 'Safety' in this sense can only be realized by the occupation of a different kind of space from that of threat and terror. Perhaps a nostalgic retreat, as in the sudden popularity of American folk music and the movie *O Brother Where Art Thou?* in the immediate wake of 9/11, and also in the remaking and recycling of movie/TV formats from or about the 1950s and 1960s.[4]

Nonetheless, the interest of the authors in this volume in the imagination of terror and violence suggests that there is no geographical limitation on how such discourses travel, or at least only those of the medium in which they are expressed. My own discussions of a relatively obscure form of terror – the *kanaimà* –

underscores this de-location, since despite regional use of the idea
it has not connected with a global discourse of terror in the way
that other local imaginings have already done, as in the case of
the vampire, zombie, or werewolf. As Stewart and Strathern (this
volume) indicate, such discourses also proliferate and expand locally
through rumour, gossip, and imagination to constitute a cultural
imaginary, and in particular they provide a sustained demonstration
of the relevance of a comparison of sorcery with terrorism and how
the field of sorcery is a key historical site for the understanding of
violent social and cultural transformations.

In the contemporary 'West' the figure of the 'suicide bomber', more
than the 'sorcerer', holds a key place in cultural imaginary, serving
as a token of the illegitimacy of political causes that generate such
acts. In Chechnya, Iraq, Sri Lanka, and Palestine, the 'suicide bomber'
evokes the imagination of an irrational and unreasoning violence
whose motivations are buried in the obscurity of religious cultism.
It important to note therefore that the 'suicide bomber' is a Western
media formulation and that martyrdom and self-sacrifice – or fighting
to the death – are much closer to the ideas that activate perpetrators.
Valuable though recent studies are they do not adequately engage
the multiple cultural imaginaries from which such acts emerge.[5] In
Japan, Iraq, Chechnya, Sri Lanka, and Palestine such acts acquire
meaning from quite distinct traditions and practices of violence. Just
as is the case for an older idea of terror, cannibalism, it transpires that
the apparent behavioural similarity of these acts actually belies their
distinct cultural meanings and trajectories. This is very strikingly
borne out by Ohnuki-Tierney's study of Japanese *kamikaze* whose
motivations were formed more through an admiring contemplation
of Western modernity than as a remnant of anachronistic and
traditional *samurai* ethics.[6]

In many ways the figure of the suicide bomber also makes
dramatically overt the identification of our bodies with the body
politic. Through the social order of power, our bodies are shaped, and
defined. They are also joined to locations and landscapes such that
destructions of sites of civic identity become felt as bodily invasions,
from which the invader must be repelled, purged, and cleansed. So
too in the absence of specific kinds of bodies – suspects, offenders,
terrorists – or in the lack of physically distinguishing features for
such categories, the site of a 'War on Terror' or against other kinds of
'enemies within' must become internalized as an aspect of 'mind' and
'attitude'. In this way we can come to appreciate how acts of violence
are necessarily, and sometimes only, acted out in imagination.

This volume has emphasized the fruitful link to be made between
'traditional' forms of terror and violence, such as sorcery, and the
contemporary depictions of terrorists, suicide bombers, and other

anti-social threats; but earlier commentators on sorcery were no less aware of the significance of the imaginative order. As one missionary in Guyana wrote:

At times I was warned that they were going to 'piai' me, that is, to cause sickness or death by their art; information which gave little uneasiness. For though the Obiah men of the negroes, and these Piai sorcerers of the aborigines, do *often cause sickness and sometimes death by the terror their threats inspire, they can only have this effect on minds imbued with a belief in them.* In order to injure others they must resort to actual poison, as in compassing the death of Mr. and Mrs. Youd [my emphasis].[7]

The subsequent expansion of global media has ensured that many more minds can become imbued with a conviction of the reality of present terror, just as previously an elaborate theatre of public punishment and execution imbued minds with a lesson as to how the destruction of the bodies of the condemned was integral to the reproduction of society, paradoxically achieving the incorporation of society through the exclusion of its victims.

It is also significant, then, that colonial depictions of other rituals of bodily destruction, particularly as encountered in the colonial occupation of America, put great stress on the collective participation of the community in the destructive production of the victim. This was done as a way of illustrating the barbarity of the ritual exercise of 'cannibalism', so that both commentators and illustrators repeatedly alluded to the participation of women and children in the cannibal moment. It is striking that it was this community participation in the incorporating cannibal moment that shocked the early modern Europeans, not its cruelties and torments. By contrast an exclusion, not inclusion, of the victim is envisaged in the European tradition of torture and execution as an adjunct to judicial process. Such is now the fate of detainees at Guantanamo USAF base in Cuba whose marked bodies and tortured minds leave them in a limbo of non-being, excluded from the society of human rights and law. As Edmund Leach noted nearly thirty years ago:

We see ourselves as threatened ... by lawless terrorists of all kinds ... we feel ourselves to be in the position of the European Christians after the withdrawal of the Mongol hordes rather than in the position of the unfortunate Caribs ... at the hands of the Spanish invaders... We now know that the dog-headed cannibals against whom Pope Gregory IX preached his crusade were representatives of a far more sophisticated civilization than anything that existed in Europe at the time... However incomprehensible the acts of terrorism may seem to be, our judges, our policemen, and our politicians must never be allowed to forget that terrorism is an activity of fellow human beings and not of dog-headed cannibals.[8]

Control over bodies – both live and dead, imaginatively and physically – is a way of engendering political power, and of all the modes of controlling bodies the physical incorporation of body parts most vividly expresses this. Such a ritual and symbolic dynamic then allows us to appreciate the indigenous political significance of the 'taste of death' in anthropophagic ritual, and to begin to understand, as in the discussion of sorcery in the chapters of this volume, how our own deep traditions of violence still persist as part of a mystical and imaginative search for the final triumph of progress over the terror and violence of barbarity.

NOTES

1. A recent series of programmes on such topics made for the US Discovery Channel was thus entitled 'Culture Shock Week'.
2. Carolyn Nordstrom has aptly termed this 'the tomorrow of violence'. See her chapter in Neil L. Whitehead (ed.), *Violence* (SAR Press, 2004).
3. See review of Mark Danner, *Torture and Truth: America, Abu Ghraib, and the War on Terror* (New York: New York Review Books, 2004) by Andrew Sullivan in *New York Sunday Book Review*, 23 January 2005.
4. A point well made by Stephen Feld at a recent lecture at the University of Wisconsin.
5. Christoph Reuter (2004) *My Life is a Weapon. A Modern History of Suicide Bombing*. Princeton: Princeton University Press.
6. Emiko Ohnuki-Tierney (2002) *Kamikaze, Cherry Blossoms, and Nationalisms: The Militarization of Aesthetics in Japanese History*. Chicago: University of Chicago Press.
7. William Brett (1881) *Mission Work in the Forests of Guiana*. London and New York: SPCK and E. & J.B. Young & Co., p. 53.
8. Edmund Leach (1977) *Custom, Law and Terrorist Violence*. Edinburgh: Edinburgh University Press.

NOTES ON CONTRIBUTORS

Misty Bastian is currently Associate Professor and Chair of the Department of Anthropology at Franklin and Marshall College in Lancaster, PA. She has published numerous ethnographic articles on gender, religious practice and popular media in Nigeria, as well as historical pieces on the 1929 Igbo Women's War and mission Christianity during the Nigerian colonial period. She has also co-edited a volume, with Jane L. Parpart, *Great Ideas for Teaching About Africa* (Lynne Rienner, 1999).

Elisabeth Kirtsoglou, Ph.D., is a Lecturer in Anthropology in the University of Wales Lampeter and author of the book *For the Love of Women: Gender, Identity and Same-Sex Relationships in a Greek Provincial Town* (Routledge, 2004). Her research interests focus on identity, gender, and politics.

Joyce J.M. Pettigrew, Ph.D., is currently Senior Fellow, Queen's University of Belfast. She worked as an anthropologist in rural areas of the Punjab over a period of 30 years and is the author of *Robber Noblemen* (Routledge & Kegan Paul, 1975); *The Sikhs of Punjab, Unheard Voices of State and Guerrilla Violence* (Zed Books, 1995); and editor of *Martyrdom and Political Resistance* (VU University Press, Centre of Asian Studies, Amsterdam, 1997).

Michele Stephen, Ph.D., is a Senior Lecturer in Anthropology at La Trobe University, Melbourne. She is editor of *Sorcerer and Witch in Melanesia* (Rutgers UP, 1987), co-editor of *The Religious Imagination in New Guinea* (Rutgers UP, 1989), and author of *A'aisa's Gifts: A Study of Magic and the Self* (California UP, 1995). Her most recent book is *Desire, Divine and Demonic: Balinese Mysticism in the Paintings of I. Ketut Budiana and I. Gusti Nyoman Mirdiana* (Hawaii UP, 2005).

Pamela J. Stewart and **Andrew Strathern** are long-time research collaborators. They are both in the Department of Anthropology, University of Pittsburgh and affiliated with the Department of Anthropology, University of Durham and the Research Institute of Irish and Scottish Studies, University of Aberdeen. They have published widely on their work in the Pacific, Europe, and Asia in journal articles and books. Their most recent co-authored books include *Witchcraft, Sorcery, Rumors and Gossip* (Cambridge UP, 2004) and *Empowering the Past, Confronting the Future* (Palgrave Macmillan, 2004); their most recent co-edited books include *Expressive Genres and Historical Change: Indonesia, Papua New Guinea, and Taiwan* (Ashgate Publishing, 2005) and *Asian Ritual Systems: Syncretisms and Ruptures* (Carolina Academic Press, forthcoming 2005). Their most recent research is on the topics of cosmological landscapes, religious conversion, ideological indoctrination, and intimidation.

Susanna Trnka is a lecturer in the Department of Anthropology at the University of Auckland in New Zealand. In addition to editing a special issue on ethnographic perspectives of the 2000 Fiji Coup (*Pacific Studies*, December 2002), she is currently working on a book on the impact of 19 May 2000 on ideas of community in Fiji. Her previous research was on gender and state transformation in the Czech Republic and resulted in the book *Young Women of Prague* (Macmillan Press, 1998), co-authored with Alena Heitlinger, and the edited volume *Bodies of Bread and Butter: Reconfiguring Women's Lives in the Post-Communist Czech Republic* (Prague Gender Studies Centre, 1993).

Neil L. Whitehead is Professor of Anthropology & Religious Studies at the University of Wisconsin-Madison. His most recent works include *Dark Shamans* (Duke UP, 2002), *In Darkness and Secrecy* (Duke UP, 2004) and *Violence* (SAR Press, 2004). He is currently working on issues of cannibalism and ethnopornography.

INDEX

lontar (sacred texts) 201, 202,
225n.10
looting 41, 43, 117, 120, 133
Lough Swilly 162
Lovell, E. W. 168n.10
Lovric, Barbara 216, 226n.12,
226n.16
Lutz, Catherine 54n.1

McKittrick, David 168n.4
MacIntyre, A. 62, 63
McVea, David 168n.4
McVeigh, Timothy 235
Macedonia 68, 78
Makrydimitris, A. 80
Makushi 171
Malkki, Liisa 10, 129–30
Manorcunningham 143
Marshall-Fratani, Ruth 44
Martin, Garry 11
martyrdom 27–8
Masonic halls 152
mass destruction, weapons of 14,
235
maũa 20, 23
Mbembe, Achille 44
media representations 10
in Fiji 118, 125–6, 139n.10
in Ireland 145, 147, 168n.6
in Nigeria 44–52
in Punjab 97, 113n.8
mediascape 52
newspapers in Athens 65
of disruptions of normalcy 234–5
of terrorist violence 234–5
of violence in 'tribal' societies
234
television 68
Mehta, Deepak 118
memory 7, 13
political 31–7
militias 55n.11
missionaries, in Amazonia 173,
179
'modernity' 183–4
Monaghan, County 142
Montaigne, Michel de 177
Mount Hagen 16, 17, 18, 25
Mouzelis, N. 67, 80
Moville 151
Muaniweni 131, 135

Muslims, in Kano 41, 42
and Shari'a law 42, 47, 50
and violence 50–1
'anti-Sufism' among 54n.7
see also, 'yan daba
mutilation 13
Myanmar (Burma) 28

Nage 228n.36
Naitasiri Province 117
narratives, of conflict 33, 34–5
of victims in Fiji 118
regarding the police in Fiji 134
rural versus urban 125, 135–6
struggles for meaning in 136–7
ubiquity of in Upahãr Gaon
123–9
narratives of violence (Northern
Ireland)
ballad of Stumpie's brae 162–5
burning of church hall 151–2
burning of Masonic hall 152
Claudy bombing 146–9
'ethnic cleansing' 154
of border violence 153–5
of conflict over land 154
Omagh bombing 149–50
nation-state, as ideal 28
as constituted 71
Nausori 121, 131
Needham, Rodney 193
Negri, Antonio 52
Newtownbutler 153
Newtowncunningham 143
Nigeria 41–59
'non-place' concept 53
Nordstrom, Carolyn 29, 238
North Atlantic Treaty Organization
(NATO) 78
Northern Ireland 33, 142, 143
Norton, Robert 120
nostalgia 34

oaths 26
Obasanjo, Olasegun 43, 48, 55n.10
Obeyesekere, Gananath 213
Oksapmin 23–4
Ohnuki-Tierney, Emiko 236
Omagh 34
Omagh bombing 149–50
Omissi, David 113n.7

www.ingramcontent.com/pod-product-compliance
Lightning Source LLC
Chambersburg PA
CBHW032124020426
42334CB00016B/1065